HISTORY OF THE COMMUNIST PARTY

History of the Communist Party in Britain 1941–1951

NOREEN BRANSON

Lawrence & Wishart
LONDON

Lawrence & Wishart Limited
99a Wallis Road
London E9 5LN

First published 1997
Copyright © Noreen Branson, 1997

The author has asserted her right under the Copyright,
Designs and Patents Act, 1988, to be identified
as author of this work.

British Library Cataloguing in Publication Data.
A catalogue record for this book is available from the British Library.

ISBN 0-85315-862-2

Photoset in North Wales by
Derek Doyle & Associates, Mold, Clwyd.
Printed and bound in Great Britain by
Biddles Ltd, Guildford.

CONTENTS

CONTENTS

PART III   The Labour Government's Last Term 1950–51

INTRODUCTION

The first two volumes of the history of the Communist Party of Great Britain were written by James Klugmann and published between 1968-9. From then on he was engaged in extensive research for a further work; however, he died before it could be written. Making much use of his research, I took responsibility for the next volume which covered the years 1927-41 and appeared in 1985. Soon after I began collecting material on the Party's role in the 1940s, but while I was doing so the Communist Party of Great Britain came to an end and was replaced by the Democratic Left organisation.

During these years we have seen the disintegration of the Soviet Union and the collapse of socialist regimes in eastern Europe. Yet, as the peoples of these countries are discovering, reversion to capitalist market economies is not leading to a better life. On the contrary, many of their former gains have disappeared; they are seeing rising unemployment, poverty and insecurity; the growth of racial and religious conflicts; the rebirth of neo-fascist organisations; and nationalist controversies often leading to civil wars.

In such a situation, those on the Left who want to move forward to a socialist society which is both humane and democratic need to analyse what went wrong in the Soviet Union and the other socialist countries. But it is also necessary to look at the record of communist movements in capitalist countries, examine the beliefs and aims of their members; their achievements as well as their failures.

In Britain the Communist Party was never very large, yet it had influence much wider than its size would imply. For many decades it was portrayed as 'the enemy'; though never officially classed as 'illegal' its members were subjected to much discrimination and harassment. Moreover, its aims and activities have been much distorted by some historians. In this book, I aim to set the record straight for the ten years between 1941 and 51, covering wartime activities, the period of the post war Labour Government, and the start of the Cold War.

Four people read my initial draft – Jim Fyrth, Monty Johnstone, Betty Lewis and George Matthews. I am more than grateful to them for their expert help and suggestions. I received valuable information from Tamara Philipps (formerly Tamara Rust) for my chapters on the position of women, and from Eddie Dare and Steve Parsons on the anti-communist purge in the civil service. Margot Heinemann supplied me with material for the section on professional workers, though sadly she did not live to read the final draft.

A valuable source of information was the 'Communist Party History Group' – now the Socialist History Society – particularly its collection of personal recollections of communists in the armed forces and of those who participated in the 1946 squatters' movement. Bill Moore, George Barnsby and Tony Atienza were among those who gave me much assistance. I also received useful suggestions from Francis Beckett, Yvonne Kapp and Kevin Morgan.

Finally, I am most grateful to the librarian at the Labour Party headquarters at Walworth Road who gave me access to the wartime Labour NEC minutes; to the staff in the Marx Memorial Library and, above all, to those in charge of the Communist Party archives from which much of the material for this book was collected.

1

1941–2. A NEW STAGE IN THE WAR

In May 1942, the Communist Party of Great Britain held a national conference at the Stoll Theatre in London. The war had been raging for over 2½ years and the conference was called to discuss how victory over the fascist enemy could be won. It was fully understood that the defeat of the fascist powers – Germany, Italy and their ally Japan – was essential if the party's long term aims for the socialist transformation of society were ever to be achieved.

In previous months, membership of the party had shown a dramatic rise – from 22,000 at the end of 1941 to 53,000 four months later. There were 1,323 delegates at the conference representing branches and factory groups. Onlookers were struck by the youth of those involved; over 500 were in their twenties and around another 500 in their thirties, only a handful were over 50.

'We are proud to welcome the new members' said Harry Pollitt, the party's general secretary. 'But we are proud of the old guard, who were in at the birth of this party.' He urged that there should be no counterposing of the new members to the old. 'We are all members of the same great party' he said. 'We have all the responsibility of helping each other, exchanging our experiences, of assisting in reading and studying, of giving our arguments freely and gladly for other comrades to use. The essence of communism is its ability and capacity for collective work.'[1]

The occupations of the delegates highlighted the party's industrial roots. Nearly 700 came from the key war industries: engineering, mining, railways and transport, shipbuilding, electrical and building trades. Topics discussed included the campaign to open a second front in Europe, the need to increase war production, the demand for freedom for colonial countries and the fight to lift the ban on the party's newspaper, the *Daily Worker*.

THE WAR SITUATION

At the time of the conference, the war had reached a new stage. Early in 1940, one country after another had been forced to surrender to Nazi Germany. Denmark and Norway had been overrun, followed by Holland and Belgium. Finally, in the summer of that year came the fall of France and the evacuation of the British Expeditionary Force from Dunkirk. As a result of this, Britain herself was threatened with invasion. It did not come; instead, there was an increase in air combat (which became known as the 'Battle of Britain') followed in September by the 'blitz' – the continuous bombing raids on London and other towns for the rest of 1940, and well into 1941.

Initially, the Communist Party had called for a 'war on two fronts'; against fascism, and also against the Chamberlain government (which had appeased Hitler). But after pressure from the Communist International, it changed its policy, characterising the war as an 'imperialist war' which it could not support. By 1940, it was campaigning for a 'peoples' government' to replace the supporters of fascism in the ruling circles and bring about a 'peoples' peace'. However, on 22 June 1941 had come a dramatic change in the war. Nazi Germany invaded the Soviet Union, and Winston Churchill – Britain's Tory Prime Minister – announced that the British would give whatever help they could to the Soviet people. On 13 July 1941, an alliance between Britain and the Soviet Union was formally announced.

It had long been agreed at Communist International congresses that if any imperialist power attacked the Soviet Union (the world's first – and, at that time, only – socialist country) the workers in every other land must be mobilised to help ensure victory for the Red Army. So, on 22 June Communist Party leaders immediately issued a statement demanding solidarity with the Soviet Union, but reiterating its call for a 'peoples' government'. However, as a result of Churchill's declaration, there was much disagreement among the party leaders, with Pollitt urging support for the Churchill government, while R. Palme Dutt (then the party's acting secretary) disagreed, and secured the backing of the majority on the party's Political Bureau. But then a message was received from Comintern headquarters arguing that the demand to replace the Churchill government with a peoples' government would encourage extreme right-wing pro-Hitlerite and anti-Soviet elements in Britain. So it was that, a few days later, the party announced that the defeat of Hitler was the supreme issue and that it would support the Churchill government in any steps it took towards collaboration with the Soviet Union.[2]

The party was, of course, jeered at for its 'somersault'. The truth was that every other political party was somersaulting also. The country which had for twenty-four years been treated as 'the enemy' had now to be welcomed as an ally.

THE IMPACT OF THE RUSSIAN RESISTANCE

Government circles in Britain did not expect that the alliance with the Soviet Union would last very long. They took for granted the weakness and inadequacy of any nation which tried to abolish capitalism, so they assumed that the German attack on Russia would afford them only a temporary respite. If a powerful capitalist nation like France could not withstand the Nazi onslaught, then it seemed obvious that an inefficient socialist country like Russia would be speedily overcome. As Prime Minister Churchill recalled after the war was over, 'almost all responsible military opinion held that the Russian armies would soon be defeated and largely destroyed.'[3] Such views even appeared publicly in newspapers. 'It is possible' said the *Daily Mail* the day after the USSR was invaded 'that the Soviet Empire may crumble to pieces at the impact of war. The German army may smash the Russian military machine with the same speed and thoroughness with which they smashed the French. Should this be so the lull may last no longer than six to eight weeks.'

Initial retreats on the Russian front appeared to lend substance to such a view. However, unlike all the other countries invaded by Hitler's troops, the Soviet Union did not collapse. The Russians fought back and by November 1941 had halted the German advance. And during that winter of 1941-2 they were to launch a major counter-offensive.

In Britain, these events provoked a sensational change in political attitudes. Ever since the 1917 revolution, Soviet Russia had been treated as the enemy without, and communists as the enemy within. In the minds of the British ruling class, the very existence of a country which had abolished capitalism and set about building socialism constituted a threat to their own supremacy. For if such a country could succeed, it might encourage British working people to follow the same road.

Alone among political parties in Britain, the Communist Party had consistently stood for solidarity with the Soviet Union and had remained convinced that if the first workers' state was smashed, this would put back the cause of world socialism for many decades. For this stand, communists had been continuously attacked, not only by Conservatives and Liberals, but by trade union and Labour leaders. Sneered at and derided by press and radio, they had been singled out for police persecution, and had received prison sentences for their activities. Right-wing figures who dominated the Labour Party treated the communists as untouchables.

Now, for the very first time, the Soviet Union had to be treated as a friend, not an enemy, by those in power. The implications of this u-turn were not at first grasped by some servants of the establishment. At an open air meeting in Plymouth on Sunday 6 July – two weeks after the German invasion of Russia – the police acted according to previous custom and practice, and confiscated all copies of a Communist Party leaflet headed 'Solidarity with the Soviet Union'. It was said they did this on the orders of the Chief Constable, who presumably was unaware that times had changed. The police action greatly enraged the 400 people attending the meeting, who responded by buying up all the communist literature that was left on sale.[4]

Soon after this incident, on the 12 July, military police in Cheltenham took it upon themselves to move on soldiers who had stopped to listen to speakers at a meeting called by the local Communist Party. When Communist MP William Gallacher protested about this, he received a letter from Captain Margesson, Minister of War, regretting that 'incorrect' action had been taken by a 'non-commissioned officer on his own initiative'.[5]

The BBC had adopted the habit of playing the national anthems of Britain's allies before the 9 o'clock news on Sunday evenings. When it failed to add the Soviet Union's national anthem (at that time 'The International') to its list, it was met with furious protests. As was afterwards revealed the BBC was acting on orders from on high.[6] As a consequence of this dispute, the BBC stopped playing national anthems altogether; however, it began to bow to popular opinion in other ways. Thus the works of the Finnish composer, Sibelius, which had been given much prominence during the Finnish war, were rapidly replaced by the music of Russian composers such as Tchaikovsky.

Behind the scenes, Churchill instructed the Ministry of Information 'to consider what action was required to counter the present tendency of the British public to forget the dangers of communism in their enthusiasm over the resistance of Russia'. This continued to be a major preoccupation for the establishment.[7]

The opponents of communism quickly found themselves submerged in a rising tide of thankfulness and admiration for the Red Army, and for the Russian people who were displaying quite unbelievable fighting capacity. Thousands of people all over the country began to attend Anglo-Soviet solidarity meetings; local Anglo-Soviet Committees were set up, often under the auspices of businessmen and members of Chambers of Commerce. When the Prime Minister's wife launched an appeal for an 'Aid to Russia' fund, it met with an unprecedented response. A short film on life in Soviet Russia was shown in many cinemas whose managers arranged for it to be followed by speakers appealing for the fund. Such speakers found their words drowned in applause.

Inevitably, communists were much in demand as speakers for such occasions. This was not surprising, since people outside the party who knew anything at all about the Soviet Union were few and far between. 'A sudden rise into respectability can be almost as disconcerting as the more familiar reverse process', was the comment of one couple involved in the campaign. 'We, whose heads and hearts have been somewhere around the right place these twenty-five years, suddenly find ourselves addressing large and influential audiences on the achievements of the Soviet Union. His Worship the Mayor is in the chair, the leaders of local society are on the platform, where the grand piano, presently to accompany both "God save the King" and the "International" is prophetically draped with the Union Jack and the Red Flag, sociably intertwined.'[8]

THE CAMPAIGN FOR A SECOND FRONT

From the summer of 1941, communists regarded the opening of a second front in Europe as the key to Hitler's defeat. It was, as Pollitt told the conference in May 1942, 'the decisive issue upon which victory or defeat depends'.

The arguments in favour of a second front were indeed obvious. So far, Hitler had always succeeded in picking off his enemies one at a time, and had thus managed to avoid fighting simultaneously on both eastern and western fronts. Now he was concentrating all his major forces on the Russian front, and had left only a few second-rate divisions in northern Europe, thus providing opportunity for attack. Moreover, although the British air force and navy were fully occupied in combatting the enemy, together with some army servicemen who had been posted to North Africa, most of the men in the army were stationed in Britain, doing no fighting at all. There was now at last a chance to smash Hitler; who could say what might happen if such a chance was missed? 'It would be the workers who would suffer most if Hitler won the war' said the well-known communist and member of the woodworkers union, Leo McGree, while addressing an after-work meeting of 3,500 Liverpool shipyard workers in September 1941. 'If we lay down and let the Russians do the fighting, then we are in for terrible times.'9 The meeting passed a resolution demanding the opening of a second front in Europe. Such meetings were taking place all over the country; reports of them appeared regularly in the *Industrial and General Information* bulletin which the party produced after the *Daily Worker* was banned.

At last, on 11 June 1942, following the signing of an Anglo-Russian treaty of alliance came a Foreign Office communique stating that 'full understanding had been reached with regard to the urgent tasks of creating a second front in Europe in 1942'. However, it didn't happen. As leading party member R. Palme Dutt pointed out in the *Labour Monthly* of October 1942, though the Americans wanted a second front in Europe in 1942, Prime Minister Churchill was refusing to agree; he wanted to concentrate on other targets.

Churchill was to get his way, with the result that the second front in Europe was delayed for two years. Some historians have since claimed that Hitler could have been defeated and the war ended much sooner had it not been for this delay.10

Instead, towards the end of October 1942, the British launched a new attack against the German army in North Africa. 'This offensive will receive the unstinted support of the people' Ted Bramley, secretary of the London Communist Party, told a rally in Trafalgar Square where 50,000 people had gathered on 24 October to support the second front campaign. But Bramley emphasized that, welcome as the North African move was, it was only a second front in *Europe* that could bring about Hitler's defeat.

Meanwhile, in November 1942, the Russians started a counter-attack which was to end in the encirclement of 300,000 Axis troops near Stalingrad.

THE ROLE OF THE 'MEN OF MUNICH'

Party members always believed that a major hindrance to the opening of a second front was the 'Men of Munich' – namely, the people who had collaborated with Chamberlain in his pre-war appeasement of Hitler, or who had had pro-fascist leanings at that time, together with those who desperately wanted to avoid fighting alongside the Soviet Union. It had been clear, ever since the German attack on Russia, that there were some in high places who did not enjoy the prospect of a Russian victory. Jack Tanner, president of the Amalgamated Engineering Union, caused a sensation at the Trades Union Congress in September 1941 when he referred to a speech by the Minister for Aircraft Production, Moore-Brabazon, in which he had suggested that if Russia and Germany destroyed each other, Britain would become the dominant power in Europe. 'The impression is still very strong that certain elements desire to switch the war against Russia' said Tanner. Asserting that the Russians needed supplies of all kinds, he asked whether they were likely to get all that could be given them when the Minister of Aircraft Production held such views.[11]

Tanner's revelations were headlined in the press and demands for Moore-Brabazon's removal flooded in, particularly from aircraft workers. In the House of Commons, Churchill implied that the minister's remarks had been 'misconstrued'. 'The Minister of Production had given an explanation of his speech' said Gallacher. 'It was "extemporare" – he had not been thinking what he was saying. But because he was not thinking what he was saying, his inmost thoughts came out.'[12]

Moore-Brabazon was not the only 'Man of Munich' in a high position. A pamphlet entitled *The Second Front* by Bill Wainwright (a young party member who worked at the party's headquarters at 16 King Street) listed others. There was Captain Margesson, Minister for War, who had been Chamberlain's chief whip at the time of Munich and who explained in a newspaper article – and therefore to Hitler – why Britain could not make any military move at that time. There was Lord Croft, also at the War Office, who had once described Spain's fascist dictator Franco as 'a great Christian gentleman', and whose sister, Lady (Edward) Pearson had, before the war, founded a branch of the British Union of Fascists.[13] There was Lord Moyne, Colonial Secretary and Leader of the House of Lords, who explained to that body why it would be 'madness' for Britain to mount a second front.[14]

There was Lord Halifax, formerly Chamberlain's Foreign Secretary, now ambassador to the United States, who had announced to the world that Britain could not invade the Western Front for lack of equipment. There was the Chancellor of the Exchequer, Sir Kingsley Wood, who had been secretary of state for Air in Chamberlain's pre-war government.

Though denouncing the 'clamour' for the second front[15] Churchill did, at the beginning of 1942, take steps to reorganise the government. On 22 February it was announced that Moore-Brabazon, Margesson and Lord Moyne were all to be replaced, while Kingsley Wood was dropped from the War Cabinet – moves which, according to IGI, were 'greeted with relief, enthusiasm and hope by workers everywhere'.[16]

'ORGANISE PRODUCTION FOR VICTORY'

It had been understood from the beginning that a second front could not be mounted unless adequate weapons and equipment were available. This meant that the main topic discussed at the 1942 communist conference was how to increase output in the war industries and in those on which weapons production depended, such as coal, steel, shipbuilding and so on. Until the attack on the Soviet Union, the priority for party members had been building up workplace organisation, improving wages and conditions, and protecting rights already won, some of which were being threatened. But after the campaign for a second front began, problems of output became a major concern.

It was a sphere in which communists could make a significant contribution. Before the war, they had been the driving force in the creation of a shop stewards movement in the aircraft industry. An Aircraft Shop Stewards National Council had been set up, with a journal, *The New Propellor*, which aimed to expand trade union organisation in the workplace, to establish links between shop stewards in different plants belonging to the same company, and also between shop stewards committees functioning in different firms, but in the same district. In 1940, the organisation had been extended to cover factories other than aircraft, and an 'Engineering and Allied Trades Shop Stewards National Council' had been set up to replace the earlier body. Secretary of the new National Council was a party member, Len Powell, and its journal, *The New Propellor*, continued to be edited by a communist of long standing, Peter Zinkin.

The influence of the party had been grudgingly recognised in a confidential Home Office memorandum in 1941: 'in industry, the Communist Party has obtained a representation among shop stewards out of all proportion to the strength of the party in the factories'.[17] Now this influence was to be directed towards solving production problems.

From August 1941 onwards, the Shop Stewards National Council was campaigning for the creation of Joint Production Committees at factories. On these committees, both workers and management would be represented, and their function would be to consult and advise on ways of overcoming production difficulties.

In his report to the 1942 conference, Pollitt stressed the need for effective state control of war industries, and for 'independence of controls from private business interests in the commodity or industry concerned' and for 'labour participation in the controls', 'both centrally and regionally, as well as through Joint Production Committees in the factories and places of work.' He said that it was necessary to 'fight for the election of the most militant and politically conscious representatives to the Production Committees so that they are not viewed with suspicion by the workers'. Arguing that Production Committees could lead to improved methods of organisation, he said: 'Those who say in the drive for increasing production that we are only "playing the bosses game" are being refuted by the powerful growth of the Shop Stewards Movement, and the opening of the way to their further great progress.'[18]

The party, indeed, always argued that participation in Joint Production Committees could go hand in hand with a great strengthening of workplace organisation. In this it was to be proved quite right.

THE FIGHT FOR THE DAILY WORKER

At the time of the party conference, the campaign to remove the ban on the *Daily Worker* was reaching a high point. The ban had been imposed in January 1941 under Defence Regulation 2D which enabled the Home Secretary to suppress any newspaper which was 'systematically fomenting opposition to the war'. Initially, the Cabinet had hesitated over such a move, but when, in October 1940, Labour leader Herbert Morrison was made Home Secretary in the Coalition Government, there could be no more uncertainty. Morrison had always been the most ardent anti-communist witch-hunter in the

Labour leadership, and now he saw his chance. He personally proposed that the *Daily Worker* should be suppressed and secured the agreement of the Cabinet for such a step.[19]

Following the ban, the party had set up an 'Industrial and General Information News Agency' run by some former members of the *Daily Worker* staff, whose function was to supply news stories to the press and send a daily bulletin to shop stewards and others, thereby maintaining the *Daily Worker*'s network of worker correspondants. At the same time, a campaign to lift the ban was launched under the auspices of the 'Daily Worker Leagues' whose national organiser was George Allison. Even before the Soviet Union was invaded, some 800 organisations had passed resolutions demanding that the ban be removed, including annual conferences of some important trade unions such as the Amalgamated Engineering Union.

When, in June 1941, the Soviet Union was attacked, and the Communist Party expressed its support for the government in any act designed to defeat Hitler, it was obvious that the grounds for banning the *Daily Worker* no longer existed; if allowed to reappear, it would not now be open to the accusation that it was 'fomenting opposition to the war' since the Communist Party was doing everything possible in support of the war effort. It was widely assumed that the paper would be allowed to be published again; however, these assumptions were quickly proved to be unfounded. Morrison, when asked in the Commons on 24 July 1941 whether he was now prepared to lift the ban, refused to do so, saying disdainfully that he welcomed the decision of the Communist Party to aid Russia 'by giving the war effort assistance which they previously were not willing to give to their own country' but that 'it would be premature and rash to treat the latest of these sudden conversions as proof of a lasting change of heart'.

Morrison was apparently among those who expected the Russian resistance to be short-lived. According to Gallacher, he told people who interviewed him on the matter not to encourage the campaign to lift the ban because Russia might go out of the war at any time, and the *Daily Worker* would reverse its policy again.[20]

After it became clear that an immediate Russian collapse was not a realistic prospect, Morrison was obliged to shift his ground. On 2 October 1941, he told a questioner that 'the view of the Government is that the Communist Party is not loyal to this country.' To which Gallacher retorted: 'Is the Minister expressing the opinion that the friends of Hitler were loyal to this country? Is it not the case that there is no legal reason why the *Daily Worker* should be suppressed at the present time?' He got no answer and, despite the fact that the legal justification for the ban had disappeared, Morrison continued for the next ten months to resist demands for lifting it. He consistently refused to meet deputations of shop stewards and others on the question, though, after the Executive of the Mineworkers Federation had protested at the ban, he found himself obliged to discuss the matter with a group of miners' MPs. On 27 November, an MP asked him to circulate a list of the national trade unions which had urged him to lift the ban. He thereupon printed an incomplete list of 18, which led to William Rust, the paper's former editor, to name another 13 which Morrison had omitted. Rust pointed out that the membership of unions now pressing for the ban to be withdrawn totalled 2,185,065.

The Daily Worker Leagues sponsored some huge district conferences at which the engineering and miners' unions were officially represented, and they issued broadsheets which by 1942 reached a combined circulation of 2 million. The campaign received support from newspapers such as the Liberal *News Chronicle* and *Manchester Guardian*, the *Daily Mirror* and, towards the end, even the right wing *Daily Express* – perhaps because its owner, Lord Beaverbrook, who had been Minister of Aircraft Production, was aware of the positive role played by communists in the aircraft factories. However, Morrison's stand received support from those who had reservations about any alliance with the Soviet Union. 'The Munichites fought us to the very end' said Bill Rust after it was all over.[21]

Morrison remained adamant throughout the campaign but on 28 May 1942, he suffered a spectacular defeat; the Labour Party annual conference supported a resolution calling for the lifting of the ban. Moved by Percy Collick of the train-drivers' union ASLEF, the resolution was carried on a card vote by 1,244,000 to 1,231,000.

A few days later, in response to questioning from a number of MPs, Morrison made clear to the House of Commons that his position remained as before, and that he was not prepared to accede to the demand to lift the ban, even though this was now the official policy of his own Party.[22] However, the National Executive of the Labour Party met on 5 June and agreed that something should be done: so they sent Morrison a copy of the resolution asking for a detailed reply or, alternatively, that he receive a deputation from among them.

Morrison answered by repeating all the old arguments – that the

Communist Party had originally discouraged cooperation in the war effort; that, though the party had now changed its line, it was not unreasonable to be cautious 'in view of the variations and uncertainties of the Party's attitude'. He said that if a deputation came to see him 'I fear that I could not add to what I have said in this letter. In the circumstances, the Executive may not wish to pursue that alternative'.

But the Executive did pursue it and on 2 July, had a lengthy interview with Morrison[23] who at last decided to change course. He raised the matter with the Cabinet and got their agreement for the lifting of the ban. He was by this time, aware that if he continued to suppress the *Daily Worker* he risked an almost certain vote of censure at the Trades Union Congress to be held in September. At the last possible moment, he took steps to avoid such humiliation. On 26 August 1942, the Order banning the paper was revoked.

The *Daily Worker*'s printing plant had been demolished in an air-raid just after the ban was imposed. Nevertheless, it took no more than ten days to purchase an old printing press near Grays Inn Road in London, to issue a call for £50,000 to pay for it (the sum was collected within three months) and to mobilise new staff, even though many of its former staff were now in the forces.

On 7 September 1942, the first day of the TUC annual congress, the paper reappeared. 'Out again' wrote Bill Rust, once more established as its editor. 'They key turns joyously in the lock of Cell 2D and the prisoner bounds joyously into freedom.' As the headline put it: 'The Blackout is over.'

2

RELATIONS WITH THE LABOUR PARTY AND THE COMINTERN 1941–3

The tendency for hostility to communists to recede as a result of the Russian achievements on the fighting front, was a matter of continuing concern to the Labour leaders. The issue arose as early as July 1941, following a letter from R. Palme Dutt to Labour Party headquarters suggesting consultation on 'associated action in the prosecution of the war'. The proposal was of course rejected by the National Executive Committee and a public declaration that 'no association with the Communist Party is possible' was issued jointly with the TUC on 31 July.[1]

It soon emerged that this declaration was being disregarded in many localities where Labour Party members were cooperating with communists in campaigns to promote Anglo-Soviet solidarity. Such joint activity was in violation of long-standing rules, one of which, adopted in 1934, stated that 'united action with the Communist Party or organisations ancillary or subsidiary thereto without the sanction of the National Executive Committee is incompatible with membership of the Labour Party'. Thus many organisations, such as the League Against Imperialism, or the Relief Committee for the Victims of German Fascism had, during the '30s, been put on a 'proscribed' list; no member of the Labour Party could belong to them and those who appeared as speakers at their meetings could be threatened with expulsion.[2]

Initially, most of the public meetings called to promote Anglo-Soviet friendship were either arranged directly by local Communist Party branches, or were organised under the auspices of the Russia Today Society, a body long since placed on the forbidden list by the Labour leaders. From 1941 onwards, thousands of people were flocking to these meetings, and soon an Anglo-Soviet Medical Aid Fund was set up, with the Dean of Canterbury as one of its chief promoters. The Dean had always been a close associate of the Communist Party, so it was not surprising that the Labour leaders instantly denounced it as a 'body ancillary to the Communist Party' and added it to its fast-growing list of proscribed organisations.

But the Labour leaders' dilemma was not confined to such bodies. A key aim of the Communist Party was to broaden the campaign so as to involve not only sections of the labour movement but groups from outside. To this end, party members often took the initiative in getting local Anglo-Soviet Friendship Committees set up, on which councillors, businessmen from Chambers of Commerce, members of employers' organisations, and even representatives from local Conservative bodies might serve. The Labour leaders had never tried to prevent their members associating with Conservatives (after all, they themselves were collaborating with Conservatives in the Coalition Government), but the involvement of communists in such local committees made them taboo. So, in November 1941, some elaborate 'guidelines' were sent out from headquarters which, in effect, advised Labour Party members not to appear on public platforms or address meetings unless these had been called under the auspices of *either* the Labour Party, the Ministry of Information, or – in certain special cases – by the 'civic authorities'.[3] Even before these 'guidelines' were despatched, it was clear what the results would be. Thus, in October 1941, the Tory Mayor of Hendon, in north London, had been persuaded to call a meeting of all local organisations in order to set up an Anglo-Soviet Friendship Committee. The two joint secretaries appointed at its inaugural meeting were a councillor from the Conservative Party alongside a well-known local communist, Marjorie Pollitt. People serving on the committee included five representatives of local churches, two local employers, two 'traders' and two trade unionists representing the local trades council. The one organisation conspicuous by its absence was the local Labour Party.[4]

At the Labour Party annual conference in May 1942, a speaker from Monmouth complained that the guidelines had caused chaos in the localities and were unworkable. 'In many parts of the country, mayors and chairmen of councils have, in response to public demands, inaugurated Anglo-Soviet Friendship Committees' he claimed. 'When a Mayor does that sort of thing, he cannot issue a public appeal to people to support such a committee, and say that only those people who are not members of the Communist Party shall join.'[5]

An attempt was made at this conference to remove the ban on Labour-Communist cooperation; a speaker from the Rusholme Labour Party in Lancashire argued the case, saying:

> Decide what you will, in practice we are more and more working together with the members of other parties, including Communists. We ask for these matters to be left to our discretion.[6]

The attempt was unsuccessful, unlike the demand to lift the ban on the *Daily Worker* which was supported by a sizeable proportion of the trade union block vote.

However, the Labour leadership's difficulties continued, as was shown only one month later when Labour's national agent reported to a sub-committee on the following items:

(a) correspondence with Sidney Silverman (Labour MP) who had addressed a meeting in company with D.N. Pritt (expelled Labour MP) and Ted Bramley (Secretary of London Communist Party)

(b) correspondence with Luke Hogan (Labour leader on Liverpool City Council) who had appeared on Communist Party platforms;

(c) correspondence with Eleanor Steward (Labour NEC member) concerning the appearance of two Labour MPs on Communist Party platforms in Glasgow

(d) correspondence concerning the association of members of the Gloucester Labour Party with Subversive Organisations

(e) correspondence with York Labour Party on its association with the Russia Today Society at a meeting addressed by D.N. Pritt.[7]

At the end of 1942, the Communist Party announced it would renew its application for affiliation to the Labour Party. The Labour leaders were faced with a further fight to maintain the political isolation of the Communist Party.

THE AFFILIATION CAMPAIGN

Though affiliated trade union membership of the Labour Party remained at a high rate, the number of individual members had fallen from over 400,000 in 1939 to less than 220,000 at the end of 1942.

According to Labour's NEC, this decline was due to war conditions – the difficulties in collecting dues and the drain on membership from military call-up – and also to the absence of elections.[8] The truth was that any party whose primary objective was electioneering, was bound to suffer when no elections were taking place. Young people tended not to join the Labour Party – indeed, onlookers at the 1942 Labour Party annual conference were struck by the ageing appearance of many of the delegates.

In contrast, the Communist Party was growing fast. It had never given priority to electioneering, but was always endeavouring to spread the socialist message, and to generate public interest in the political and economic issues of the day. So, despite some overall loss due to military call-ups, its membership did not fall, largely owing to the continual recruitment of young people. By December 1942, the membership was recorded as 56,000 – one member for every four individual members of the Labour Party.

The Communist Party in Britain was however, faced with a quite different problem from any which confronted Communist Parties in other countries. Unlike the Social Democratic Parties on the continent, the Labour Party had originally been set up by the trade unions. Though it was a loose federation which included 'socialist societies' and individual members, the trade unions had always had the dominant voice in Labour Party policy. At the 1943 Labour Party Annual Conference, the trade union delegates controlled 80 per cent of the card vote. The voting structure was as follows:

Organisation	Number	Number of delegates	Card Vote
Trade unions	59	364	2,210,000
Socialist societies	5	5	6,000
Co-operative society	1	6	26,000
Labour parties	444	449	474,000
Federations	17	17	17,000
	526	841	2,733,000

Note: The card vote of each delegate from local labour parties counted as at least 1,000 even when the number represented was much less. The actual individual membership in 1943 was 218,783. The card vote of trade union delegates was based on the numbers paying the political levy.[9]

Throughout its existence, the Labour Party had remained the party of the trade unions. Yet trade union activists who were communists were debarred from direct participation in their trade union's own political party. The Communist Party's predecessor, the British Socialist Party, had been affiliated to the Labour Party as one of its 'socialist societies'; but the Communist Party had never been allowed to follow in its footsteps. The largest among the group of 'socialist societies' had originally been the Independent Labour Party which had disaffiliated in 1932. By 1940 the group had dwindled to five, the biggest of which was the Fabian Society with less than 2,000 members. But these socialist societies still had the right to table resolutions for Labour Party annual conferences, to argue their point of view in the localities, their members also being allowed to stand as Labour candidates.

The Communist Party's attempt to become an affiliated 'socialist society' had been rejected in the 'twenties and again in 1936. Now the Central Committee decided to try again. So, on 18 December 1942, Harry Pollitt sent a letter to J.S. Middleton, Secretary of the Labour Party, asking him to place the application for affiliation before the Labour Party Annual Conference in June 1943. In this letter, he said that the experience gained in the struggle against fascism had shown the tremendous part that a united working class movement could play, not only in winning the war, but in solving the problems of reconstruction when peace had been restored. He said: 'The Communist Party is fully prepared to accept all the obligations of being affiliated to the Labour Party and to loyally carry out all the decisions reached at its annual conference.' He proposed that representatives of both parties should meet to discuss the matter.

There could be little doubt what the reaction of the Labour Party's National Executive would be. At its meeting on 27 January 1943, Sam Watson (who represented the Miners Federation) suggested that the Communist Party be asked whether, if they became affiliated, they would still consider themselves bound by the instructions of the Communist International. He was supported by Emanual Shinwell MP, but his proposal was defeated by 16 votes to 2. Harold Laski (one of the Labour left at constant loggerheads with his colleagues) then urged that Communist Party representatives be invited to meet the NEC to discuss the matter. He was supported by Barbara Ayrton Gould, but his motion was lost by 15 votes to 4. The NEC then decided – again by 15 votes to 4 – that they could not recommend acceptance of the affiliation proposal.[10]

In his reply to the Communist Party telling them of this decision, Middleton advanced one reason only: that, as a section of the

Communist International, the CPGB was 'unable to accept of its own free will the decisions of the Annual Party Conference' because it was subject to the constitution and rules of the Communist International which could not be reconciled with those of the Labour Party.

It was of course true that most of the Communist Party leaders believed that policies adopted by the ECCI must be adhered to, as was shown by the decisions taken in 1939 and 1941 on the attitude to the war. However they had for some years been planning a revision of the rules which would mean that the party was responsible for its own decisions. In answer to Middleton, Pollitt insisted that the Party 'determines its policy on the basis of the decisions of its democratically elected Congresses, and through the democratically elected Central Committee which appoints its officials.' He argued that acceptance of the Labour Party's constitution by the CPGB would involve no conflict with the terms of the CI constitution, and suggested that the difficulties raised by Middleton should be subject to negotiation.

In response, Middleton rejected the argument that the CPGB decided its own policies, and quoted the Communist International's own rules under which the policies of each of its 'sections' were decided by its World Congresses, while, in between, the ECCI gave instructions which were obligatory on all these sections. 'The Communist Party is neither independent, self-governing, nor self-supporting' he wrote.

In his answer, dated 18 March, Pollitt took up the timeworn allegation that the CPGB was not 'self-supporting' – in other words, that it was financed from Moscow. 'The Communist Party of Great Britain and all its activities are entirely financed by the voluntary support of its members and wide sections of the people ... who are in sympathy with its aims' he wrote.[11]

Middleton was indeed faced with the same problem which had proved such an awkward stumbling block for Herbert Morrison – Home Secretary – when he found that the Home Office, with all its resources, had been unable to discover any evidence that the party or its paper were then being financed from outside sources.[12] All the same Middleton was determined to keep that particular story going.

Pollitt challenged Middleton to 'examine the dues paid by membership of the Communist Party in comparison with what the Labour Party received', and also emphasized the financial support from workers in factories and at demonstrations in addition to the huge sales of communist literature. 'There is no hidden mystery here, but, on the contrary, a splendid public political achievement' which, he said 'could be emulated by the Labour Party if it carried out the same forms of mass activity.'

On 21 February 1943, the *Daily Herald* published a Labour Party statement reiterating accusations concerning the Comintern, but adding others. In reply, the Communist Party dealt with the argument that its policies were different from that of the Labour party, pointing out that, on the contrary, the party supported the socialist aims set out in Clause 4 of the Labour Party's constitution (i.e. common ownership of the means of production, distribution and exchange). To the charge that communist activity in working class organisations was 'disturbing and disruptive', the party underlined the contribution its members had made in strengthening trade unions and extending payment of the political levy. In response to the allegation that the communist policy in 1939-41 (when it characterised the war as 'imperialist') could have led to the victory of fascism, the party responded by stating that it had always been in the forefront of the fight against fascism unlike the Labour Party which had supported non-intervention in Spain and applauded Chamberlain at the time of the Munich agreement.

By this time the party's campaign for affiliation was well under way, and it was claimed on 10 March that 1,432 organisations had passed resolutions in support. Most of these were of course trade union branches, but everyone knew that such resolutions could go before local Labour parties and could lead to pressure on higher committees.

The Labour leaders were alarmed at this growth in support, so from mid-March the *Daily Herald* began to publish regular articles, letters and leaders devoted to undermining the communist case. A 2d pamphlet 'The Communist Party and the War – a record of hypocrisy and treachery to the workers of Europe' was issued from Labour's headquarters, while its Press and Publicity Department (which, during 1942 had produced only one leaflet and appeared to be in the doldrums) suddenly came to life and published three leaflets entitled respectively: 'Where is the Communist Party Balance Sheet?' 'Communist Propaganda and Labour Party Facts' and 'Shall Communists Smash the Labour Party?'

Despite this, several union conferences went on record in support of communist affiliation, and by mid-May, organisations which had passed such resolutions numbered over 3,000.

The chief argument used by the Labour Party Executive continued to be that, owing to its relationship with the Comintern, the Communist Party was a puppet manipulated from abroad. But, in May 1943 the foundation on which the whole argument against affiliation had been built up suddenly collapsed, when it was announced that the Presidium of the Executive Committee of the Communist International was proposing the dissolution of that body.

THE PARTY AND THE COMINTERN

At the time of the CI announcement, the Communist Party in Britain was about to adopt changes in its own rules which might counteract allegations that it was under orders from abroad. (Such changes had indeed been in preparation some four years earlier, timed for the 16th Congress planned for October 1939. But then the war had started and the congress had to be postponed). Early in 1943, it was decided that the 16th Congress should be convened. Initially announced for April, it was put off until July 1943 so as to take place after the Labour Party conference. In preparation for the conference and to ensure that it was a subject for discussion, the Central Committee in March 1943 once more circulated new draft rules which, on paper, would appear to alter the party's relationship with the Comintern.

The CI constitution had been adopted in 1928. According to Clause 1 the Communist International was a 'World Communist Party' and the various parties affiliated to it, including the Communist Party of Great Britain, ranked as 'sections' of this 'world party'. According to Clause 8, the supreme decision-making body was the World Congress at which all parties ('sections') were represented. In between congresses, the Executive Committee of the Comintern (ECCI) on which the British Party had had two representatives during the 'thirties had the right to give instructions to all its 'sections' and its decisions were binding.

This constitution had never been formally changed since, though after the 7th World Congress in 1935, the rules had been interpreted more flexibly than before, and the various parties had in practice assumed responsibility for decisions relating to their own countries.

The rules of the Communist Party of Great Britain had been adopted in 1932 and had also never been formally revised, though in practice they had changed a lot – for example, the factory and street 'cells' and 'Local Party Committees' provided for in these 1932 rules had by 1936 given way to workplace or ward 'groups' joined together in local 'branches'. The draft rules circulated in 1939 had not only incorporated these structural changes already in operation, but had also updated those sections relating to the Comintern.

Thus, in the 1939 draft the party was no longer classed as a 'section' of the Communist International, while the obligation on members to accept the programme, structure, and decisions of the CI (embodied in Clause 2 of the 1932 rules) was deleted. Indeed the Communist International was not referred to until Rule 11 where, under the subhead 'affiliations', the following words were proposed:

> The Communist Party of Great Britain is affiliated to the Communist International which consists of the Communist Parties of all countries. It participates in Congresses of the Communist International and is represented on its Executive Committee. Resolutions and decisions of the International Congresses shall be considered and acted upon by the National Congress, or between congresses, by the Central Committee.

The new draft, circulated in March 1943, went even further than that of 1939 in asserting the party's independence. In Rule 1 it was laid down that 'The Communist Party of Great Britain is part of the British Labour Movement' and the Party's own aims were then listed. The first of these was 'to strengthen the organisation, political understanding and activity of the whole working class and to win support for the conquest of power and the development of socialism'. Rule 6 stated that decisions of the Party Congress or of the Central Committee elected by it, were binding on all members, and Rule 11 emphasised that 'the National Congress is the highest authority of the party'. There was only one mention of the Communist International: in Rule 12 the party was said to be 'affiliated to the Communist International which consists of Communist Parties of all countries' but then went on to say that it aimed to be affiliated to the Labour Party and to other bodies 'where the association is in the best interests of the working class'.

These draft rules were despatched to party branches in March 1943 for discussion and amendment. Unbeknown to the CPGB the action coincided with meetings taking place in Moscow at CI headquarters where a proposal to dissolve the Communist International altogether was under consideration. There were no British representatives present at these discussions; the war had made their presence impossible. However, on 13 May 1943, the proposal was finally put before the

Presidium of the ECCI and agreed to. On 15 May, a resolution advocating the dissolution of the CI was despatched to those Communist Parties which could be contacted.

This resolution stressed the positive contribution made by the Comintern in the past, but said that its organisational structure no longer allowed it to respond to the increasing complexity of problems in individual countries. The resolution stated that, long before the war, it had become clear that any international centre was bound to meet with insuperable obstacles in attempting to solve the problems of the movement in each individual country. It pointed out that a number of other parties had already suggested the dissolution of the CI but that, under war conditions, it was impossible to convene a congress to discuss the matter. It therefore submitted the proposal to its 'sections' for approval separately. By 8 June, the 31 Communist Parties able to communicate with the CI had expressed their support and, on 19 June, the dissolution was formally announced.

Among the 31 which approved the dissolution was, of course, the British party. The Central Committee agreed to the CI's proposals on 24 May, and said that it would recommend their acceptance to its coming congress. Its decision was to be endorsed by the Party's 16th Congress held in July.

The Impact of the CI Dissolution

Faced with the fact that its main argument against communist affiliation had disappeared, Labour's NEC found itself obliged to fall back on what Pollitt had previously described as 'a stale rehash of all that has gone before'.[13] An emergency meeting of the NEC was convened on 28 May from which a statement was issued reiterating opposition to affiliation on all the old grounds e.g. (1) that communists believed in 'dictatorship' not parliamentary democracy (2) that if the communist's anti-war line in 1939-41 had succeeded, Britain would have been crushed by fascist hordes (3) if affiliated, communists would have access to every Labour Party meeting, and would aim to make the Labour Party adjust itself to communist attitudes (4) only disruption would result (5) if the Communist Party believed in unity, it should dissolve itself.

By 11 June, 3,484 organisations had passed resolutions in support of affiliation including 15 union executives, 190 trade union district committees, 2,765 trade union branches, 136 trades councils, 241

Labour Party organisations (including 91 Divisional Labour Parties).

The Labour Party Conference opened in London on Monday 14 June, and the debate on affiliation took up most of the ensuing Wednesday morning. The motion in support was moved by Will Lawther on behalf of the Mineworkers Federation who objected to suggestions that communist affiliation would 'break our Party'. He said that was not the experience of the Mineworkers Federation in meeting with members of the Communist Party as trade unionists. And he paid tribute to the work of communist Arthur Horner, who was president of the South Wales Miners. The motion was seconded by W.C. Rowe, representing the Leek (Staffordshire) Divisional Labour Party, who argued that what stood in the way of unity was 'prejudice, the mortal enemy of freedom'. The secretary of the Constructional Engineering Union, J. Stanley, said that his own union had recently made rapid strides as a result of the activities of the communists on his Executive.[14]

It was of course a foregone conclusion that the motion for affiliation would be lost. Though those voting for it included some important trade unions – not only the mineworkers, but the Amalgamated Engineering Union, the train drivers union – ASLEF, the Society of Pottery Workers, the National Union of Public Employees, and half a dozen smaller unions – it was obvious that the two General Workers Unions which were dominated by the right wing and commanded between them a block vote of nearly 600,000 would be against. Moreover, the party had not succeeded in winning over two large unions in which it had considerable influence: the National Union of Railwaymen and the Distributive Workers Union. The upshot was a vote of 712,000 for the motion, but 1,951,000 against. In other words, one quarter of the votes were cast in favour.

THE COMMUNIST PARTY CONGRESS

The 16th Congress of the party took place in London on Saturday and Sunday, 3/4 July 1943. There were 406 delegates, of whom 300 were men and 106 women. The average age was 33. 399 belonged to trade unions and of these, members of the Amalgamated Engineering Union were the most numerous, followed by the Transport and General Workers Union, the Clerical and Administrative Workers Union, the railway unions, and the mining unions.

William Gallacher MP in his opening address from the chair, stated:

'This Congress meets at a time when the fate of humanity is in the balance'. He spoke of the 'heroic and epic defence of Stalingrad' which had been followed by a winter offensive ending early in 1943 with the 'crushing defeat and elimination of the German Sixth Army'. 'The defeat of the Germans before Moscow in the winter of 1941 should have been the signal for heavy blows from this side; unfortunately, our political and military leaders were expecting the fall of Moscow, not the defeat of the Germans' he said. The defence of Leningrad during 17 months 'should have inspired our leaders to action'; 'instead they waited and kept on waiting, speculating on how long the Red Army or the Soviet Union would remain in the war.'

Both Gallacher and Pollitt argued that the triumph of the Red Army at Stalingrad, together with victories of the allies in north Africa, demonstrated that, with a speedy second front in Europe the danger of a prolonged war could be averted. 'The whole future progress of civilisation demands the complete extermination of every vestige of fascist thought, power and organisation' said Pollitt. 'To prevent this, Hitler and the friends of fascism in Britain and America will play for time, will try and prolong the war, with the aim of achieving a compromise peace. That aim, the second front in Europe alone can destroy.'[16]

The Congress discussed and endorsed a memorandum on trade union policy in the war against fascism. It condemned the government's repressive actions in India, and pledged solidarity with the colonial peoples. A major item concerned the social, economic and political measures needed on the home front (including legislation on social insurance, housing, health and education) which would not only help to satisfy immediate needs, but could pave the way to a new Britain after the war. 'There can be no separation, no sharp dividing line, between the war and after the war' said Dutt. 'The future grows out of the present.'[17]

New rules were adopted. Though they incorporated all the major changes suggested in the draft which had been sent out the previous March, there had been numerous other amendments suggested by branches since it had been circulated, and many of these were also accepted. Thus it was decided that, as the organisation was no longer part of a 'world party' the name 'The Communist Party' would replace the former one, 'The Communist Party of Great Britain' (though some years later the old name was to be reinstated).

Another verbal change meant that what had hitherto been known as the 'Central Committee' was to be termed the 'Executive Committee'.

Much more significant than any change in terminology was the fact that the names of the 30 members elected to this Executive were, for the first time since the 1920s made public. The party thus disposed of what remained of its semi-secret practices, and emerged as a party solely responsible for its own actions.

3

INDUSTRIAL WORK 1941–4

Ever since the party came into existence, the workplace had been regarded as the most important area of activity. It was at a time when two-thirds of the occupied population were manual workers, classed as 'skilled', 'semi-skilled' and 'unskilled'. Most of the trade unions were divided into these occupational categories, and one of the party's priorities was the fostering of workplace solidarity between different groups and different unions with the aim of gaining concessions out of the employers. But party activity did not end here. Linked to the struggle around 'bread and butter' questions was the fight for political understanding, the endeavour to stimulate action on current political issues while explaining what was wrong with capitalist society, and the need to replace it with a socialist system, and how this could be achieved.

From June 1941 onwards, the defeat of Hitler was seen as the paramount political issue of the day; a victory for the fascist powers would put back the cause of socialism for generations, while their downfall could open up prospects of socialist advances everywhere. But Hitler could not be defeated without weapons; it followed that actions which would impede their output must be avoided – indeed, everything possible must be done to increase arms production. Did this mean bowing to the wishes of the employers? The party argued that it often meant the opposite since, for many employers, the need to safeguard their firms' post-war position took precedent over current production problems.

THE WARTIME FRAMEWORK

Only with great difficulty had the British economy been brought on to a war footing which, among other things, necessitated the planned allocation of scarce resources. In May 1940, the government had armed itself with wide powers of control which had been directed primarily at the workforce. For example, under the Essential Work Order, those employed in 'scheduled undertakings' – mainly engineering, shipbuild-ing, chemicals, coalmining etc – were legally prohibited from changing their jobs, while those in 'non-essential' work could be directed into 'work of national importance'.

But the controls imposed on employers were a good deal less restrictive than those applied to the workers, as was emphasised in an 'Urgent Memorandum on Production' produced by the Communist Party in March 1942. The inadequacies of a system geared to the profit motive and dependent on 'market forces' was glaringly revealed in the arms industries where planned production had become essential. Here, the responsibility for the placing of contracts was in the hands of a number of seemingly uncoordinated government departments. The Ministry of Supply was mainly responsible for weapons and equipment required by the army, the Admiralty for the needs of the navy, and the Ministry of Aircraft Production for those of the airforce. These bodies tended to compete with one another for limited industrial capacity, and the firms concerned were not above playing off one government department against another. The wartime controls were in many instances manned by representatives of the leading companies involved, who thought in terms of furthering their firms' own interests. Many were determined to hold on to their trade secrets and were not prepared to share technical information.

Since early 1941, managerial inefficiency had been the focus of much public criticism. Some of it was attributed to abuse of the notorious 'cost plus 10 per cent' system whereby a firm received what it had spent in carrying out a contract *plus* an agreed percentage of that cost in profit. So the higher the total cost, the higher the profit, which meant that it might actually benefit a firm to keep the workforce hanging about idle on overtime and Sunday pay.

THE RISE OF JOINT PRODUCTION COMMITTEES

By August 1941, the engineering shop stewards' journal, the *New Propellor*, was reporting that demands for the creation of joint production committees were coming from many works. In Manchester, it said, seventy-one delegates, representing forty factories, had held a conference at which complaints of mismanagement and inefficiency were made. Many similar meetings were being reported from elsewhere and, on 19 October 1941, the Engineering and Allied

Trades Shop Stewards National Council held a conference on the subject. It was attended by 1,237 delegates representing over 300 workplaces which between them employed about half a million workers.

The conference was chaired by Joe Goss, a shop steward's convenor and member of the London District Commitee of the Communist Party. The opening address was delivered by another well-known party member, Walter Swanson, convenor of shop stewards at Napiers factory. 'Every one of us has to approach the problem of production from a new angle' he said. 'And we believe we will get the best results from our conference, not merely by discussing the waste, mismanagement, and inefficiency of present methods of control and direction of production, but what we can do and will do to increase production from our side and, in doing so, help to effect changes which will go right through industry even to the top.' He made a call for the formation of Joint Production Committees.[1]

The discussion which followed was highly revealing. A Manchester aircraft worker claimed that thousands of hours were being wasted through lack of work and that there was little evidence of intelligent planning. This was supported by a delegate from Coventry who said that men and women were waiting around doing nothing for days on end; similar stories came from Southampton and Clydeside shipyard workers. Many examples were given of bad planning within factories and consequent hold-ups, together with failure to repair machines which had broken down.

The conference, which received wide publicity, adopted a list of proposals for the removal of grievances (such as bad ventilation and sanitation, inadequate canteens etc) to be submitted to the appropriate government committee. But the setting up of production committees in every workplace was seen as the most important aim.

A few on the far left disagreed with this call, alleging that participation of shop stewards in 'Joint Production Committees' signified class collaboration. Thus Rachel Ryan, a delegate from West London, argued that where JPCs were set up 'the bosses will attempt to use them as a means to paralyse any independent action on the part of the working class'. This was not the view held by the majority of the delegates; it was, however, an argument being publicised by some members of the Independent Labour Party and by some Trotskyist groups who were accusing the Communist Party of abandoning the class struggle. In the December issue of the *Labour Monthly* Johnny

Campbell – a leading communist – joined issue with 'leftists' on this subject. He suggested that the vast changes in industry could not be met by clinging to restrictive practices. 'The working class will enormously increase its political and industrial strength if, instead of hanging back, it takes the lead in mobilising the people for an overwhelmingly powerful anti-fascist war effort.' In this forecast he was to be proved right; Joint Production Committees did not lead to any weakening of trade union organisation; on the contrary, shop floor trade union organisation was to emerge by the end of the war, far more powerfully entrenched than ever before.

In fact, the main opposition to Joint Production Committees came from the employers who initially resisted them, looking on them as an interference in their 'right to manage'. In November 1941, the AEU Executive invited the Engineering Employers Federation to discuss the matter, but at the subsequent meetings the employers made clear that they were not prepared to agree to the proposal. According to the reminiscences of Wal Hannington (the former leader of the unemployed workers movement who was by this time National AEU organiser) the employers' representative at these discussions insisted that he 'was not going to be a party to handing over the production of the factory and problems concerning production to shop stewards or anyone else; there could be no divided authority in running the works.'[2]

However, in February 1942, the Ministry of Supply agreed with the unions to set up Joint Production Committees in Royal Ordnance factories. After this and – it was widely assumed – as a result of government pressure behind the scenes, the engineering employers at last gave in, and on 18 March 1942, agreement was reached for JPCs which would have an equal number of representatives from management and workers; the workers' side was to be elected by a ballot vote of all the workers in their respective departments; their functions were 'to consult and advise on matters relating to production' – for example, maximum utilisation of existing machinery; upkeep of fixtures, tools etc. It was specifically laid down that the committees should *not* discuss wages or other matters dealt with through existing machinery.

Although the Employers' Federation signed this agreement, many of its members resisted its application, and JPCs were only set up after much pressure from the workforce.

THE COAL INDUSTRY

Coal mining was crucial to arms production. The steelworks depended on coal; electricity power stations, on which all factories depended, were fuelled almost entirely by coal; so were the railway engines needed to transport supplies. Yet, by 1941, the coal industry was in a state of crisis, producing far less than before the war. This was mainly due to the fall of France in June 1940; an important coal export market was cut off, and the colliery owners had closed pits which had been producing for export. Moreover, as the party's memorandum pointed out, they were concentrating work on less productive seams in order to save the most profitable seams for after the war. As a result, thousands of miners had become unemployed; many left the coal fields, some being called up into the armed forces, with most being transferred into other employment where they were usually better paid and working in far more congenial surroundings. By 1941, the number of miners had fallen from the pre-war level of 760,000 to 697,000. As new war factories came into operation, the demand for coal began to outstrip the supply. In the spring of 1942, the government took belated action and, under the Essential Work Order, coal-miners were prohibited from leaving the pits, while ex-miners working elsewhere were ordered to return. However, far fewer were brought back than expected; moreover, a ruling that ex-miners be released from the armed forces was resisted by the military authorities. A desperate move to allow those newly called up to opt for coal-mining was a failure because hardly anyone wanted to go down the mines. In the end, it was decided that one in ten of new conscripts was to be *directed* into the mines, instead of into the armed services. They became known as 'Bevin boys.'

In the autumn of 1941, Communist Party miners met to discuss what should be done; changes in the way Pit Production Committees functioned was seen as a priority. These had been in existence since 1940, but had been used by colliery managers to concentrate on matters such as 'absenteeism', thereby side-stepping serious discussion on production deficiencies. It was one of the arguments used by some on the left who thought participation of miners in the committees signified class collaboration. Arthur Horner, Central Committee member of the Communist Party, and president of the South Wales Miners Federation, replied to such allegations at his union's annual conference in April 1942. He said that collaboration with a government which was organising the struggle against fascism was not a denial of the class struggle – on the contrary, failure to fight against this menace would mean deserting the working class and all it stood for.[3]

In the summer of 1942, the government was forced to make changes. It was decided that Pit Production Committees were to stop dealing with individual cases of absenteeism; this enabled the miners' representatives to concentrate on more pressing issues, such as better maintenance of haulage roads and elimination of defects in machinery. As Horner was to point out, most of the coalowners were deeply hostile to the committees. 'They believe (and it may be rightly) that if the workers succeed in making these committees work successfully, this will greatly strengthen the case for national ownership of the coal mines at some future date'.[4]

By 1942 discontent in the coalfields was growing, and when the mineowners rejected a claim from the Mineworkers' Federation for a minimum wage of £4 5s, the government finally decided to intervene. It set up a Board of Investigation, and the upshot was the introduction of a national minimum weekly wage: for face workers this was to be £4 3s, thus lifting coalminers' wages from 59th to 23rd place in the Ministry of Labour's list.

At the same time, the government was forced to introduce a scheme for controlling the industry. It fell far short of the Federation's demands for a National Coal Board and District Boards to be composed of equal representatives of men and management. Instead, a cumbersome system which became known as 'dual control' was introduced, under which a Ministry of Fuel and Power was set up with Regional Controllers to exercise supervision. However, as the coal owners still owned the mines, there was no fundamental change in the financial structure, and relations between the coalowners and their employees remained as before. Indeed, the Ministry of Fuel and Power became known among miners as the 'Ministry of Fuel *without* Power'.[5]

Throughout, the party argued that the solution to the coal mining problem was nationalisation of the mines, which was now seen, not just as an aim for the future, but as an urgent necessity if the coal shortage was to be overcome. The case for immediate nationalisation was set out by Harry Pollitt in a pamphlet *Take Over the Mines* which, in 1944, appealed to the public to use political pressure to bring it about. The campaign did not succeed, but it undoubtedly played a part in influencing public attitudes in the general election at the end of the war.

THE PARTY AND STRIKES

In 1943 came a wave of strikes in the engineering industry. Most of them were of short duration; one of the longest was at Barrow-in-Furness where, on 17 September 1943, 9,000 workers employed by Vickers Armstrong stopped work and remained on strike for 18 days. The workforce was already subject to a 'premium bonus' system which was much resented. The strike arose because of the management's interpretation of a new National Arbitration Tribunal Award under which the Barrow workers had expected wage improvements, but found to their dismay, that this was not to be the case – indeed some would actually suffer a wage decrease. The decision to strike was taken at a meeting of 5,000 workers and, despite an instruction from the Executive of the Amalgamated Engineering Union *not* to strike, the Barrow AEU District Committee supported the decision, whereupon the AEU Executive suspended the District Committee from office.

For some time, the party had been arguing that a strike was not always the most appropriate weapon; indeed, the need for war production made it possible for grievances to be remedied and advances made by other means. The mobilisation of public support, with deputations to MPs and government ministers, could bring about government intervention.

But when, in Barrow, this argument was put by local party members, they incurred much hostility, while the Barrow Strike Committee expelled from its deliberations two party members. However, in the end it was to be a party member, George Crane, who was to bring about a settlement of the dispute.

Crane was a founding member of the Communist Party and had served for many years on its Central Committee. A former shop stewards convener at Rover Aero factory and later at EMI, he had been elected (by a vote of 36,158 to 25,327) as a national organiser of the AEU in March 1943. Now the AEU Executive sent him to Barrow to try to settle the dispute. Here he engaged in a prolonged round of discussions with the Vickers management and the shop stewards committee, and succeeded in hammering out an agreement to replace the firm's 'premium bonus' system with a more acceptable one. After this, the strike was called off.[6]

At the time, Communist Party member Trevor Robinson was shop stewards convenor at the English Steel Corporation works in Sheffield, which was part of the Vickers combine. Robinson and his colleagues got help from the Shop Stewards National Council in convening a conference of representatives from all Vickers factories. Delegates from most of these factories participated, including those from the Barrow works. There was a prolonged discussion on the different systems of payment within the combine, whereby different management boards aimed to play one factory off against another. The upshot was the creation, for the first time, of a Vickers Combine Committee.

The event was reported in the December issue of the *New Propellor*, while an editorial stressed the fact that the press had used the Barrow strike to attack the unions.

In retrospect a little later Harry Pollitt commented:

> It would not be difficult for me to prove that, as a result of our production policy we have gained more vital advances for the workers than any strike has ever been able to obtain. Certainly our policy has been unpopular at times – we can take the case of Barrow: during their strike, thousands of workers opposed our point of view, but now they see that we were correct, and the gains could have been won without any stoppage of the output of vital munitions of war.[7]

On 18 April, 1944, a new defence regulation, IAA, was issued introducing more drastic powers for dealing with those who incited others to strike. It had the support of both the TUC and the British Employers Confederation. The new regulation was seen as being directed against Trotskyist organisations which were trying to encourage strikes wherever there was a grievance.

Two days earlier, the Executive Committee of the Communist Party had warned of 'the necessity to be on guard against any attempt of reactionary interests to utilise the pretext of Trotskyism ... to introduce any wider measures which would be harmful to the democratic rights and liberties of the working class movement'.[8]

When Regulation IAA was published, it appeared that this warning was amply justified. Gallacher put down a motion complaining that the House of Commons should have been consulted before the regulation was issued (the House was in recess at the time) and asserting that the government already had sufficient powers for dealing with any undesirable or dangerous agitation. His motion was not called and when, on 28 April, Aneurin Bevan moved the annulment of the regulation he was defeated by 314 votes to 23. However, 109 Labour MPs abstained. Gallacher was of course, among the 23 who supported Bevan's motion. In the event, after the opening of the second front in June 1944, there was a marked decline in the number of strikes, and Regulation IAA was never used.

GROWTH OF WORKPLACE ORGANISATION

The rise in trade union organisation and in shop stewards' activity continued. On 12 March 1944, the Shop Stewards National Council (of which Len Powell was still secretary) held a national conference in the Stoll Theatre in London. According to the April issue of the *New Propellor* (still edited by Peter Zinkin) it surpassed in scope and influence any previous gathering of its kind. 1,800 delegates from 450 factories and shipyards were present. It was chaired by Trevor Robinson, and the opening statement was made by Finlay Hart, a party member who worked at a shipyard on the Clyde. 'Our country is not the same as it was when last we met in this Stoll Theatre in 1941' he said. Describing the vast increase in output by the engineering trades, he said that the rise in production had taken place mainly because of the consistent drive by the shop stewards despite the obstacles placed in their way by the employers. Stressing the need to prevent victimisation of shop stewards when the war ended, he said:

> Let us firmly determine, along with our comrades in the armed forces, to make our voice heard now for the retention of vital controls after the war on prices, profits, distribution of commodities and investment of capital. Let us make our voices heard for the nationalisation of the land, mines, banks and other key industries, for a policy that will ensure jobs and security for all.[9]

During the war, membership of the Amalgamated Engineering Union nearly trebled, rising from 354,000 to 908,000. As the official history of that union said later:

> The prodigious growth in membership and influence of the AEU was by no means an automatic process. It rested largely on the painstaking work and feats of organisation performed by stewards up and down the country, who gave up much of their limited spare time and energy and frequently sacrificed their earnings to devote their attention to improving the conditions of their workmates.[10]

And, as the non-communist president of the AEU, Jack Tanner, said just after the war was over: 'It is, I think, generally known that a very large proportion of the leading shop stewards in the engineering industry are communists'.[11]

RELATIONS WITH THE TUC

Though the main concentration was towards the workplace, communists were beginning to get elected to leading positions in many trade unions. Among miners, there was not only Arthur Horner, president of the South Wales Miners, but Abe Moffat, who was elected president of the Scottish Miners in 1942. In the AEU Joe Scott was voted on to the Executive Council in 1942 after several attempts in earlier years by Executive members to keep him out. By 1943, another party member, Gilbert Hitchings, had also been voted on to the AEU Executive. In 1941 Wal Hannington was elected national organiser in the AEU; in 1943, he was joined in this office by George Crane. Tim Burns was on the Executive of the train-drivers union ASLEF; in 1944, a founding member of the party, Jim Gardner, was elected general secretary of the Foundry Workers Union. In that year, John Horner, the general secretary of the Fire Brigades Union was to join the party.

The TUC leaders were much concerned about the growing support for the Communist Party. TUC Circular 17, originally issued in 1934, had requested all unions to prohibit the election of communists to official positions. This circular had had success in some unions. But by now it was virtually a dead letter.

The same was not the case with Circular 16 (known as the 'Black Circular') under which union branches were forbidden to elect communists as their delegates to local trades councils. These trades councils offered an opportunity for representatives of different unions in a locality to meet together, discuss problems and participate in activities around local issues ranging from trade union recruitment, health and safety at work, housing and rents, to broader political questions. For over eight years the TUC General Council had banned participation of communists in these trades councils. But in 1942 it had become clear that the General Council might be forced to lift the ban.

In a desperate bid to stem the left wing tide, the TUC General Council focussed on a new target: the Labour Research Department. The General Council decided that the time had come to put the LRD on the 'proscribed list'; it secured the agreement of the Labour Party NEC for this move, and a joint circular banning the LRD was sent out in April 1942. The ostensible reason for this action was that the LRD was 'to a considerable extent subject to communist influence and control.'

The LRD was in fact an independent research body founded in 1912 by Beatrice Webb as part of the Fabian Society. Its main function was to supply its affiliated organisations – most of which were trade union bodies – with facts and figures about wages and conditions, company profits, social services and legal rights at work. In 1942, its affiliated organisations numbered 592, including 60 national unions, many shop stewards committees, local trade union branches, trades councils and local Labour parties. Its executive was elected annually in a postal ballot of its affiliated organisations. Among those regularly reelected were several leading communists, including two of the LRD's former secretaries: R. Page Arnot and Emile Burns.

The decision to ban the LRD was accepted by the Labour Party Annual Conference held in May 1942. But at the Trades Union Congress the following September, it ran into much opposition, and was agreed to only because the Mineworkers Federation, which opposed the ban, failed to cast its vote as a result of a muddle.

At that same 1942 congress, a motion urging the withdrawal of the anti-Communist Circular 16 was moved on behalf of the AEU and was the subject of prolonged debate. A number of well-known communists took part, including George Crane of the AEU, Jim Hammond of the Mineworkers Federation and Jim Godfrey from the traindrivers union ASLEF. The motion was defeated, but by a very narrow majority.

However, during the ensuing year, the campaign for the withdrawal of Circular 16 was intensified, and some important unions which had voted for its retention were obliged to change their attitude as a result of decisions at their 1943 annual conferences.

While all this was going on, the TUC leaders had made another move, this time an attempt to limit the growing influence of the *Daily Worker* which had been contacting trade union branches and Labour Parties in an effort to build up its network of 'worker correspondents'. A circular was sent out by the TUC General Council 'warning' trade union general secretaries of the *Daily Worker*'s approach to their branches in the hope that they would 'take appropriate steps to deal with the matter'.[12]

It did not appear that much notice was being taken of this circular, and by the time of the congress in September in 1943, it had become clear that the TUC leaders were in a quite untenable position. In order to avoid certain defeat, Sir Walter Citrine, the general secretary, made a public announcement that Circular 16 was to be withdrawn. At the same time, a proposal that the ban on the LRD be lifted was agreed to without discussion.[13]

For the next two years, the TUC General Council was obliged to leave anti-communist campaigns to the Labour Party. Indeed, in 1944, a communist was for the first time to be elected to the TUC General Council. This was Bert Papworth, nominated by the largest union of all, the Transport and General Workers Union. Papworth had been a leader of the London Busmen's Rank and File Movement in the 1930s; after the 'Coronation strike' of 1937, he had been expelled from the union as part of the witch-hunt mounted against the left by Ernest Bevin. In 1941, he had been allowed back into the union, and was quickly elected to its executive council. 'His busmen comrades call him "Pappy" ' wrote Walter Holmes in the *Daily Worker* but 'he is anything but what that might imply.... The TUC General Council certainly won't find its first communist member, A.F. Papworth, a sleeping partner.'[14] This prophecy turned out to be correct.

4

THE FIGHT FOR EQUALITY FOR WOMEN

During the war, women began to play a rather more prominent part in the Communist Party than before. More of them were being elected on to their local branch committees, chairing meetings, acting as branch secretaries, treasurers, membership organisers, taking charge of literature sales, and so on. They also figured more frequently as speakers at open-air meetings. At the 1943 Congress, 106 out of 406 delegates were women – 26% – a much higher proportion than in pre-war years.

The conscription of men into the armed services meant that women took over as local activists. However, the major change was the entry of women into work formerly regarded as a male preserve.

THE PRE-WAR BACKGROUND

Between the wars, just over one-third of all women were in paid employment. The majority of those who went to work were young and unmarried; only ten per cent of married women did so. As Joan Beauchamp observed in 1942: 'Paid work for women was regarded as an interim occupation for unmarried girls ... or as a sad burden on widows and other women unfortunate enough to have no male breadwinner to look after them'.[1]

The majority of married women did not want to go out to work, mainly because their quality of life would be impaired. Although the spread of knowledge concerning contraceptives during the 1920s meant that wives had been relieved of the incessant child-bearing of earlier decades, the standard of comfort in most homes still depended on the presence of someone during the day. Heating came from coal fires which needed constant attention; few had refrigerators, so daily shopping was required; washing had to be done by hand and hung up outside to dry; many houses had no bathrooms or constant hot water; the smoke from chimneys meant that incessant dusting was required. So, if both husband and wife were out at work all day, they came home to uncomfortable surroundings. The reluctance of women to work was exacerbated by the low pay they received. By the time the extra costs of laundry sent out, fares to work, dinners and teas out were deducted, the small amount of money left did not compensate for the trouble.

Out of the 6.8 million – mainly single – women employed in 1931, over a million were in domestic service, learning skills regarded as vital for married women. About half a million were in clerical work which was skilled but relatively poorly paid, and which offered little chance of promotion. Many others served as shop assistants. Otherwise they went into low paid work in textiles or clothing, or into the mass production processes being introduced into engineering – indeed, whole factories had been reconstructed so as to be based primarily on the work of women, who were regarded as a source of cheap labour. There had always been a clear divide between 'women's work' and 'men's work'. And since most women expected this work to be temporary, few of them joined trade unions.

Higher up, in professions such as teaching, or in the civil service, women often did the same work as men for much lower pay. There was, moreover, a 'marriage bar' which prevented women who married from continuing with their profession.

The Communist Party had always stood for the emancipation of women, for equality between the sexes and – in particular – for equal pay. It was assumed that the inequalities were the product of the capitalist system. Only when that system was abolished could real equality be established. As R. Palme Dutt had put it in 1934:

> The subjection of women and the forcible compulsion of the majority of women to economic dependence on marriage as their sole means of livelihood, are bound up with the existence of private property society, and can only be ended with Communist social organisation.[2]

The conviction that a socialist society would bring about the emancipation of women was reinforced by what was happening in the Soviet Union where, by law, women were entitled to equal pay and were employed in many jobs which were in Britain reserved for men; where creche and nursery facilities were provided at workplaces, and canteens and communal restaurants relieved women from cooking at home. Since the struggle to overthrow capitalism was the priority, communists in Britain had reservations about feminist movements which were regarded as 'bourgeois'; moreover, they thought it was crucial to involve men in the struggle for equal rights for women, seeing feminist movements as divisive.

THE ENTRY OF WOMEN INTO WAR INDUSTRY

Much of the pre-war discussion about equal pay for women had focused on the possibilities offered by a socialist world in the future. During the war, it suddenly became a matter of urgency: this was because women were entering industry in huge numbers.

At the beginning of 1942, female conscription was introduced. Women aged 18 upwards became legally obliged to register; some of the young among them were taken into the Women's Auxiliary Services, becoming 'Ats', 'Wrens' or 'Waafs'; some went into the 'Women's Land Army' to do agricultural work; most were directed into jobs in the war industries, or into those vital to war production such as transport. An unmarried woman could be compelled to leave home in order to work in another part of the country. Married women could not be ordered to do this, but could be directed into any jobs within daily travelling distance of their homes. Those with children under fourteen living at home were exempted from such directions; otherwise, they had to plead a special case.

At that time, many party members were organised in factory groups, and in November 1941, a syllabus for a four-lesson course for the use of such groups was sent out from party headquarters entitled *Marxism and Industrial Workers*. While Lessons 1 and 2 concentrated on the fight against Hitler, its relationship to the class struggle, and the need to increase production, a large part of lesson 3, entitled 'The Workers' Responsibility' was devoted to the need to draw women into production, and to give them help and training. 'Whilst the principle of equal pay for equal work (the rate for the job) must be enforced, less skilled workers can be helped by more skilled to do the job. Women must also not only be organised, but drawn into trade union representation on production committees, shop stewards' committees, union branch committees, etc.'

The first two questions which, it was proposed, the tutor should put to the class were '(1) What are the main problems of the women in your factory? (2) What steps have been taken to overcome them (a) in the factory and (b) through other organisations in the locality?'

The truth was that most women were facing a good deal of prejudice on the part of men who saw them as a threat to their hard won standards. Communists argued that the answer to this threat was to help women to organise, to persuade them to become active in the trade unions and to fight for women to be paid 'the rate for the job' – ie the same as men. In all this they were facing a hard battle.

Apart from the fear that the influx of women would undermine existing wage standards, there was a widespread conviction that women were not capable of doing jobs that men normally did. This conviction was not confined to the workplace; it was plainly visible in the higher reaches of the trade unions, and was constantly attacked in the *Daily Worker*. An example of this was seen on 10 October 1942, in a leader under the headline 'Make Way for Women':

> At this crucial moment of the war, with manpower urgently needed for offensive strategy, old-fashioned prejudice against employment of women keeps bobbing up. The obstructionists are not only to be found among reactionaries, but also among those who should know better. Mr Marchbank, general secretary of the NUR in an interview yesterday on the shortage of manpower in transport, said that the employment of women was no solution 'in view of the limited range of jobs they may be expected to do.' Why so limited? In the Soviet Union there are women engine-drivers, trains with full crews of women, women station-masters, women regional traffic superintendents. Are British women less capable than Russian women?

Although it accepted women into membership, the National Union of Railwaymen had an agreement with the railway companies that they should be employed in the 'starting grades' only; for this, they would be paid the rate for the job, but would not be offered the opportunity of promotion to more skilled work. In a pamphlet issued in 1943 by the Communist Party entitled '*Clear the Lines*' the treatment of women was severely criticised. 'The majority of women on the railways have been dumped, so to speak, in starting grades and left there with little effective training, without any incentive ... Women should receive real training, opportunity for promotion and decent working conditions.'

In that summer of 1943, the labour shortage became so acute, that the employment of women in other than 'starting grades' was acceded to, and some of them began to be trained as 'signalmen' and guards. But though the number of female railway clerks was rising, the railway companies refused to pay women clerks the 'rate for the job'. In the railway workshops, where women began to show much competence in jobs hitherto regarded as suitable for men, they had to serve a much longer probationary period than men before receiving an equal rate of pay.[3]

It was in the engineering industry that the equal pay issue became most pressing. The largest trade union in the industry was the Amalgamated Engineering Union (AEU). Originally an organisation catering for highly trained 'fitters and turners' it had, from 1926 onwards, opened its doors to semi-skilled and unskilled men, but was still clinging to what Joan Beachamp had described as 'the suicidal policy of refusing to enrol women'.[4] In May 1940, despite the fact that women were still not allowed to enter its ranks, the AEU had negotiated an agreement with the employers under which if, after a probationary period of 32 weeks, a woman could do the job formerly done by a man without additional supervision, she would be entitled to the male rate.

This agreement did not achieve anything like what was expected of it for two main reasons. Firstly, it did not cover work done by women in the pre-war period when they had been taken on as cheap labour in the new mass production processes. For women sent into this kind of work, the employers were able to argue that the AEU agreement didn't apply. The second reason for its failure was the numerous evasions to which the employers resorted, such as making small changes to a job description which allowed them to argue that it could not be directly compared with that previously performed by a man, or that a woman, even after 32 weeks, still required more supervision than her male predecessor. As Wal Hannington, then an AEU national organiser observed: 'Women have shown themselves capable of doing work which before the war was generally considered to be entirely outside their range of ability, but many employers continue to exploit them as cheap labour simply because they are women. A more reactionary and disgraceful outlook it is difficult to conceive.'[5]

One of the reasons why the employers were able to get away with this was the reluctance of unions to accept women as members. It was not until 1942 that the Electrical Trades Union at last started to do so; it was not until 1943 that the AEU, having belatedly changed its rules, also began to accept women into its ranks. Before this happened, the more determined among the male shop stewards had been trying to recruit women into the only available ones: the two general workers' unions. Inevitably, the admittance of women into the AEU provoked some inter-union rivalry, which hardly encouraged them to join.

SHOP STEWARDS MOVEMENT

The party's main influence at the time was in the shop stewards movement. Here there were major debates on the women's questions and, on 5 October 1941, the Shop Stewards National Council called the first ever conference of women shop stewards in London. There were 35 female shop stewards present, representing 32 London factories, together with 21 trade union representatives. Peggy Stanton, a convener in a West London aircraft factory, opened the discussion suggesting that the hostility to women felt by the men was partly due to what happened after the last war when the men came back to unemployment and the dole. The women must be organised in unions and must prove to the men that they were there to help maintain the conditions that had been won by the men after a long hard fight.[6]

A fortnight later the Shop Stewards National Council held its national conference attended by 1327 delegates. A number of women shop stewards were present, one of whom, Flo Mitten – a communist employed in a Manchester engineering works – described what women were up against. She said:

> I represent a factory employing over 3,000 women. The management in their usual way were quick to take advantage of using women for their own interests and their own betterment, but the men in the industries surprisingly enough stuck their heads in the sand and refused to see the possibilities that women had ... I tackled the women and said: 'Haven't you joined the trade union?'. They said the men didn't want them in the trade union so they never bothered. One of them had been there for 32 years working alongside men. She was not in the trade union because the men did not ask her.

Walter Swanson said in his opening address to the conference:

> It is of the utmost political and military importance that we now accept our own direct responsibility for teaching women how to do the most

skilled jobs, and drop all our prejudices and fears about the introduction and training of women.

He went on:

> We men must do all we can to help the women to secure equal pay for equal work, adequate welfare and nursery facilities, with provision for shopping and transport.

Among the points agreed to by the conference was the need for equal pay and to break down the reluctance to train women.[7]

During the ensuing months the number of female shop stewards rose steadily. Among party members who became shop stewards' convenors were Peggy McIlven (later Peggy Aprahamian) at Standard Telephones; Muriel Rayment in EMI; Nell Coward at a Royal Ordnance Factory in Liverpool; Agnes MacLean at a Rolls Royce factory in Scotland.[8]

In April 1942 the Shop Stewards National Council organised another conference of women shop stewards – this time in Birmingham; representatives came from factories in the Midlands. Anne Wheeler, a communist and shop steward in a London factory, spoke to the meeting on behalf of the National Council pointing out that the minimum rate for women – 43s – was far too low.

The Shop Stewards magazine *The New Propellor* had already been giving prominence to a new Royal Ordnance Factory agreement reached between the AEU and the Ministry of Supply, which provided that the *minimum* rates for women on skilled work but still needing supervision should be equal to that paid to semi-skilled men. What this could mean if applied outside the ROF factories would be a rise in the minimum women's rate from 43s a week to 62s in London and 59s outside London. The women in a Cossors factory asked the Shop Stewards National Council to campaign for this agreement to be operated elsewhere: the council circularised all shop stewards committees and many mass meetings were held on the issue.

However, the general workers' unions failed to back this campaign; instead they came to an agreement with the Engineering Employers Federation for a new 'grading system' which, though it provided for a paltry increase, would help keep women's wages down.

WOMEN'S PARLIAMENT

The Party was seeking ways of broadening the movement for women's rights and in the summer of 1941 Ted Bramley, London District Secretary, discussed the matter with Tamara Rust, a member of the London District Committee and responsible for women's work. The idea of setting up a so-called 'women's parliament' was mooted and the suggestion passed on to the organisation known as the Peoples' Convention which had been listed as a 'proscribed organisation' by the Labour leaders.

The outcome was the formation of a 'London Women's Parliament' which held its first 'session' on 13 July 1941 in the Conway Hall. Present were 345 delegates from factories, trade unions and cooperative organisations; the actress Beatrix Lehmann delivered the opening address; 'Bills' on women's work, welfare and wages were discussed by the 'MPs' present with Nan Macmillan – a teacher and long-standing party member – acting as 'speaker'.[9]

This first 'session' was held under the auspices of the Peoples Convention, a left-wing organisation formed in 1940 which had campaigned for 'a new government really representative of the people'; and had been listed as a 'proscribed organisation' by the Labour leaders. By the end of 1941, this organisation had been dissolved, but the London Women's Parliament gained strength. Its honorary secretary was a Labour councillor, Diana Pym, who soon after joined the Communist Party. Its secretary was the communist, Frida Grimble, a former teacher, while Tamara Rust was its treasurer and convenor of its organising committee. It described itself as 'a movement which coordinates the work of many organisations and groups of women ... It is definitely not a separate organisation with members ... It enables representatives of existing organisations to get together and forge a policy to deal with problems common to them all'. Explaining that it was *not* a feminist organisation, it said: 'The parliament wants men and women to work together as partners.' It was also stressed that the 'parliament' did not owe allegiance to any political party, but aimed to provide a platform for all sections of opinion among women. Its function was to hold 'sessions' (ie conferences) of elected delegates to discuss specific issues and decide on action to be taken.

The 'parliament's' organising committee consisted of 43 women nominated by supporting organisations including a doctor, a nurse, a bus conductress, a welfare superviser and a canteen manageress. Among others were civil servants, teachers and factory workers.

On 14 June 1942, its '3rd session' took place at the Bedford Theatre in Camden Town. No less than 983 delegates were present, most of whom represented factories and trade union organisations. The 'Bills' discussed were on women's wages; part-time work; training; wartime nurseries, and the position of women in the armed services.

Nan Macmillan took the chair; Peggy McIlven opened the session. Four of the five 'Bills' were moved by women 'MPs' as was customary but, in the case of the wages 'Bill' which proclaimed that the discrepancies between male and female rates of wages 'can no longer be tolerated', the usual practice was discarded and the debate was opened by a male guest, Walter Swanson, shop steward from Napiers, who said that he realised that the demand would only become a reality if both men and women campaigned for it and lifted it into the spotlight of parliament and public opinion. He said: 'The women's parliament has a most vital part to play in order to bring about the position where the economic and social status of women is equal to that of men.'[10]

The 'women's parliament' movement was not confined to London; it also developed elsewhere, particularly in Lancashire, South Wales, Yorkshire and Scotland.

The movement caused concern on the General Council of the TUC and on 18 December 1942, a circular (No 35) was sent out by TUC general secretary, Walter Citrine, advising all unions and trades councils 'not to support "women's parliaments" set up in various districts.' It pointed out that the women's parliament organising committee operated from Napier House – the address of the Peoples Convention which had been a proscribed organisation until its demise; that the Parliament's Honorary Secretary had been a strong supporter of the Peoples Convention; that the 'Bills' drawn up for discussion were sent to various government departments, to unions catering for women, and to women MPs. It alleged that the women's parliaments 'are attempting to deal with many matters which are the subject of negotiations by individual unions or the trade union movement generally, and have intervened on matters which are essentially the responsibility of the trade unions.'

'The latest example of heresy hunting in which Transport House finds time to indulge comes from the General Council of the TUC' observed Emile Burns on 9 January in *World News and Views*. 'It has issued a solemn warning against "women's parliaments" because they have "Bills" dealing with wages.'

In the event, the warning did not have much effect. At the 4th session of the London Women's Parliament held on 14 November 1943, over 800 turned up, including 244 delegates from factories, 220 from trade union bodies including branches, district committees, National Executives and trades councils; 30 from coop organisations, 70 from various women's organisations, and 155 from political organisations (including Labour, Liberal and Communist Party branches). The session was filmed by the Ministry of Information and received wide publicity in the newspapers, including conservative papers like the *Daily Mail*, which commented: 'These women from factories, transport depots, hospitals, wartime nurseries, schools and homes stood on the stage in the glare of arc-lamps and delivered speeches that, in brevity and sincerity, were models for any politician.'[12]

The change in the climate of opinion became clear when, shortly afterwards, on 28 March 1944, Conservative MP Thelma Cazalet-Keir, achieved a majority in the House of Commons for an amendment to an Education Bill providing for equal pay for men and women teachers. The prime minister, Winston Churchill, indignantly turned the issue into one of confidence, and two days later the Commons reversed its decision. The result of this crisis was the establishment of a Royal Commission on equal pay.

More and more people were also facing the fact that women were perfectly capable of doing the jobs which had formerly been considered only suitable for men. The *Daily Worker* was giving a great deal of space to the contribution being made by women in the war industries, and when Ernest Bevin, the leading trade union figure who had become Minister of Labour in the coalition government at last conceded that one woman was equal to one man, the paper published a triumphant leader:

> In producing the tools for victory, British women, according to Mr Bevin, have astounded the government experts. Under the influence of obsolete prejudice, the experts believed that in war industry it would take three women to do the work of two men. In fact, the respective outputs have proved equal. We hope that Mr Bevin will bring these facts to the notice of the Royal Commission on Equal Pay. For here is the proof that the lower wages received by women in most industries are not due to inferior efficiency, but to the fact that unscrupulous employers have taken advantage of the weak trade union organisation existing among them. This weakness is due in considerable measure to the doubts and prejudices of male workers who feared the competition of women.[13]

PARTY ORGANISATION AMONG WOMEN

At the 16th Party Congress held in August 1943, five women were elected on to the new Executive Committee which almost immediately decided to set up a National Women's Advisory Council to give leadership on women's questions. Secretary of this council was Tamara Rust.

Most of the council's members were working in industry; nevertheless they managed to visit the party's various District Committees to discuss work among women and help in the setting up of women's sections of the party. Paper rationing made it difficult to launch a new women's journal; however, a former paper used for tenant's work was taken over and transformed into a small monthly magazine *Woman Today* which at its peak reached a circulation of 12,000.

After the announcement of a Royal Commission on equal pay, a pamphlet was produced by Tamara Rust entitled *Equal Pay for Equal Work – your questions answered*. It pointed out that in 1944 the average man got £6 1s 4d a week and the average woman £3 2s. It argued that the men got more 'because they organised themselves in trade unions and forced the employers to pay.'

The party put in its own evidence to the Royal Commission. Stressing that the aim was to end 'the exploitation of women as cheap labour' it asserted that 'The fundamental objection to the present state of affairs is that wages are fixed for women as a special group, and that the major factor in determining their wage rates is their sex and not their work.'

The memo surveyed the wage rates for women in various types of employment, pointing out that even in clerical jobs, in which men and women had long been doing identical work, the rates for women were lower than those for men, and their opportunities for promotion far more limited. It urged the government to apply the principle of equal pay to all public employment and to encourage its application elsewhere.

The issue of equal pay came up at the 17th Party Congress in October 1944. 'In my factory where there are about 5,000 women employed ... only about 110 are receiving the rate for the job' said Norah Walsh from Manchester, while Vida John from London showed how equal pay covered only those jobs where men and women were on the same work; hundreds of thousands of women were not getting a living wage.[14]

Tamara Rust raised the broader question of what would happen after the war. She said that 55 per cent of the women in industry wanted to remain there after the war; 45 per cent of those in engineering wanted to do so. But, she said:

> It is not only the question of whether women will remain in industry or go home. It is a much deeper question ... of how to ensure that their skill which they have so widely shown during the war is to be transferred to all aspects of the life of the country ... We must see to it that all the leading positions in our democracy are not taken up by the men ... The fight for women's demands is a joint fight of men and women because until this fight is won it will hold back the progress of the people'.[15]

5

THE PARTY AND THE ARMED FORCES

In 1941, most of the party members in the armed services were stationed in Britain. But during 1942 many of them were posted to the Middle East, and participated in the offensive against Rommel's army in north Africa, and in the invasion of Italy in 1943. Others were sent to India from where the attack on the Japanese in Burma was launched. Others did not leave Britain until the Normandy landings in June 1944.

From the start it was understood by most members that when called up, they must not take with them their party cards. This practice was intended to safeguard them against being charged with an offence against the King's Regulation 541 which laid down that soldiers were not permitted to play an active part in the affairs of a political party. Similar rules applied to the Air Force; those covering the Navy were rather different.[1]

However, after the Russians entered the war, increasing numbers of men who had not been in the party before call-up began applying to join it. Most were told that they could not do so. That indeed was the experience of Wolfe Wayne who, together with a group of friends serving with him in the Army, wrote to 16 King Street in the Spring of 1942 asking to join the party. In reply, he got a letter from Harry Pollitt telling him he could not be enrolled as a member. Wolfe Wayne was one of those who joined the party as soon as the war was over, and served as one of its full-time organisers before going on to become a polytechnic lecturer.

Some of those who were already in the party before call-up objected to this rule. Sam Fisher, a teacher in civilian life, when stationed near St Albans, travelled to London and complained to Bob Stewart, who was working at King Street, that he had recruited several new members and had then been told they could not be issued with party cards. The upshot was that arrangements were made for two of his recruits to be registered at a secret address in London where their cards were held for them. Fisher's case was exceptional. Most would-be recruits had to wait to join until they were demobilised.

The 'party card' problem was, of course, a side issue. Most of the members called up managed to contact other members, met in groups to exchange views, sought to spread the socialist message, mainly by personal contact, but also by selling pamphlets, distributing leaflets and passing on copies of the *Daily Worker*, and participating in discussions laid on by the Army Education Corps or by other organisations. As one member later recalled: 'Members took advantage of many types of discussion groups. At Catterick we attended the YMCA and made its discussion group our centre, until Intelligence got on to us'.[2]

Wherever they were, party members aimed to win understanding of the need to defeat fascism, and for this purpose to improve the fighting capacity of those involved. But they also aimed to spread socialist understanding, and helped to promote discussion on the kind of Britain people wanted after the war; how the poverty, hunger and unemployment experienced during the 1930s could be prevented from returning in the post-war years. Indeed, they understood that expectations for a better future were an important factor in maintaining morale.

In these endeavours, they naturally faced acute hostility from above: it was perfectly obvious that those in charge were obsessed with the desire to limit the spread of left-wing ideas. However, not quite all those in higher ranks adopted such an attitude; there were some commanding officers who showed themselves prepared to cooperate with people on the Left. A few party members, or those close to the party, reached high positions. One example was the scientist Desmond Bernal who had been singled out for special responsibilities by Admiral Lord Mountbatten.

CHANGING HABITS IN THE ARMED FORCES

Background to the problems communists faced was the supremely undemocratic structure of the armed forces. Since the First World War, their main use had been for the policing of colonial territories. At home they had been used for the protection of strikebreakers at times of industrial unrest. The officers in charge had been drawn almost entirely from the governing class; most of them had been educated at fee-paying schools such as Eton, with particular bias in favour of the younger sons of the aristocracy. The lower ranks had been primarily recruited from among unskilled, unemployed workers. Once in the army, they were kept apart from civilians and were subjected to repressive regimes under which their sole duty was to obey orders. Elementary democratic rights – for instance, the right to make a collective complaint about conditions – did not exist. There was no freedom of speech or discussion; politics were banned.

After the introduction of conscription in 1939, both structure and practice underwent certain modifications, and as more and more civilians were called up, the highly autocratic system began to be shaken to its foundations. Those in charge faced some embarrassing contradictions. Their supremely undemocratic organisation was supposed to be fighting for democracy. And, from June 1941 onwards, it was fighting on the same side as the Soviet Union, previously regarded, along with all communists, as 'the enemy'.

Army education was one of the arenas where these contradictions were highlighted. Education had played a minor role in the peacetime services but after the retreat from Dunkirk in 1940 when the majority of serving soldiers were stationed back in Britain, a War Office Committee became convinced that educational activities could help boost morale and relieve boredom.[3] In consequence the Army Education Corps, which had almost gone out of existence, was revived and arrangements made for courses of lectures on a wide variety of subjects. Most of the lecturers were civilians, and the courses proved popular. Then, in 1941, the Army Bureau of Current Affairs (ABCA) was created. It issued regular bulletins on current events, concentrating in part on the latest happenings on the fighting fronts, but also dispensing information on political and social affairs. The object was to provide material for officers to give weekly talks to the men under their command, and to offer opportunities to them for discussion.

However, both the Army Education Corps and ABCA were seen by some on high as offering a threat to their supremacy. Concerted efforts were made to ban lectures by people thought to be on the left. The philosopher, Dr John Lewis, was employed full time as a lecturer for the Army Education Corps, but when those in charge became aware of his views, he got the sack. One of those stopped over and over again was D.N. Pritt MP, who had been expelled from the Labour Party in 1940 for his support of the Russians during the invasion of Finland and who was constantly invited to give lectures on the Soviet Union.[4]

Two months after the formation of the ABCA, Prime Minister Churchill wrote to the Secretary for War saying: 'I do not approve of this system of encouraging political discussion in the Army among soldiers ... there cannot be controversy without prejudice to discipline.'[5] Churchill did not achieve his aim of closing down ABCA but when, on 19 December 1942, a summary of the official report on social insurance, written by its author Sir William Beveridge himself, was issued as an ABCA pamphlet, it was, within three days, withdrawn on the orders of the War Office.

DISCRIMINATION AGAINST COMMUNISTS

So obsessed were the authorities with the need to undermine communist influence that they took steps to prevent some party members from getting into the armed services at all.

Under the National Service (Armed Forces) Act, all men between 18 and 41 were made liable for conscription, and each age group in turn was required to register. The process started with the younger age groups, and by June 1941 had reached men aged 40. When the men registered, they listed their existing occupation and their preference of the three fighting services. Unless they were in a 'reserved occupation' and therefore exempt from call-up, they would then be summoned for a medical examination, followed by an interview, after which the call-up papers would arrive, telling them where to report for duty. But in 1941 and 1942, there were quite a number of party members who went through the whole process, including medical examinations and interviews, but whose call-up papers never arrived.

One of these was Phil Piratin, a communist councillor in Stepney, East London, later to be elected as a communist MP. After his interview and medical examination, he assumed he had been accepted for service in the RAF for which he had opted: he waited and waited, but his call-up papers never came. Another example was Henry Parsons, who had been head of the party's publishing firm, Lawrence & Wishart, and had subsequently acted as business manager of the *Daily Worker*. After it was banned in January 1941, he spent a year working for a catering firm. When his age group became due for call-up in 1942, he registered, had his interview, and was told he was to be drafted into signals. But his call-up papers never came. Jack Cohen, full-time party organiser in Coventry, registered for military service, went through his medical examination, but was never called up. The same thing happened to Michael Shapiro who, before the war, had been secretary of the Federation of Tenants and Residents Associations, and to Ivor Montagu, author of a book, *The Traitor Class*, published in 1940. Alan Winnington, who was later to act as *Daily Worker* correspondent during the Korean war, was interviewed and accepted as a trainee fighter pilot in the RAF but after waiting three months, he received an official communication from the RAF: 'services no longer required.'

It was obvious that blacklists had been circulated directing that leading communists must be prevented from entry into the armed services. However, the exclusions were somewhat haphazard, and not very numerous. The main aim of commanding officers was to keep a check on the activities of communists who *were* called up and to prevent their promotion. One example of this was the experience of Malcolm Dunbar who, during the 1930s, had fought against Franco's fascists in Spain. In the British Army, he was never allowed to rise above the rank of sergeant.[6]

Another example was Gabriel ('Bill') Carritt, who had previously worked as national secretary of the League of Nations Youth Movement. Stationed as a gunner with an anti-aircraft rocket gun unit in Salford, he applied to go to an Officer Training Unit, was accepted and graduated as one of the best on the course. But he was not accepted as an officer. He insisted on seeing the colonel to find out why, and the colonel eventually explained that 'orders from higher up stated that since I was a communist, my name could not be put forward.'[7]

Again, Jack Gaster, a solicitor by profession, was appointed to a newly established Army Legal Service with the rank of captain. But, as he later recalled 'the War Office intervened and cancelled my appointment. I was indirectly told by the CO that this was "political". Surprise, surprise.'[8]

Despite these efforts, a few party members managed to slip through the net to become officers. One of these was Bill Alexander, who had been commander of the British Battalion in Spain and during the war was a captain in the Reconnaissance Corps, in Italy, France and Germany. However, any further promotion was blocked by a directive from above. John Angus, also one of the volunteers in Spain, got further; he was to serve in Burma and reached the rank of major. This was also true of James Klugmann who arrived in the Middle East as a private in the Pioneer Corps. On the troopship out, he became known as 'The Prof'; he ran classes on fascism, the causes of war, dialectics, the social and economic justification for socialism. Soon after arrival, he was unobtrusively transferred to Cairo to take charge of a group of Yugoslav-born Canadian miners who were waiting to be parachuted into Yugoslavia to join up with the Partisans led by Tito. Klugmann planned this first parachute mission, and in the end rose to the rank of major. As one writer said of him:

> Officially he was classified as a dangerous red, to be kept continuously under observation, and on no account to be posted out of the country. Somehow, it did not work out that way. Although everywhere Klugmann went, his papers, like Mary's little lamb, followed after, 'almost invariably they arrived after someone had conveniently posted me elsewhere' he would explain, almost apologetically, with a grin.[9]

Endeavours to keep watch on 'dangerous Reds' went on incessantly. Despatches were sent to commanding officers, enclosing dossiers (often inaccurate) on the pre-war political activities of the individuals concerned, and asking for reports on their present behaviour. Clearly, any pre-war anti-fascist was an object of suspicion, although such people were in practice more dedicated to the defeat of the Nazi enemy than many others in the forces.

One of the party members subjected to this process was Clive Branson, who was also among those never allowed to rise above the rank of sergeant. Branson had been posted to the 54th Training Regiment of the Royal Armoured Corps at Perham Down, near Andover. In July 1941, he was asked to give a lecture on the International Brigade (IB) in Spain (in which he had served); it was a great success, and he was immediately booked for a further lecture – this time on 'Cromwell's army' – and was meanwhile invited to give his lecture on the IB at Tidworth nearby. However, an order came from the Southern Command that Branson was not to lecture again on any subject, anywhere. In October 1941, he was suddenly transferred to the 57th Training Regiment at Warminster ('the reason is known to everyone here as political' he said in a letter home) where a little later he was selected to go on a gunnery instructor's course. But before this began, he was suddenly transferred – again, for political reasons – to the 52nd Training Regiment in Dorset, and was soon after posted to India.[10]

Branson's experience was similar to that of many party members who became aware that reports on their alleged political records were following them around. One of these was R.J. Spector who, after the war wrote a pamphlet for the National Council for Civil Liberties on *Freedom for the Forces*. As he put it: 'A Cambridge University Honours graduate in Modern Languages, and of working class origins and opinion, I was debarred from occupying any suitable job, let alone appear before a War Office Selection Board for the commission for which the selection officer had recommended me because of my pre-war left-wing record ... At my second unit, I was tipped off by a friendly officer that I was 'blacklisted' and at a subsequent unit my OC admitted to me the existence of a blacklist comprising (in his words) "communists and other peculiar people".'[11]

In one or two cases, the Party members concerned managed to see the reports on their activities, usually with the connivance of the officer in charge. One such was Wally Macfarlane who, as a member of the Transport and General Workers Union, had been active as a shop steward and in 1936 had been awarded a TUC medal for trade union recruitment. While on service in Burma, he arrived at battalion headquarters for duty one evening and found, lying on the table, a file marked INTELLIGENCE OFFICERS FILE: SECRET. 'It was clearly an invitation to read it ... so I did just that' he later recalled. 'To my surprise, it was a War Office Dispatch from London calling for a report on 5259214 Pte Walter Macfarlane, as I then was. Security MI5 wanted to know if I was fraternising with the natives and if so whom? To make clear what they were after, and the motivation, there was a dossier on my political activities in Civvy Street and surprisingly, on my wife Ruth.' The dossier was, as Macfarlane found, 'a hotchpotch of fact and fiction'. For example, in 1934 he had been for a three-week holiday in the Soviet Union; this was presented as a year with the Lenin Institute in Moscow. His trade union activities were classed as 'trade union penetration'.[12]

Another party member who got a glimpse of the report which followed him around was Fred Westacott, a skilled toolmaker and former secretary of the Welsh Engineering Shop Stewards Movement. He was called up into REME (Royal Electrical and Mechanical Engineers) and spent most of his army service in Italy. During this time he began to suspect that he was being watched; proof of this came when the war was over, and the unit was breaking up. A new major took over who had left-wing sympathies. He asked Westacott to do a job in his office, and deliberately left on his desk a file marked *Top Secret*. It was addressed to Westacott's previous commanding officer and began: 'I am writing to you regarding 14574600 Cfn Westacott FC ... This man has been known to the Security Authorities in London as a branch official of the Communist Party ... Since joining the army he was closely watched ...' The letter said that the authorities were 'anxious to know whether he comes into contact with secret information to which it is undesirable he should have access and I shall be glad if you will let me know on what type of work he is employed.' The letter was signed by G.Eyres Monsell – who later became a Tory MP.

Those in charge were much less anxious to investigate the activities of former fascists. As Westacott recalled: 'At the time in question we had a corporal who admitted he had worked full time for Mosley's Blackshirts. There was no enquiry about *him*.'[13]

ACTIVITIES IN THE ARMED SERVICES

In 1941-2 most serving soldiers were stationed in Britain. For the party at that time, the need for a second front in Europe was the overriding issue; those members who had been called up were doing their utmost to spread the message, and to convince others in the ranks that this was the priority if Hitler was to be defeated.

Such endeavours were taking place all over the country. The experience of Joe Berry was not untypical. Berry was in the RAF as an aero-engine fitter; he was being moved from one base to another. In mid-1942 he was sent to Henlow maintenance unit in Bedfordshire. Here Communists and Labour left got together to promote the slogan 'Open the Second Front Now'. They sold the *Daily Worker*, together with pamphlets, helped to get speakers for camp lectures, organised contingents to attend meetings in surrounding towns and villages and even got one to go to a Trafalgar Square 'Second Front' rally. In the end, they persuaded the air commodore in command to permit the launch of a wall-newspaper which provided a mix of camp news, cartoons, satires and *Daily Worker* politics.[14]

Such activity was, of course, meeting with disapproval from on high, as was shown by the experience of Bill Brooks who was in the 15th Battalion of the Royal Fusilliers stationed in Barnstable. Brooks was editor of a wall newspaper *Rapid Fire* and he and his group were, as he put it 'working might and main to try and get the morale up and the political discussion going, military preparedness and so on ...' With the full co-operation of their commanding officer they organised a big debate demanding the immediate opening of the second front, and special training so that the battalion could take part in it. The commanding officer was delighted – he was one of those who wanted to get into action. But within a fortnight of the debate the battalion was disbanded. 'The CO was in tears, pleaded in vain with the War Office to preserve the battalion' Brooks later recalled. Everyone suspected that it was disbanded because of the political activity.[15]

The experiences of Hymie Fagan illustrate the problems faced by many party members. Born in Stepney in 1903, Fagan had initially worked in a tailoring factory but had risen to prominence in the Communist Party, and was well-known as the author of a book about the peasants' revolt, *Nine Days that Shook England*. He was in the Pioneer Corps and was stationed at Blandford Camp in Dorset. Early on he was tipped off that regular monthly reports about him had to be sent to the War Office. He formed a small party group which met weekly in the house of an ATS member, and started an unofficial discussion group which many men began to attend. Fagan suggested that they should organise a petition for the opening of a second front, that the petition should be circulated among the troops and sent to Prime Minister Churchill. While on 48-hour leave, he contacted D.N. Pritt MP, who advised him that, if he was charged with 'mutiny', he (Pritt) would certainly attend the court-martial.

Fagan typed out the petition forms, and had collected about ninety signatures when he was arrested. Brought before the commanding officer, he was told he would be faced with a court-martial; meanwhile, he would be confined to barracks and the petition forms confiscated. So he told the CO that the forms had already been sent to Churchill, at which the CO exclaimed 'Oh my God, the fat is in the fire'. In fact, the petition forms were still in Fagan's pocket but, told to wait in the outer office, he managed to hand them over surreptitiously to another party member telling him to send them at once to Churchill in Downing Street. When brought back again to the inner office it became clear to Fagan that the CO had been on the phone to the War Office. He was thereupon told he must await a court-martial. But it never came. As Fagan later observed, it seemed that those in charge 'knew what a stir would be created if D.N. Pritt appeared to defend a communist soldier charged with circulating a petition calling for the second front.'[16]

When posted abroad, the political activities continued. Many party members were responsible for running ABCA classes and helped to organise and edit 'wall newspapers' and regimental bulletins. For example, Colin Siddons set up a discussion group at the Tura Caves some miles out of Cairo; the group had a wall newspaper GRIFF with an editorial committee which met once a week. Siddons was one of those who ran an ABCA class. Fred Westacott, when based in Italy, was the assistant editor, and later the editor, of his unit's newspaper *The Chronicle*. Selwyn Evans, who was for a time in Shillong at a transit centre for troops on their way to the Burma front, helped form a left wing discussion group and brought out a wall newspaper. Peter Kingsford, who had joined the party in 1936, was at the Army School of Education in India, where he trained officers and men to take ABCA courses. Joe Vandenburg, from east London, a sergeant-major, was stationed at Almazar in Egypt; he produced a paper for his unit, *The Almazar Star*, and was soon appointed ABCA officer to give regular lectures on the current ABCA pamphlets. Arthur Gibbard, another warrant officer in Egypt, was also an ABCA officer and helped to produce a magazine. Izzy Pushkin, a former tenants' activist in East London, was on the staff of the formation college at Poona.

'MOCK' PARLIAMENTS

One of the high points of political activity was reached with the formation of the 'forces parliament' in Cairo. Large sections of the army and the RAF were stationed in Egypt, and the Army Education Corps had set up a cultural centre in Cairo for leisure activities of the men stationed nearby, or on leave from desert fighting. Entitled 'Music-for-All', the building included a large meeting hall.

Communists in the Mediterranean Expeditionary Force were behaving as always: contacting one another by word-of-mouth recommendations, meeting as groups to discuss the political situation, what issues to take up, how to promote the spread of socialist ideas via wall-newspapers, etc. They were active among those who were organising meetings, 'brains trusts', lectures and debates at the Music-for-All centre. At one such meeting in the autumn of 1943 it was suggested that a 'mock parliament' should be set up. The proposal was agreed to by those in command; the organisation of it was in the hands of an adhoc committee for which party member Sam Bardell acted as secretary. Among others actively involved in organising it were Dave Wallis, a corporal in Signals and Michael Katanka who had worked for Command headquarters at Heliopolis. But most members of the organising committee were not party members, though they had left-wing views.

The 'mock' parliament started its meetings. Initially it was not divided into parties. Every time it met the hall was crammed. On 1 December 1943, there was a debate on a 'Distribution Trades Nationalisation Bill' which was adopted by an overwhelming majority.

Early in 1944, the committee decided that the 'mock parliament' should be run on party lines, for which purpose a mock 'general election' would be held. This took place on 2 February 1944; in line with their aim of Labour–Communist unity, communists did not stand independently. 'The reason that there wasn't a communist selected to stand at that Cairo Forces Parliament is that we decided that the first requirement was for a Labour government to be returned ... it was necessary to make sure there was a Labour majority' recalled Don Brayford, one of the participants. Arthur Attwood later described the mock election in his camp: 'We went all round the camp on the back of a lorry putting our case. The party member withdrew in the interest of unity ... the Labour chap romped home'.[17]

The end result of the mock election was a clear majority for Labour. The 'parliament' continued with its meetings which attracted about 500 participants. But, in April 1944, the Army authorities closed it down, while several of those who had served on its parliamentary committee were hastily 'posted' elsewhere. On 25 April, D.N. Pritt MP questioned Grigg, the Secretary of State for War, about this instruction that the Forces Mock Parliament must be banned, but Grigg brushed the matter aside, saying that he was 'expecting a report'. Following which Communist MP Gallacher asked whether it was not the case that those in charge were concerned 'not so much that the troops are discussing politics, as that they are discussing the wrong kind of politics?' He got no reply. However, in July Grigg told the Commons that the meetings of the disbanded Forces Parliament were a 'species of political exhibitionism which it was right for the Commander-in-Chief to restrict.'[18]

'Mock parliaments' were not confined to Cairo; they emerged in several locations. Thus, in that year of 1944, after the battles of Khima and Imphal, during which a Japanese offensive was repulsed, the men who had been in the front line were brought out to be rested. They were up in the hills, with no leisure facilities, so Wally Macfarlane was asked by the company commander to organise a 'model parliament'. This he did, and over four weeks they debated four subjects: Equal Rights for Women; State Control; What to do with Germany after the war; Should India have Independence? Following these debates, there was continuing discussion among the serving men.[19]

The landslide victory which Labour was to achieve in 1945 was in no small measure the result of an overwhelming vote from those in the armed services. There was little doubt that communists could take some of the credit for bringing about this victory.

6

WARTIME STRUGGLES FOR COLONIAL FREEDOM

Since its formation, the party had always been involved in struggles for colonial freedom. The subject was treated as a matter of importance at the 1942 conference and at each of the wartime congresses held later.

In 1939 the British Empire covered about 550 million people: one quarter of the human race. Of these, only 70 million white people were self-governing. They lived in Britain or in the Dominions: Australia, Canada, New Zealand. Of the non-whites, much the largest number – about 400 million – were in India. The remaining 80 million were in parts of Africa, the West Indies, Burma, Ceylon, Malaya and so on. All of these countries were subject to British rule and though, in some cases, there was a pretence that 'self-government' was on the way, in actual fact moves in this direction had been cosmetic.

This was demonstrated in the case of India where, during the 1930s, elections to provincial assemblies had at last been permitted. At these elections, the Indian National Congress, a body fighting for independence, had achieved a sweeping victory. But the powers of these assemblies were severely limited and India continued to be governed from the centre under a 'Viceroy' appointed by the British Government. When the war broke out, India was declared to be at war with Germany without any consultation with representatives of the Indian people. The Indian National Congress reacted by asking the British Government to apply to India the principles of liberty and national independence for which it claimed to be waging war. This request was rejected. So, in October 1940, the congress embarked on a civil disobedience campaign – whereupon almost all its leaders, including Nehru, were arrested; by May 1941, there were 20,000 people in prison for their advocacy of the Congress cause.

In August 1941, Prime Minister Churchill and the United States

President, Roosevelt, signed a joint declaration known as the 'Atlantic Charter' which stated that they 'respect the right of all peoples to choose the form of government under which they will live.' However, Churchill himself indicated on 9 September 1941 that the statement 'all peoples' did not apply to those of India, Burma, or any other parts of the British Empire.

Following the entry of Japan into the war in December 1941 came speedy Japanese advances into Malaya, the fall of Singapore, and the start of attacks on Burma. It was clear that India would soon be under threat. To counter this, in March 1942, the coalition government sent Sir Stafford Cripps to India to make a new offer to the Indian Congress leaders. This consisted of a changed but still extremely undemocratic constitution to be brought in *after* the war was over. Not surprisingly, the Congress leaders rejected this offer and Cripps returned empty-handed.

THE PARTY IN THE FIGHT FOR INDIAN INDEPENDENCE

Just after Cripps returned from India, the party published a pamphlet by Ben Bradley entitled *India: What We Must Do* which confirmed that the Cripps proposals for a changed constitution after the war were totally undemocratic, and argued that the demands of the Indian National Congress for the formation of a Provisional National Government *during* the war should be supported. As Bradley put it: 'how can the Indian people take seriously our declarations that we fight for freedom against fascism, when we lock up in our prisons thousands of the most convinced and capable anti-fascists?' Bradley urged that every Labour, trade union, and cooperative organisation should demand that India have its own national government, and that workers in the factories and pits should send telegrams to the Prime Minister voicing this demand.

At the 1942 Party Conference, the issue was given much prominence and an emergency resolution was adopted urging that negotiations be reopened with the Indian National Congress for the formation of a representative national government and calling upon all working class organisations to fight for a change in policy. 'We regret that Sir Stafford Cripps lent the political standing and prestige of his name to take terms to India which represented simply the old historical policy of British imperialism 'Divide and Rule', said Pollitt.

Endeavours on the left to persuade the government to change course did not succeed, with highly unfortunate results. The Indian National Congress persisted in demanding withdrawal of British rule, arguing that a free India would throw all its resources into the struggle against Nazism, fascism and imperialism. But, at a meeting held on August 8 1942, it also announced that, if its appeal was ignored, a campaign of non-violent struggle would be launched. Representatives from the Indian Communist Party (which had just gained legal status after being banned for many years) argued against this proposal, saying that it would injure the anti-fascist cause, but they were defeated. However, the campaign for non-violent civil disobedience never got going because, on 9 August, the Congress leaders were once more arrested and imprisoned. the result was a spontaneous outbreak of rioting and violence.

In Britain, though they had not agreed with the Congress proposals for civil disobedience, communists denounced the arrests, claiming that they would provoke more violence. They reaffirmed their demand for a reversal of the government's policy and for recognition of India's right to independence.[1]

However, the government received approval for its actions in India from the TUC General Council and Labour's National Executive.[2] At the Trades Union Congress in September this stand was challenged by some on the left. They included Bill Whittaker of the Burnley Weavers Association who was a member of the Central Committee of the Communist Party. But the attempt to reverse the policy on India was defeated.[3]

The matter was again discussed at the Communist Party's 16th Congress held in July 1943, at which a resolution was adopted demanding the release of all anti-fascist Indian leaders and for the formation of a representative Indian national government.[4] The debate was opened by Joe Scott of the AEU and among those who spoke was the Indian, Krishna Menon, a member of the Indian National Congress, who was present as a fraternal delegate. He was one of the leaders of an organisation known as the India League, which was based in London and which campaigned for Indian independence, and to which party members gave much active support. Some years later, after independence was at last achieved, he was to become Nehru's Foreign Minister in the Indian Government.

Among the books produced during the war were *India Today* by R. Palme Dutt, published by the Left Book Club in 1940, and a Penguin

Special, *Problems of India* by D. Shelvankar, a member of the party's Colonial Committee. According to Clive Branson, who had been posted to India in the summer of 1942, both these books were banned from being sold in Bombay, though Hitler's *Mein Kampf* was prominently displayed there on bookstalls.

After Branson was killed in Burma in 1944, his letters home were published in a book entitled *British Soldier in India*. It exposed the terrible oppression suffered by the Indian people, the appalling attitudes of the British towards them, and discussed the political problems of the time. It received a wide sale.

HOW THE PARTY MAINTAINED LINKS

Before the war, the party not only campaigned for Indian freedom, it also managed to maintain direct links with the Indian Communist Party, despite the difficulties involved which were highlighted in the notorious 'Meerut Conspiracy' case in 1929. This was when Ben Bradley and Philip Spratt were arrested and jailed along with 29 Indian activists for 'conspiracy to deprive the King Emperor of sovereignty over British India.'

From then on links between the Communist International and the Indian Communist Party had been maintained largely through undercover operations organised by the British Party. Couriers would go out and meet surreptitiously with the Indian Party leaders, handing over documents and taking back others. Michael Carritt, who worked for the Indian Civil Service, but who joined the British Communist Party while on leave in 1935, was among those who helped maintain contact, along with the Rev. Michael Scott, Chaplain to the Bishop of Bombay.[5]

After the war broke out, such direct links became virtually impossible. However, indirect links were forged as troops were sent out to India and communists among them made contact with the Indian Party.

Branson was one of the party members in the armed forces who held frequent meetings with members of the Indian Communist Party in Bombay and later in Calcutta. Another was Bill Carritt, brother of Michael Carritt mentioned above, who was sent out to India in the spring of 1944. He spent his leave at the offices of the Communist Party of India where he had many talks with P.C. Joshi, then its general secretary. As he later recalled, 'all Communist Party members in the forces in India who wished, gave their leave money to the CPI, who provided accommodation and hospitality in return.[6]

Jim Fyrth, who served with the 50th Indian Tank Brigade from the end of 1944, also spent much time contacting the Indian Communist Party. He, and other party members he knew, would get to Bombay whenever they could and go to the Raj Bhuvan, the CPI headquarters and commune in Sandhurst Road. There they met up with other British comrades and with Indian leaders such as Joshi and Dange (the veteran trade union leader). They would have discussions on Indian affairs and world events, and, on one occasion, arrangements were made for Fyrth to meet Gandhi, and the leaders of both the Bombay Congress and of the Bombay Muslim League. The people at Sandhurst Road gave Fyrth names and addresses so that wherever he went in India, he could get in touch with the local party, even in quite remote places.[7]

By this time, many party members were writing to the *Daily Worker* about what they were seeing in India. Thus, on 22 March, 1945, a letter from a corporal described his experiences in Bengal as follows:

> The other day I met and talked with some Indians not far from Arakan. This is the first occasion I have been able to speak to Bengal peasants – and what an experience. For heaven's sake tell our comrades at home that they've got to work their fingers to the bone to assist these victims of a bankrupt imperialism. The mud huts, the disease, prostitution – in a word, the social and moral degradation of the Bengal workers and peasants make a terrible indictment of the British Raj. The British people cannot escape responsibility for the situation in 'Mr Amery's India'.

(The Conservative MP L.C.S. Amery was at that time Minister for India and Burma in the Coalition Government).

The *Daily Worker* was indeed devoting considerable space to the appalling conditions in India, and one ex-lance-corporal, who had arrived home after 18 months service there, commented on how correct these articles were. He said that 'in Bombay, starvation and over-crowding existed everywhere.... As a result of travelling all over India, we came to the conclusion that India was a land of beggars'.[8]

AFRICA, ASIA, THE WEST INDIES, CYPRUS

It has sometimes been suggested that the party's anti-colonial activities were largely confined to India. This is untrue. The party tried to mobilise support for all the oppressed peoples of the Empire and their struggles for freedom and democratic rights.

Most of the party's work in this sphere was coordinated through its Colonial Information Bureau, set up in 1937, with Ben Bradley as its secretary. The bureau issued a regular *Colonial Information Bulletin* to subscribers which, in 1940, changed its name to *Inside the Empire*. It was one of the publications discussed by the secret Cabinet Committee on Communist Activities in January 1941, the question at issue being whether it should be suppressed. In the event, no action was taken against it other than a continuing ban on its export.[9] However, due to the blitz, it went temporarily out of existence, only to reappear in March 1943. The subjects covered in this particular issue illustrate the wide range of localities on which it concentrated. They included a description of the Indian famine; an outline of the Communist Party of South Africa's campaign against the colour-bar and the 'pass laws'; an item on the imprisonment of a newspaper editor in Sierra Leone (West Africa); an article on the wages paid to miners in Jamaica. Other subjects were forced labour in Kenya, Northern Rhodesia and Nigeria; Irish immigration; trade unions in Canada and notes on Cyprus.

Winning the war against fascism was the party's overriding concern in March 1943, and in an editorial heralding the paper's reappearance, Ben Bradley made the somewhat questionable assertion that the colonial peoples understood that progress to self-determination was dependent on a victory over fascism. However, the main stress in the bulletin was on the 'tremendous responsibility' of the British people 'to show in action their recognition of the rights of the colonial peoples to democratic liberties.'

During this period, the work of the party's Colonial Committee was much extended. It had 16 members. Among them was Reginald Bridgeman, pre-war secretary of the League against Imperialism, who had been expelled from the Labour Party and, though not formally a member of the Communist Party, always worked closely with it. The committee also included the Indian author D.K. Shelvankar; Desmond Buckle who came from West Africa; a Greek Cypriot, E. Pappianou (who was later to become secretary of AKEL, the Communist Party in Cyprus); Desmond Greaves from Ireland. Other members were Arthur Clegg, prominent in the China Campaign Committee; Jim Shields, a former editor of the *Daily Worker*; Malcolm McEwen, a journalist on the *Daily Worker*; Maud Rogerson, a north London activist; George Rude, later to become well known as a historian; Lazar Zaidman, prominent in Jewish organisations; Horace Palmer, a music teacher who helped edit *Inside the Empire*; Freda Cook, who came from Australia; Douglas Walton from South Africa; Arthur Oleranshaw, who had fought in the International Brigade in Spain.

This committee helped to draft a memorandum which was adopted by the Party's Executive Committee, and was in November 1944 issued as a pamphlet entitled *Colonies: The Way Forward*. It did not deal with India (for which the party's demand for independence was long established) but concentrated on the other colonies, including those in Africa and the West Indies, together with Cyprus, Malta and Palestine, and territories then under Japanese occupation such as Burma and Malaya. Based on this memorandum, a study syllabus was issued by Ben Bradley on 'Colonies and the Future' and a conference was held on the subject in March 1945 while the war was still on, at which speakers from Nigeria, Northern Rhodesia and Cyprus participated.

In both these publications, it was argued that the victory over fascism would present the most favourable conditions for colonial liberation, because fascism represented the most vicious racial superiority and denial of freedom and democracy. It was also argued that self-rule for the colonial people was in the interests of the great majority of British people. Those opposing it were the small but powerful section of monopoly capitalists who made super profits from the economic and political exploitation of the colonies. 'Our task is, therefore, to win the Labour and progressive movement as speedily as possible to support the demands of the colonial peoples.'

It was pointed out that none of the colonies were self-governing; civil liberties were severely restricted, and even where some limited form of representative institution existed it had no real power. Economically, all colonies were subordinated to British interests, either directly by companies enjoying concessions, or by settlers appropriating the best land and resources, or indirectly under trading forms whereby production was carried on for big outside companies, who bought up entire crops for sale outside the country concerned.

The common assumption that the colonial peoples were 'not yet fit' for self-determination was strongly attacked. It was stressed that such arguments were not only used by those who had an interest in maintaining the subjection of the colonial peoples, but that they were sometimes used also by philanthropically concerned spokesmen.

'These are extremely dangerous arguments, and can lead to false and dangerous conclusions.' It emphasised that self-determination was in the interests of all people and quoted Marx: 'No nation can be free if it oppresses other nations.'

It was pointed out that, in order to win support of the countries such as Burma, the Japanese pretended to offer freedom. A firm declaration that Britain would grant freedom to Burma would win the Burmese people as allies.

The policies of the Labour Party were criticised, since although its colonial policy contained many valuable proposals on health and education the 'question of self-determination is shelved to a dim future, and the colonial peoples are treated as 'primitives' whose territories have to be administered as a 'trust' '.

There was continual reference to Clause 3 of the Atlantic Charter which asserted the right of all peoples to choose their government, and to Churchill's argument that it did not apply to British colonial territories. Again, in his booklet *How to Win the Peace*, published in September 1944, Harry Pollitt stressed the need for the application of this charter to the peoples of India, Africa, the East and West Indies, Malaya, Burma and Ceylon. This demand was endorsed by the 17th Party Congress held in October 1944, and shortly afterwards, the work of the party's Colonial Committee was extended. A colonial department was established at the party centre with Michael Carritt in charge. When the war ended in August 1945, meetings of demobilised soldiers who had served in India, the Far East or the Middle East began to be held to make use of their experiences, and an Indian and a Middle East newsletter was circulated.

RACIAL DISCRIMINATION AT HOME

It had long been understood that one of the obstacles to the cause of colonial liberation was racial prejudice – the notion that non-whites were not capable of governing themselves. This prejudice became more marked as the war progressed.

At the time when the war broke out, very few black people were living in Britain, but as the war continued more began to enter the country. Some had been brought in from the West Indies to work in war factories; others were stationed in Britain as part of the American or Canadian armed forces.

In October 1943 an 'Educational Commentary' issued twice

monthly by Marx House in association with the *Daily Worker* was headed 'the Colour Bar – a Barrier to Progress'.

It asserted that the colour bar had raised its 'ugly head' recently in many places. It cited the case of 'twenty-six-year-old Amelia King' whose family had lived in Britain for five generations, and who had been turned down by the Land Army because she was black. 'Miss King is both mentally and physically fit, but her skin is dark.' It went on to mention a well-known West Indian cricketer, Learie Constantine, who had booked rooms for himself and his family at a London hotel, but on arriving was asked by the manager to find 'other accommodation' as 'certain of his guests objected to being in the same hotel as a man of colour.'

It said: 'There are other "incidents" of colour prejudice happening daily that go unrecorded in this country'; these included the banning of dance halls and saloon bars, and sometimes even public reading rooms, to black troops; frequent refusals to them of hotel accommodation; difficulties experienced by black seamen in finding lodgings.

It went on to condemn the idea that white people were basically superior to black people. 'This prejudice was first spread to provide a justification for the conquest and subjection of the 'backward' coloured peoples, the annexation and exploitation of their territories by white traders and capitalists ... to this day a social prejudice against coloured people is deliberately worked up to provide a cover for economic exploitation and political reaction. It is perpetuated by capitalist exploiters who use it to condemn the Negro to serve as a source of cheap labour.' And it stressed that such racial prejudice formed an important part of the stock-in-trade of Hitler's 'Fifth Column'.

It quoted Professor J.B.S. Haldane's study of the subject in which he had concluded that blacks were not inferior to whites either intellectually or physically.

And it emphasised the need 'to fight consistently and ruthlessly any expression of colour or racial prejudice, no matter in what form it rears its ugly head.'

During 1944 and 1945 the *Daily Worker* continued to draw attention to the colour-bar question. For example a letter from a Manchester reader said: 'I am a Negro and I want to protest against the treatment of coloured men who are British subjects serving in the Army and the RAF and in industry. We have pledged ourselves to serve against

Hitler and his gang. Some of us will never return from this service. Yet some of the treatment we get makes us wonder what we are fighting for.'[10]

Another letter described how young women, recruited into the ATS (Auxilliary Territorial Service) had been warned not to associate with coloured troops.[11]

After the war, when black people were to come to Britain in much greater numbers, the problems of racial prejudice were to become much greater. But it was not until the 1960s that any attempts were made to put legal curbs on racial discrimination.

7

FRIENDS OR ENEMIES? 1943–4

Despite their efforts to increase war production and to improve fighting capacity in the armed forces, communists were habitually portrayed as 'the enemy' by those on high. In this connection, much use was made of what became known as the 'Springhall case'. It was on 28 July 1943 that 'Dave' Springhall (his actual name was Douglas Frank Springhall) was sentenced to seven years' imprisonment after a trial held in secret at the Old Bailey.

Springhall – formerly a seaman – had been on the Central Committee of the party since 1932. He had acted as full-time London District Secretary; had served as a Political Commissar to the British Battalion of the International Brigade in Spain; in 1938, he was for a brief period editor of the *Daily Worker*, and in 1939, had been in Moscow as British representative at Comintern headquarters. At the time of his arrest on 17 June 1943 he was working as national organiser at the Communist Party headquarters at 16 King Street.

The charge against him was 'of obtaining from Olive Sheehan, an Air Ministry employee, information in respect to munitions of war, and obtaining from her, for a purpose prejudicial to the interests and safety of the state, information calculated to be useful to the enemy'.[1]

What Springhall had in fact been involved in at the time of his arrest was handing over to the Russians technical information arising from research into jet engines.[2] This was not made public at the time; had it been, Springhall might well have received more public support. For the affair would have demonstrated something that government circles were trying to hide: their desire to avoid any close relationship with the Soviet Union. The Russians were, after all, allies of Britain; they were engaged in destroying the German army and so preventing a German invasion of Britain. The British were busy handing over scientific and technical information of all kinds to the Americans; yet to give anything to the country which was saving their future was classed as 'prejudicial to the interests and safety of the state.' Indeed, when he passed sentence in public at the end of a trial *in camera*, Mr Justice Oliver admitted that, in view of Springhall's record, 'it was not likely that his purpose was to communicate those things to the enemy.'[3]

However, whatever the justification was in this instance for passing such information to the Russians, such action was never condoned by the Communist Party, whose function was to change the ideas and attitudes of British people through its activities as a legitimate political party. Though working at the party's head office, Springhall had not informed Harry Pollitt, its general secretary, or anyone else that he was involved in something which might lead to a charge under the Official Secrets Act. Had he done so, he would have been told to stop it, since it was easy to see that such a charge could be used against the party itself, and might even jeopardise its very existence. Indeed, the revelation of Springhall's activities caused much indignation at the party's head office.

It was immediately obvious that the right-wing Labour leaders would make maximum use of the event in the hope of stirring up hostility to communists. Thus, just after Springhall was sentenced, Labour MP, Dan Frankel, gave notice that he would ask Herbert Morrison, Home Secretary, whether, as a result of the Springhall case, he proposed to undertake an investigation into the activities of the Communist Party 'to ensure himself that its organisation is not being used for any purpose detrimental to the national interest'. In response to this, Pollitt issued a statement on behalf of the party:

> The Communist Party had no knowledge of any activity such as it has been alleged Springhall was engaged in. If it had, it would have taken disciplinary action against him. The Communist Party will welcome and give the fullest facilities for any investigation in regard to baseless allegations that it is being used for any purpose detrimental to the national interest.
>
> The Communist Party has nothing to fear or hide from any such investigation. On the contrary, the facts would prove its whole activity has only one aim – the strengthening of every aspect of the war effort ...
>
> The purpose of Mr Frankel's questions has nothing to do with the national interest. It is prompted solely with the intention of attacking the Communist Party.[4]

Frankel's question was answered by Herbert Morrison on 5 August. He stressed that Springhall had, for many years, been prominent in the leadership of the party, and went on to say:

'having regard to the nature and record of the Communist Party my hon. friend may be assured that their activities are not overlooked. I do not think any special investigation is called for, but the vigilance of all concerned will, of course, be stimulated by this case, and whenever cause for action should arise, I should not hesitate to take whatever course appeared most effective and appropriate in the circumstances.'

Asked whether he accepted Pollitt's statement that the Communist Party had no knowledge of Springhall's activities, he replied that 'the party would hardly be likely to admit to any complicity, but I think the facts speak for themselves', to which Gallacher shouted: 'What facts?' and then said: 'In view of the fact that this case was tried *in camera*, is it in order for the minister to say that the facts speak for themselves, when it is notorious that if it had been tried in public the prosecution could never have got away with the evidence? It is a dirty bit of business'.[5]

Earlier, Gallacher caused uproar and laughter in the House by challenging Morrison to be frank about 'how the character of myself or Harry Pollitt compares with his own mouldy character and that of the disreputable stooge whom he put up to ask this question'.

A few days later, the newly elected Executive Committee of the Communist Party decided that Springhall must be expelled from the party.

DISCRIMINATION AGAINST THE *DAILY WORKER*

Morrison was to continue his attempts to isolate communists and limit the growth of their influence. One example was his treatment of the *Daily Worker* which by 1944 had a daily circulation of 100,000 – this figure would have been far higher had it not been for paper rationing. But in February 1944, when there was a renewed wave of incendiary bomb air-raids on London, and the Home Office convened a special press conference to brief journalists, Morrison personally made sure that no *Daily Worker* correspondent would be present.

Morrison of course received the approval of Prime Minister Churchill for his actions; so did the War Secretary Sir James Grigg who refused to allow the paper to have an 'accredited war correspondent.' As early as 2 March 1943, the *Daily Worker* had applied to have two of its staff – Claud Cockburn and Clemens Dutt –

appointed as accredited war correspondents. But the paper was informed by the War Office that the two names submitted were 'not acceptable', no reason being given. The *Daily Worker* then submitted a further name, Walter Holmes, and this was in turn refused. In July 1943, two more names – George Sinfield and Frank Lesser – were put forward, but no answer was received.

In July 1943, after the British and American forces had driven the Germans and Italians out of North Africa, and established a base under French control, it was agreed that a party of 'diplomatic' correspondents would be allowed to visit the scene, and Claud Cockburn (who not only worked for the *Daily Worker* but edited an information bulletin *The Week*) managed to get permission to be one of the party. After arriving in Algiers, he was told by the British that he was to be expelled from North Africa, and should leave within 24 hours. In the event, Cockburn went into hiding and returned to England a fortnight later in a blaze of publicity.[6]

At the beginning of 1944, in reply to a question in the House of Commons, Sir James Grigg made clear that no writer for the *Daily Worker* would be regarded as suitable for the position of 'accredited correspondent' to the armed forces, since such correspondents received secret information and 'recent experience' had shown that 'members and adherents of the Communist Party could not be trusted not to communicate secret information to that party.'[7] The 'recent experience' to which Grigg referred was, of course, the Springhall case.

FASCISTS AND ANTI-SEMITES

In contrast to his tough attitude to communists, Morrison went out of his way to be kind to Sir Oswald Mosley, leader of the British Union of Fascists. 700 of Mosley's followers had been detained in June 1940 under Defence Regulation 18b. This regulation enabled the Home Secretary to detain without trial members of organisations which sympathised with 'the system of government of any power with which His Majesty is at war' and where there was danger that such an organisation could be used 'for purposes prejudicial to the efficient prosecution of the war'. Since the British Union of Fascists had given fervent support to the Hitler regime, and Britain was at war with Germany, regulation 18b clearly applied to its members.

However, in his first year of office as Home Secretary, Morrison reduced the number of British fascists detained, by more than half. By the autumn of 1942, this was having repercussions. An organisation calling itself the British National Party was set up and an anti-semitic campaign got rapidly under way. Anti-Jewish leaflets were distributed, anti-semitic slogans were prominently displayed in certain war factories; they implied that the war was being fought to make the Jews rich. 'It's a Jews' war' was chalked up in certain London streets. The British National Party's proclaimed aims were the release of Sir Oswald Mosley, a negotiated peace with Hitler, the expulsion of all Jews from Britain.[8]

'Everyone with eyes and ears must be aware of the recent marked increase of anti-semitic propaganda in this country; and everyone with political intelligence must be aware that this is a political phenomenon, reflecting increased Fascist and Fifth Column activity in this country, following on the release of Fascist detainees' wrote Dutt.[9] He noted that questions in the House of Commons concerning openly fascist and anti-semitic demonstrations in central London had been met with 'polite unconcern' by government spokesmen. And he attacked the government for refusing to admit Jewish refugee children from Nazi occupied countries into Britain, on the grounds that this might offend anti-semitic feeling in this country. This was an issue that had been given prominence by Claud Cockburn in *The Week* on 11 December 1942.

An article by Pollitt on the dangers of anti-semitism appeared in the *Daily Worker* on 12 December 1942, and for the next few months the Party paid a good deal of attention to the matter, aiming to counteract it wherever it appeared. A pamphlet *Anti-Semitism: What it means to you* by Gallacher was published in April 1943. This pointed out that, whenever there had been a breakdown in society through war or economic collapse, the reactionaries, 'seeking a way of turning discontent away from themselves' had tried to incite sections of the community against a helpless and defenceless minority – the Jews. He answered the common allegations made against the Jews, showing that in Britain, they were *not* among the biggest financiers; they did *not* control the press; they were *not* responsible for the 'Black Market'; the allegation that the Jews made money while everyone else did the fighting had no foundation; on the contrary, the Jews had a higher proportion of their men in the fighting services than the Gentiles. He listed the number of Jews who had been decorated for bravery and for their work during the blitz.

The call for action against the anti-semites met with some response;

resolutions were carried by various working-class organisations including the London Trades Council, condemning anti-semitism and pro-fascist activity. As John Gollan said, the object of the anti-semitic campaign was to 'turn public hatred against the imaginary Jewish enemy while preparaing for appeasement with the real enemy – Hitler.' 'They want to sow the seeds of discord, split and disunite the people by inflaming hatred against an imaginary enemy as a prelude to doing a deal with the real enemy.' He suggested that anti-semitic propaganda should be made a criminal offence.[10] But the government made no moves in that direction, and incitement to racial hatred was not to become a criminal offence until thirty years later.

MOSLEY'S RELEASE

At the beginning of October 1943, following pressure from Sir Oswald Mosley's sympathisers – many of whom were in high places – Churchill asked Morrison for information concerning Mosley's state of health.

Mosley was in fact being far better treated than most detainees, let alone normal prisoners. He was residing with his wife in a disused wing of Holloway prison where they lived in a state of relative luxury. They occupied a self-contained flat consisting of two bedrooms, a sitting-room, kitchen and bathroom. They had constant hot water and their own gas stove on which Lady Mosley cooked when she felt inclined to do so, while Sir Oswald spent time cultivating their allotment and growing vegetables in the prison grounds. They wore their own clothes, received constant visitors; food and drink were brought in to them from outside as required; prisoners from the main building waited upon them and helped to clean their flat.

Morrison passed on Churchill's request for information on Mosley's health to the prison doctors. Mosley had, in fact, for some twenty years suffered from recurrent attacks of phlebitis. In view of the way he was being treated, the doctors replied that they saw no reason for alarm. Morrison could have left it at that. He didn't. Instead he called for outside medical advice in the person of Lord Dawson of Penn, following which the prison doctors suddenly changed their minds and recommended Mosley's release.

By the autumn of 1943, rumours were widespread that Mosley was to be released from prison and, on 11 November, the *Daily Worker* devoted much space to the matter, insisting that 'the release of Mosley, no matter what the pretext, would cause widespread indignation, alarm and cynicism.' Two days later, it reported that many resolutions – particularly from war factories – had been sent to Morrison demanding the continued detention of Mosley. But Morrison ignored these warnings, and on 17 November he informed the war cabinet that he intended to release Mosley from detention on 'humanitarian grounds.' He secured approval for this action, despite furious opposition from Ernest Bevin, Minister of Labour and former general secretary of the Transport and General Workers Union;[12] his decision was announced on the same day, at a time when parliament was conveniently in recess.

'This decision will not be tolerated by the people' was the immediate reaction of the *Daily Worker*, a forecast which turned out to be justified as Morrison faced what his biographers later described as the 'biggest storm of his wartime career.'

Messages of protest poured into the Home Office and 10 Downing Street; delegations besieged government buildings, people queued in the streets to sign petitions of protest; telegrams flooded into Downing Street; threats of strike action in war factories were only averted by decisions to send instant deputations to call on Morrison. For the next few days, the *Daily Worker* was printing column after column, listing organisations which had protested against the release; on 23 November, it announced that, as it was inundated by such resolutions, it was impossible to go on printing them. Organisations were asked, nevertheless, to continue sending them in, as summaries would be published.

This fury from 'down below' had to be recognised by the Labour leaders. The executive council of the Transport and General Workers Union, the largest union in the country, asked for a reconsideration of the decision; the National Council of Labour disassociated itself from Morrison's action; the General Council of the TUC said that the release was a blunder and urged that it be reconsidered; the National Executive Committee of the Labour Party expressed its 'regret' at the decision.

However, at a meeting of the Parliamentary Labour Party, Morrison managed to secure support for his action by 51 votes to 43, and on 2 December, when the matter was debated in the Commons, a critical amendment was defeated by 327 votes to 62.

At the time it was suggested that the anger shown by ordinary people had been stirred up by communists for their own ends. In fact, this was not the case; Morrison's action provoked spontaneous fury both in the workplace and in the armed forces, for it seemed like an insult to those who were fighting and dying for the anti-fascist cause. In practice, communists were heavily engaged in trying to channel the anger into actions which would not damage the war effort. They headed off protest strikes in the war factories and the coal mines by advocating, instead, the appointment of deputations to meet with MPs and government representatives, and by launching petitions to be despatched to Downing Street.

Mosley's release reinforced the belief among communists that there were fascist sympathisers in high places. As a statement issued by the Party's Executive Committee put it: 'the release of Mosley is a blow against everything for which the people are fighting. It is a blow against the Eighth and Fifth Armies; against the people of Europe and Russia; against the men of the RAF, the merchant service and the Navy. It will bring joy only to Hitler, Mussolini and Laval and the Fifth Column in Britain.'[13]

8

THE PARTY'S POST-WAR AIMS

During the summer of 1944, the party was circulating a draft programme outlining its aims for post-war Britain. In doing this, it was responding to the mood of many people who were determined not to go back to the 'hungry thirties'. Memories were still alive of the promises made in World War I for a 'land fit for heroes'. The outcome: mass unemployment, depressed areas, under-fed children and the widening gap between rich and poor was far removed from this ideal. When, in its programme, the party asserted 'Never again must we tolerate poverty in the midst of plenty' it was echoing the thoughts of millions.

Two years earlier, party leaders had regarded talk about what should happen after the war with some suspicion, believing it could be used as a diversion from the war effort. That was the feeling in the summer of 1942. When, later that year, government plans for post-war Britain began to appear, the need to examine them became important. They included the Scott and Uthwatt proposals for the use and control of land, and the Beveridge Report which defined 'freedom from want' as its goal, and proposed far-reaching changes in the social insurance system, making unemployment benefit and sickness benefit enough to live on, together with child allowances and a comprehensive health service.

The Beveridge Report came out in December 1942, and soon afterwards the party's Central Committee met and adopted a memorandum headed 'Guiding Lines on Questions of Post-War Reconstruction' which was circulated to the membership. It was pointed out that post-war plans were 'no longer mainly the happy-hunting-ground of social theorists and cranks as an escape from current war questions' but were now the subject of proposed legislation, on which all political parties were taking up positions; it was essential for the party to participate. Several committees were therefore set up and produced memoranda on such matters as social insurance, education, housing, the health service, agriculture, transport, and coal mining. These culminated in a document entitled *Britain for the People: Proposals for Post-war Policy* issued for discussion by the Executive Committee in May 1944.

WARTIME ACHIEVEMENTS

The need to build on what had been achieved was emphasised in *Britain for the People*. For the ironic fact was that, during the war, considerable advances had been made in living standards for working people. True, they had faced death and destruction from air-raids, had lived under constant fear of attack, while large numbers had been bombed out of their homes and forced into temporary accommodation, having lost some or all of their personal possessions. And they had suffered much discomfort from fuel shortages, the inconveniences of the blackout, the lack of consumer goods, the rationing of food and clothing. Yet despite these difficulties, working people had made some astonishing gains. The basic reason for this was that, for the first time in 20 years, there had been no unemployment. This meant that people no longer went hungry as they had before the war. Under-nourishment, particularly among children, was fast disappearing. A survey of Glasgow children, revealing sharp increases in average heights and weights, underlined the changes taking place. Indeed, certain of the foodstuffs now rationed – for example, butter – were ones which many families had not been able to afford to buy before the war; they were now eating them regularly.

This trend to better feeding had been bolstered by a whole series of measures, including the spread of free milk in schools, the obligation imposed on employers to set up adequate works canteens, the introduction of non-profit making 'British Restaurants' run by local authorities, which provided good food at a low price.

As George Matthews, a young farmer and member of the party's Executive Committee, observed early in 1944: 'Today, there is widespread determination that we in Britain are never going back to pre-war conditions in which ... one third of our population was under-nourished, starvation and semi-starvation went side by side with the decay of agriculture in Britain and overseas, and food urgently needed by millions was consigned to the sea and the flames'.[1]

Full employment had also had a dramatic impact on rights at work. Although the Essential Work Order (under which workers could be directed into a job and forbidden to leave it) had initially been regarded as an attack on freedom, it made it very difficult for employers to sack people. This was one reason for a marked increase in self-confidence among manual workers. There had been a huge growth in workplace organisation, resulting in trade union recognition and much levelling-up of wage rates. Despite long hours and blackout difficulties, there were marked improvements in conditions of work. The experience of the Joint Production Committees had opened the eyes of many workers to the possibilities of participation in decision-making.

PLANS FOR A BETTER BRITAIN

In its draft programme *Britain for the People* the party stressed that gains made during the war should be maintained and used to build a better Britain. The immediate aims listed fell into nine broad categories: (1) work for all (2) social security (3) a self-contained house or flat for every family (4) no return to low wages and under-nourishment (5) a comprehensive national health service (6) universal rights to education (7) the widest access to culture (8) democracy: 'the present passive kind of democracy in which public affairs still, in practice, remain in the hands of the few must be replaced by an active democracy in which all play a part' (9) a peace settlement which will 'lay the foundations for real, international collaboration and lasting peace.'

The programme pointed out that during the war central planning and state control had led to vast increases in production, major technical and scientific developments and much greater efficiency. 'The state became the major buyer and placer of orders; it owned factories; it supplied finance to extend existing plants; it controlled investment; it allocated supply according to priority needs, and organised the distribution of goods'. Although these wartime controls were hampered by the fact that most of the controllers were drawn from firms with a vested interest in the product concerned, wartime state control had proved itself far more efficient than the 'pre-war uncoordinated scramble of vested interests.' Therefore, when the war ended, state control should be carried forward to produce abundance for the people.

To achieve this aim, the land, transport, coal and power, steel and the banks should be taken into public ownership. For the rest, the state should assume repsonsibility for planning allocation of supplies, bulk purchase, the organisation of distribution etc. The state-controlling bodies must contain sufficient representatives of the Government, the trade unions and the consumer cooperatives. 'Trade union participation in control should be established at every stage, from the workshop to the national bodies.'

These proposals were to be seen, not as ends in themselves, but as immediate measures, as steps towards the establishment of a socialist Britain. For the Communist Party 'holds the view that the only final solution is the complete ending of the class ownership of the means of production, and the establishment of social ownership and organisation of the resources of the country, of the land, the mines, the factories, the docks, the shipping, the banks and all the large-scale machinery of production and distribution.'

THE ATTITUDE TO PARLIAMENT

In one very important respect, *Britain for the People* implied a major change in the attitude of the party. This concerned Parliament.

In previous programmes (such as that issued in 1935 *For Soviet Britain* or the draft programme issued but never adopted in 1939) it had always been emphasised that socialism could not be achieved through Parliament for two main reasons: first, because there would be violent resistance on the part of the ruling class and the capitalist apparatus, and secondly, because socialism required a different kind of political system, one in which workers participated through workers' councils elected at the workplace.

Now, for the first time, the party held out a prospect, not of abolishing Parliament, but of changing it; not of destroying the state machine, but of democratising it.

With regard to Parliament itself, the Executive Committee had in 1943 set up a 'Parliamentary and Local Government Committee' which was chaired by William Gallacher, and whose purpose was to advise the Executive on proposals for post-war reform. The upshot was a recommendation for a change to proportional representation in the form of the single transferable vote, a measure which Gallacher advocated (unsuccessfully) at the House of Commons Speakers Conference on 18 February 1944. The case for change in the electoral system was obvious since a party which won only a minority of the votes could nevertheless gain a huge majority of seats in the Commons.

The proposals for the reform of Parliament and the method of electing it did not mean that the party now believed that the abolition of capitalism and the introduction of a socialist system could be achieved through Parliament alone, as had always been implied by the Labour Party leadership. As *Britain for the People* put it:

> 'The new power of the people cannot operate solely through the ballot box, by which responsibility is delegated to a few hundred or thousand individuals. Every progressive measure requires the active help and personal initiative of millions if it is to be realised not only on the Statute Book, but in the life of the people. In the long run, the people's will prevails only through their own action. This is the meaning of democracy'

It was thus recognised that the way forward involved a combination of parliamentary measures and extra-parliamentary action; they should not be seen as alternatives.

17TH NATIONAL CONGRESS

The final version of *Britain for the People* was agreed to at the party's 17th Congress held in the Shoreditch Town Hall in London in October 1944. Present were 754 delegates, over a third of whom were under 30. Once again the occupations of the delegates revealed the party's industrial base. Thus 266 were from engineering or shipbuilding, 53 were in mining, 61 came from the railways or other forms of transport, and 24 from the building industry. However, 43 were in office work, while 79 were from the professions.

Although events on the fighting front received attention – the second front had opened some months earlier – the congress devoted much of its time to discussing plans for the future. As well as endorsing the programme *Britain for the People* it debated resolutions on the conversion of industry to peace-time production and on the need to provide suitable jobs and training for those demobilised from the armed forces. Other subjects on which attention was focussed included the problems of housebuilding, wages policy and so on.

Despite losses due to call-up, the registered membership was still over 47,000.

'BROWDERISM'

'Britain for the People' stressed that plans for reconstruction after the war could not be separated from international policy. It underlined the importance of the agreements reached between Britain, the Soviet Union and the USA – particularly at the Teheran conference in December 1943 – for continued collaboration after the war in the maintenance of peace and for economic reconstruction.

The view that wartime collaboration could be continued into the peace had been strongly argued by Earl Browder, general secretary of the Communist Party of the USA. But by early 1944, he was also urging a much more fundamental change in the American party's attitudes. 'Capitalism and socialism have begun to find the way to peaceful coexistence' he said, stressing the need to 'establish the prospect that this unity will be continued in the post war period and will not explode into the chaos of inner struggles at the moment war hostilities cease'.[2] As the political report to the post war 1945 Congress of the British Party was later to point out, Browder's proposals 'assumed a basic change in the character of imperialism, denied its reactionary role, and held out a long-term perspective of harmonious capitalist development and class peace after the war, both for the United States and the world.'[3] Among Browder's new proposals was the idea that the Communist Party of the United States should call itself a 'political association' rather than a 'party' – a proposal later accepted by a USA Communist Party Congress.

At the time when Browder's views were first made public, the British Party leadership failed to make any criticism of them, and indeed implied acceptance of them. When on 22 January 1944 the full text of a speech by Browder was reprinted in *World News and Views* it was accompanied by an editorial note from Emile Burns – at that time a member of the party's Political Committee – which attacked those who regarded Browder's statement as the 'abandonment of socialism' and suggested that the way forward must be very different in different countries. It was followed up in March 1944 with reprints of extracts from the American magazine *New Masses* justifying Browder's stance.[4] Meanwhile, a feature article by Bill Rust appeared in the *Daily Worker* on 28 January giving support to Browder, though adding that the same organisational conclusions did not apply in Britain.

Later that year, in a pamphlet *Pollitt answers questions on Communist Policy* Browder was again defended in terms of 'conditions as they exist' in the USA. Though many party members raised objections to Browder's view, the British Party refrained from initiating any debate on the question.

There were two main reasons for the failure to criticise Browder's proposals. Most important was the belief that collaboration between 'the big three' – Britain, the Soviet Union, the USA – in the post-war years could remove the threat of a third world war and secure a lasting peace. These hopes continued to grow when the Teheran Conference in December 1943 was succeeded by the Crimea Conference in 1945 where it was agreed to establish the United Nations.

Another motive for avoiding criticism of Browder was the fact that President Roosevelt of the United States – one of the main people responsible for the Teheran and Crimea agreements – was facing re-election in November 1944, and Browder was urging support for him and for the Democrats so as to guarantee the continuation of his policies. As was argued in *New Masses*: 'What happens at the polls will determine to a great extent whether the Teheran agreements will be effectively implemented or whether men will come to prominent office who will move heaven and earth to shatter the perspective of peaceful cooperation for many generations to come'.[5] In the event, Roosevelt was reelected President and his supporters, the Democrats, won a big majority of the seats in the House of Representatives, severely defeating Roosevelt's opponents, the Republicans.

The attitude taken by the British Party was also partly based on the assumption that Browder had received support for his line from Moscow.[6]

It was not until the war ended in August 1945 that an article by Jacques Duclos of the French Party attacking Browder's view was reprinted in the *Labour Monthly* though it had appeared in France the previous April. By the end of July the 'United States Communist Political Association' had itself recognised that Browder's analysis was mistaken, and had reestablished itself as the Communist Party of the United States, with one of Browder's chief critics, W.Z. Foster, as its chairman.[7]

In the autumn of 1945 during the discussion leading up to the British Party's 18th Congress, there was to be much criticism of the Executive's failure to distance itself from 'Browderism' and, when the Congress took place, an amendment voicing these criticisms from the Cambridge and Portsmouth branches was the subject of debate. But the amendment was defeated, after Pollitt had claimed that the

Executive had in fact resisted attempts to import Browder's ideas into the British Party, and had privately told the American Party of its disagreement with them. He said: 'We refused to publish Browder's book in this country because we disagreed with its contents, and the American comrades were made aware of that. If you consider it is any part of communist leadership in the most difficult stages of winning the war against fascism, that we should tip you all off about circumstances of that description, so far as I am concerned, you have another think coming.'[8]

THE CALL FOR A COALITION GOVERNMENT

The hopes of the British Party concerning post-war relationships between the 'Big Three' – USA, Britain and the Soviet Union – were the main reason why, before the war ended in 1945, it issued a call for a future coalition government in Britain. This followed the Crimea conference between Churchill, Roosevelt and Stalin in February 1945 at which the determination of the 'Big Three' to maintain unity of action in the preservation of peace and democracy had been reaffirmed. Harry Pollitt described these decisions as a 'turning point in world history' offering the prospect of an alliance which could lead to a lasting peace.[9]

So, after circulating its proposal to the membership and receiving strong support at meetings called to discuss the question, the Party Executive issued a new statement, reaffirming its view that the existing government must be replaced by a 'Labour and progressive majority' at the next election, but also suggesting that, on this basis, a new 'national government' should be formed, to include representatives of all those parties supporting the decisions of the Crimea Conference, international economic cooperation and, at home, a minimum programme which would include the nationalisation of key industries.[10]

Arguing the case for this in another pamphlet *Answers to Questions* issued in May 1945, Pollitt said that 'the experience of the war has shown that national unity has been essential for winning victory over fascism. The character of the problems to be solved after the military defeat of Hitler will require national unity no less.'

The proposal for another coalition government – though with Labour as the dominant party – was based on a number of misconceptions. First, it was never expected that the Labour Party could win a majority of the size achieved at the 1945 election. Indeed, nobody had anticipated such a victory, despite the small swings in favour of Labour shown in the gallup polls. For Labour had never previously won an overall majority; moreover, accurate forecasts were virtually impossible in view of the freakishness of the British electoral system under which the number of seats won by a party seldom reflected the proportion of votes received.

A second misconception concerned the Conservative Party. It was known that an anti-Soviet bias was already emerging within that party, but it was thought that this could be undermined if some sort of coalition continued. What party members had not realised was the strength of Churchill's anti-Soviet stance which he kept under cover so long as the war with Germany continued, but which was to emerge in an extreme form soon after the war ended.

But the major misconception was, of course, the belief that the wartime alliance of the 'Big Three' could be continued with a 'peace alliance' in the post war era. These hopes were to be dashed soon after the war ended. It is possible that things might have turned out differently had Roosevelt not died in April 1945. But the attitude of his successor, Truman, left no doubt that any prospects of a post-war 'peace alliance' would rapidly disappear.

The proposal for a coalition government aroused much hostility in the Labour Party. It was jeered at as 'political acrobatics' in the London Labour Party's magazine *London News* and was used by the leaders to attack and denounce the party both before and after the July election.

After the war had ended, on 28 August 1945, the Communist Party Executive sent out a political letter to the members, in which it admitted that the proposal for another coalition government – even though with Labour as the dominant party – had been a mistake. However, as with 'Browderism' there was to be much criticism of the Executive over the matter at its post-war party congress. As Bill Rowe from the East Midlands put it, the policy of 'national unity' put forward before the election had 'disarmed the Communist Party at a critical time.'[11]

9

THE LAST YEAR OF THE WAR

June 6 1944 was 'D-Day'. The long-postponed second front was opened at last as British and American troops landed in northern France.

A few days later, people living in the south east were suddenly faced with a new kind of terror weapon: the 'flying bomb', officially called the V-I. Between 100 and 150 of them landed every 24 hours. Most of the previous bombing raids had been at night. But the 'buzz-bomb' or 'doodle-bug', as it was called, came at any time of day or night. The drone of its engine would grow louder and louder until it suddenly cut out; at that moment it would begin to fall. As it hit the ground, there would be a massive explosion. The bombs were not aimed at particular targets; they fell at random, mostly in south London. Within three weeks, 2,700 people had been killed and 8,000 injured. And, because the raids were not confined to night-time, they caused considerable disruption at work. Most factories used 'roof-spotters' who gave warning to take cover whenever a buzz-bomb was getting close. Evacuation of schoolchildren and mothers with babies was hurriedly organised. Altogether, 1.5 million people, many of whom had drifted back during the months of relative calm, left London once more.

The need for those not engaged in essential work to leave London was urgent for another reason. A far more powerful weapon, a long-range rocket bomb containing a much higher explosive power than the buzz-bomb was expected at any time. Ted Bramley, the Communist Party's London District Secretary, claimed on 11 August that far too little attention had been paid to the warning given by Churchill that London would be the primary target for what was to become known as the 'V-2'.[1]

The first V-2 fell on 8 September; in the next few months, some 1,000 were launched, of which over 500 reached London. Nothing was said about them in the press until 10 November when Churchill divulged what had been happening. The news blackout was intended to prevent the enemy assessing the V-2's effects. But it also meant that many evacuees returned to London and suffered from these raids as a result.

The rocket bomb travelled faster than the speed of sound, so that its massive explosion would be *followed* by the noise of its approach. Since people could not hear it coming they could not take cover in advance. The V-2 had extremely sinister implications for a future arms race. This, however, was far ahead. The attacks from V-Is and V-2s petered out towards the end of 1944 as the allied forces succeeded in capturing or destroying the bases from which they were launched.

In the 'reception areas', local party branches concentrated on adequate billeting of evacuees, collecting lists of people willing to accommodate them, organising sporting and other events for the children, and so on. In London, they went into action once again on the issue of shelters, reviving shelter committees. In some places they recruited volunteer squads from the factories for the repair of people's homes.

Tess Gorringe, a party member in south London who was working as a bus conductor, described what her party group was doing:

> Early in the period of the doodle-bugs, during the first ten days we were getting at least two a day. In the first five days, not even first-aid repairs were done. We suggested to the people that we should have a meeting in the street, and from that a deputation went to the mayor and had a discussion which lasted 2½ hours on the problem. Other streets followed suit and today there are 700 people in our Residents' Protection Association, speeding up bomb repairs, but not limiting themselves to this. They are vitally concerned in all the problems of post war reconstruction and what the people can do about it.[2]

DISCRIMINATION AGAINST THE *DAILY WORKER*

The *Daily Worker* was still denied permission for an 'accredited war correspondent' despite its support for the war effort. When the second front opened, renewed attempts were made to get the ban lifted. More than 50 MPs signed a petition for its withdrawal, and the matter was debated in the Commons on 3 August 1944. Sir James Grigg, Secretary of State for War, argued – as he had done from the start – that it was wrong to direct the attack against him, since he was carrying out a Cabinet decision. Grigg had previously served for thirty years as a civil servant, and was described by the *Daily Worker*'s editor, Bill Rust, as 'born in a pigeonhole and cradled in red tape.' Rust's pamphlet entitled *Gagged by Grigg* was widely read.

In August it appeared that the *Daily Worker* had managed to get around the ban on one section of the front. Clemens Dutt had gone to Algiers as one of the paper's foreign correspondents and, in 1944, was accepted by the French military authorities there as a war correspondent. So when the French forces landed in the South of France, he went with them. His first despatch appeared in the *Daily Worker* on 17 August and was enthusiastically received. But the joy was shortlived. On 21 August, Dutt was withdrawn from his post on the instructions of the British War Office, the previous endorsement by the Allied Forces HQ being described as an 'irregularity'.

At the Trades Union Congress, held in October 1944, a resolution from the National Union of Journalists protesting at the ban received unanimous support. So, in March 1945, a deputation from the TUC led by Sir Walter Citrine, its general secretary, went to Downing Street and spent an hour arguing the matter with Churchill.[3] But it was to no avail. The ban on the paper's war correspondents remained until September 1945. By that time the war was over.

From the summer of 1944 onwards, an increasing number of letters from men serving in the armed forces abroad began to appear in the *Daily Worker*'s correspondence columns, though the rules forbade publication of the names of those who wrote them. 'From all the war fronts where British soldiers are fighting, our readers write to us – from France, from Italy and from Burma' proclaimed an editorial on 17 July 1944. 'They are our war correspondents until the day that Grigg raises the ban on our representatives'. Soon such letters were coming from Belgium and from Greece.

THE EUROPEAN SCENE

The main focus of attention for the party from June 1944 onwards was what was happening on the fighting fronts – the Russian drive in the East, the advances of the British and American troops in western Europe. In many of the countries occupied by the Germans, massive resistance movements had grown up, and British troops were reaping the benefits. As Harry Pollitt observed: 'Never in world history before have we seen advancing armies received with such warmth and enthusiasm by those whom they are freeing from a black and shameful terror. This is the measure of the fundamental difference between this and all other wars ... it is a war of the peoples for the people, and by the people, so that the outcome shall be a new kind of people's world'.[4]

Behind the scenes, the resistance movements had been causing some concern in government circles, because of 'the unfortunate fact that communists seem to make the best guerilla leaders' as Foreign Secretary Anthony Eden put it privately to Churchill in May 1944.[5] The role of communists was indeed something that Churchill was forced to recognise in the case of Yugoslavia. Here British support had initially been directed towards the Chetniks, the military arm of the Yugoslav government-in-exile led by Colonel Mihailovich who was in practice doing little to resist the fascist occupiers. But in the summer of 1944, it was at last decided that British aid would be switched from the Chetniks to the broad partisan front led by communist Tito.[6] As the *Daily Worker* observed on 8 July 1944: 'All British democrats will rejoice that the long fight against the Quisling Mihailovich has ended with a victory for the Yugoslav upholders of unity and democracy.'

However, Yugoslavia turned out to be an exception. Although Churchill was careful to express ardent friendship in all public statements for the Soviet Union, which was still bearing the brunt of the fighting and dying, his government was simultaneously giving help to certain organisations engaged in anti-Soviet agitation. Among these was the London-based rump Polish government which was responsible in August 1944 for instructing its underground contacts to seize Warsaw before the Red Army reached it. The instruction was issued without consultation or coordination with either the British or Russian troops, and the result was a tragedy. A premature rising, in which many patriots participated, was crushed by the Germans, while the so-called Polish government in London used the event to spread a campaign of vilification of the Red Army for failing to help the insurgents.

EVENTS IN GREECE

Churchill's anti-communist – and indeed anti-democratic – obsession was clearly exposed in the case of Greece. Some years before the war began, the King of Greece had dissolved his country's parliament, and imposed a dictatorship under General Metaxas. When the Germans occupied Greece in 1941, the King fled from the country. But, within Greece, great resistance movements grew up, the most important of which was EAM, a 'National Liberation Front' composed of the

Communist Party, the Socialist Party, the Union of Popular Democrats, the Agrarian Party, and various other groups. By 1944, it claimed to have the support of 2 million people and, not surprisingly, it was anti-royalist. While mobilising people for active resistance to the Germans, EAM's declared aim was the restoration of liberties and free elections for a constituent assembly. Attached to EAM was a guerilla force, known as ELAS.

In the Autumn of 1944, the German Army was forced to withdraw from Greece. At the same time, British troops landed there, and were greeted with wild enthusiasm. This mood was short-lived. In the hope of protecting Britain's sea routes to India and maintaining British influence in the Western Mediterranean, Churchill installed a right-wing government appointed by the King of Greece while the latter was in exile in Cairo and, before long, British troops found themselves engaged in fighting the Liberation Army, ELAS. A protest against this, moved in the House of Commons on 8 December 1944, was defeated by 281 votes to 32, but only 23 out of 166 Labour MPs voted with the government, most of the rest abstained. At the Labour Party Annual Conference on 13 December, there was anger among some delegates whose emergency resolutions condemning the government's actions in Greece had not been allowed on to the agenda. Instead, conference was faced with what was described as a 'milk and water' resolution deeply regretting the 'tragic situation' in Greece, and urging the establishment of a provisional government which would proceed to free elections. It was carried after Ernest Bevin, Minister of Labour and Cabinet member, had given a rambling explanation of his support for the government's action. 'The British Empire cannot abandon its position in the Mediterranean,' he said.[7]

The Communist Party Executive urged a reversal of the government's policy. They argued that, 'We cannot tolerate a situation in which British soldiers are involved in action, with tanks, warships and bombing planes, against their comrades, the democratic anti-fascist fighters of Greece, who have played such a heroic part in the long struggle against Nazism'.[8]

There was, indeed, widespread indignation at the use of British troops against the anti-fascist resistance movement in Greece; as Gallacher stressed, he was receiving telegrams on a daily basis from mass meetings of factory workers demanding an end to the policy.[9] The protests were soon to be supported by letters written to the *Daily Worker* from British soldiers serving in Greece. One who wrote from

Athens said: 'As a British soldier in Greece, I have seen how the whole nation supports EAM. We may clear certain areas, we may drive them into the mountains, but they will never give in.... The whole people help ELAS with food and active assistance.' Another wrote of how the real, decent, honest people of Greece 'now find themselves refighting their fight to overthrow oppression. I protest against what is being done in the name of the British people.' Another said 'we who have fought for liberation and against the oppressors of our fellow men are being dragged into the position of oppressor to the most gallant Greek patriots.' These letters, all of which appeared on 4 January 1945, were to be followed by many more in the ensuing weeks. However, an application by the *Daily Worker* to send Ivor Montagu to Athens as a special correspondent, although agreed to by the Ministry of Information, was rejected by the military authorities.[10]

COLD WAR ORIGINS

The Greek crisis revealed more clearly than ever before the gap between what the mass of the people thought they were fighting for – freedom and democracy – and the Churchill Government's aims, the preservation of capitalist interests at home and of colonial possessions abroad, and the reestablishment of reactionary regimes in the other European countries. It also illustrated the dilemma in which Churchill and his colleagues found themselves in trying to undermine communist influence both at home and abroad while continuing to proclaim their close alliance with the Soviet Union in the fight against Nazi Germany.

Initially (as shown in Chapter 1) it had been assumed that the Germans would crush the Russians, probably in a matter of weeks. When the expected Russian collapse did not occur, the hopes expressed by Moore-Brabazon – that the Germans and Russian would destroy one another to the advantage of Britain – still lingered on in the minds of many in high places. But, after the Red Army's winter offensive early in 1943, and the German defeat at Stalingrad, such hopes disappeared.

From then on, government circles were beset by what one (anti-communist) historian has described as 'two recurrent but mutually exclusive fears'.[11] The first of these was that the Russians might rest on their laurels after driving the German invaders off their soil, thus leaving Hitler free to transfer forces to the Western front – perhaps even tipping him the wink to do so. Churchill was privately expressing such fears as late as April 1944. In the event, the opposite happened. Two weeks after the Normandy landings on 6 June, the Russian summer offensive against Germany was launched. By the middle of July the Red Army had swept the Germans out of Russia and had overrun large parts of Poland.

So it was that the anxiety that the Russians might be defeated was rapidly replaced by a different fear: that the Soviet Union might defeat the Germans almost single-handed and so end up as the dominant power in large parts of Europe. As the war neared its end Churchill tried desperately to ensure that the Russians were stopped as far east as possible, and even made some frantic attempts to prevent them reaching Berlin before the British-American forces did so. In this effort, he was to be unsuccessful.[12]

VE DAY AND THE GENERAL ELECTION

On 7 May 1945, the Germans surrendered. As the news filtered through at midday, those working in Fleet Street and the Strand began tearing up bits of paper and flinging them out of the windows so that passers-by found themselves ankle-deep in a swirl of white litter; soon it was announced that May 8th would be Victory in Europe day, a national holiday.

But the holiday had already begun. By afternoon, buildings were festooned with flags: the Union Jack, the Hammer-and-Sickle, the Stars and Stripes, mingled with flags of many other countries; strings of bunting decorated houses in the back streets. By early evening, Trafalgar Square was packed with people dancing and singing 'Knees up Mother Brown' and 'It Ain't Going to Rain No More.' Crowds swarmed on to the roofs of cars, blowing whistles; ships lying in the London docks set off their sirens. That night, innumerable bonfires were lit at street corners. The blackout was over at last.

Even though the war with Japan was still on, many in political circles expected that the defeat of Hitler would lead to a rapid return to party politics. Churchill was anxious that such a return should be delayed. On 18 May, he wrote to the Labour leaders proposing the continuation of the coalition until the defeat of Japan. He made clear that if this was not agreed to, he would call an immediate General Election. Attlee, Bevin and Dalton were in favour of continuing the coalition, but the majority of Labour's NEC rejected this proposal, and their stand was overwhelmingly supported at the Labour Party Annual Conference on 21 May. Thereupon Labour withdrew from the coalition.

The Labour leaders then urged that the election should be held in the Autumn when a more up-to-date register of voters would be available, but Churchill turned this down. He formed a 'caretaker' government, without the participation of Labour, and announced that Parliament would be dissolved on 15 June. The General Election was to take place on 5 July, though the ballot boxes would not be opened until 25 July, so as to give time to collect the service votes, since those in the armed forces abroad were entitled to cast their vote either by post or by proxy.

Having failed in its aim of proportional representation, the Communist Party had earlier suggested that there should be local conferences of progressive organisations to choose the candidate to represent them in order to prevent splitting the anti-Tory vote. This proposition had been turned down at the 1944 Labour Party annual conference. At the 1945 conference, on behalf of the Amalgamated Engineering Union, Jack Tanner made a further attempt to get discussion on the issue of 'progressive unity' in the General Election, but was ruled out of order. His endeavours to overthrow this ruling were defeated by a narrow majority of 1,314,000 votes to 1,219,000.[13] The unions supporting Tanner's move included the National Union of Mineworkers, the two main railway unions, NUR and ASLEF, the National Union of Distributive Workers, the Electrical Trades Union, and the Fire Brigades Union. In all these, the party had by this time built up considerable support. But both the big general workers' unions were among those who voted against it: the Transport and General Workers Union and the General and Municipal Workers Union.

In view of the need to avoid splitting the anti-Tory vote, the Party Executive had already decided in April that its list of prospective parliamentary candidates should be reduced from 52 to 22 – later there was one further withdrawal and the number of seats contested was 21. In all other constituencies party members went into action in support of Labour candidates, most of whom welcomed this help. In some areas, party premises were used as Labour party committee rooms.

Many people remembered Lloyd George's 'coupon election' after World War I and feared that Churchill would gain a similar victory. In the event, the opposite happened. The Conservatives lost 175 seats. Labour won the biggest majority in its history: 393 seats out of 640 – a majority of 146. There was an immense swing to the left. However, the results also revealed how unrepresentative is the 'first-past-the-post' electoral system, since Labour's percentage of the poll was less than half at 47.8 per cent. The number of candidates who lost their deposits because they failed to win one-eighth – 12½ per cent – of the poll rose to 168 – far more than in any previous election. They included not only 12 Communists, but 64 Liberals, together with Scottish and Welsh nationalists, members of the 'Commonwealth' Party, Independents, and so on.

Of the 22 Communist candidates, two were elected. William Gallacher was once more returned for West Fife, with 17,636 votes, while Phil Piratin, who had served as a communist councillor in the East London borough of Stepney since 1937, was elected MP for the small Mile End constituency, with 5,075 votes. There was deep disappointment that Harry Pollitt failed to get in at Rhondda East, where he received 15,761 votes, or over 45 per cent of the poll, but was narrowly defeated by the Labour candidate. Among other communists who failed to get in were Bill Rust in Hackney South who got 24 per cent of the votes; G.J. Jones in Hornsey (21 per cent); Bill Carritt in the Abbey division of Westminster (17.6 per cent); Johnny Campbell in Greenock (17.1 per cent); Howard Hill, Brightside, Sheffield (13 per cent); Bob Cooney, Glasgow Central (12.7 per cent)

In most of the seats contested, few party members had believed that communist candidates had much chance: they were aware that some communist supporters might cast their vote for Labour so as not to let the Tories in. In one case, that of R. Palme Dutt, who stood for the Sparkbrook constituency of Birmingham, the contest was little more than a symbolic gesture. Sparkbrook was chosen, not because of any strong communist support, but because it was the seat held by L.S. Amery, a right-wing Tory who had served in the government as Secretary of State for India and Burma. During his campaign, Dutt highlighted the party's aim of colonial freedom. He received many messages of support from organisations and individuals in India, including the leader of the civil disobedience movement, Mahatma Gandhi, and the Congress leader, Pandit Nehru. Messages also came from Burma and Ceylon. Dutt got only 1,813 votes (about 7 per cent of the poll) but fortunately, Amery was defeated by the Labour candidate who got in with 14,965 votes.

As soon as the election results were known, the Party Executive met to discuss their implications and issued a statement. 'Labour's victory at the General Election has been greeted with joy by democratic people all over the world' it said. Pledging 'whole-hearted support' to the

Labour Government both in relation to the war against Japan and in carrying out the great social changes for which the people voted, it stated: 'The electoral victory is only the beginning. The real battle lies before us'.[14]

10

THE LABOUR GOVERNMENT AND THE OUTSIDE WORLD 1945–6

On 6 August 1945, ten days after the Labour Government was installed, a single American plane flew over a Japanese city, Hiroshima, and for the first time dropped an atomic bomb. Within a few minutes, some 80,000 people were dead, a similar number injured, and two-thirds of the city was gutted by fire. Three days later, a second atomic bomb was dropped by the Americans, this time on Nagasaki. On 10 August Japan offered to surrender, and on 14 August the final terms were agreed. They were ratified on 2 September. The war with Japan was over.

Weeks before the Hiroshima bomb was dropped, the Japanese rulers, who knew they were beaten, had sued for peace and appealed to the Russians to mediate on their behalf. This appeal was rejected because the Soviet Union's leader, Stalin, had previously promised Britain and the USA that his country would declare war on Japan three months after the German surrender. It has since been suggested that one of the objects of the Americans in dropping the bomb was to force Japan's surrender before the Soviet Union entered the war in the Far East in order to limit possible Soviet gains in the region.[1] Another motive was undoubtedly the desire of the American military to demonstrate the power of their new weapon before the war ended. Whatever the aims, it was a devastating event, and the development thereafter of nuclear weapons was to overshadow international relations for the next half century, and to threaten the whole future of the human race.

Initially the true significance of the Hiroshima bomb was not fully appreciated on the left. The *Daily Worker* went as far as to suggest on 7 August that the bomb would expedite Japanese surrender and thus save 'valuable lives'. However, it did express certain fears for the future. In a leader headed 'Blessing or Curse?' it said that the event 'registered the opening of a new stage in evolution of warfare and at the same time a vast problem for human civilisation.' And it said: 'The moral that the victorious nations must cooperate to build a just and enduring peace should be obvious ... For a new war waged by great states possessing this terrible power of destruction would indeed mark the end of all civilisation.'

A few days later, the likely pattern of coming events emerged in a contribution from the defeated Conservative leader, Churchill, in the debate on the King's speech. 'The decision to use the atomic bomb was taken by President Truman and myself at Potsdam. I am in entire agreement with the President that the secrets of the atomic bomb shall, so far as possible, not be imparted, at the present time, to any other country in the world.' He went on to say that 'For this and many other reasons, the United States stand at this moment at the summit of the world. I rejoice that this should be so.'[2]

Neither Labour's Prime Minister Attlee, nor his newly-appointed Foreign Secretary, Ernest Bevin, expressed any disagreement with Churchill on the atom bomb question. However, unknown to the general public, Attlee decided that Britain must develop her own independent nuclear weapons. A secret Cabinet Committee, from which most Cabinet members were excluded, was set up to oversee the programme, and from late 1945 onwards, research and experimental work went ahead at Harwell. This decision followed the refusal of the American President to share atomic information with Britain, as previously promised, even though British nuclear physicists had originally been involved in developing the bomb. Later, when Hugh Dalton, Chancellor of the Exchequer, and Stafford Cripps, President of the Board of Trade, tried to stop production of the bomb on financial grounds, their arguments were swept aside by Bevin, who asserted that it was important for the Union Jack to fly over a British bomb.[3] The fact that Britain was producing its own nuclear weapons was not made public until October 1952, one year after Labour lost office.

By 1949, the Communist Party was to be actively engaged in an international movement to ban the bomb. But at its 18th Congress held in November 1945, the main focus was on other aspects of Labour's foreign and colonial policy. However, a resolution was adopted which declared that the discovery of atomic energy opened up great possibilities if used in the interests of social progress. But it urged the immediate sharing of atomic bomb secrets between the 'Big Three' and that ultimate control of the bomb should be vested in the Security Council of the United Nations.[4]

LABOUR'S FOREIGN POLICIES

The appointment of the right-wing Ernest Bevin as Foreign Secretary was an indication that the Labour Government's approach to international affairs was to be no different from that of their former Conservative colleagues. So it was not surprising that Churchill expressed his gratification at Bevin's appointment. 'We are sure he will do his best to preserve the great causes for which we have so long pulled together' he said during the first debate in the newly elected House of Commons. He also made a furious attack on the Soviet Union's actions in Eastern Europe: 'It is not impossible that tragedy on a prodigious scale is unfolding itself behind the iron curtain' he said,[5] thus echoing the voice of the former Nazi propaganda chief, Goebbels, who had first coined the term 'iron curtain' when dealing with the threat to Nazi Germany posed by the Soviet Union. It was a term which would be used by the British establishment for the next forty years.

Bevin, in his first speech as Foreign Secretary, made clear his agreement with much of what Churchill said. 'The basis of our policy is in keeping with that worked out by the Coalition Government' he promised.[6] He criticised the provisional governments' set-up in the Russian-occupied East European countries while the war was still in progress. In these provisional governments, the anti-fascist resistance movements, which had arisen during the German occupation, were strongly represented. But Bevin said of them that 'one kind of totalitarianism is being replaced by another.'

Bevin's true attitude to democracy had been revealed in the case of Greece where (as shown in Chapter 9) he had approved the installation of a government of the far right with monarchists and fascists reinstated in key posts.

The foreign policy debates in August 1945 confirmed the Communist Party's worst fears about the Labour Government's attitude to international affairs. 'Mr Bevin's recent speech does not correspond to what the masses voted for at the General Election' was the comment in a political letter issued by the Party Executive on 28

August. 'The fight against Tory reaction needs to be conducted on Foreign policy no less than on Home policy'. But the new government had already made clear that its guiding principles would not only include support for reactionary regimes in Europe, but would also be aimed at the retention of Britain's colonial possessions, the return to France and Holland of their previous colonies and, above all a reversion to the pre-war line-up under which the Soviet Union was once more to be regarded as the *real* enemy. The fact that it was the Soviet people who had made the greatest contribution to the defeat of the *actual* enemy, Nazi Germany, was to be ignored and, indeed, forgotten.

The new aim of a divided Europe was criticised in a *Daily Worker* editorial as early as 18 September 1945. 'One profound lesson of the war is surely that the democratic powers should pursue a policy for Europe as a whole and not permit division between East and West' it said. 'But today the air is thick with cries for what is described as a Western Bloc, a grouping of Western European countries under Anglo-French leadership'.

By November 1945, Hungary and Bulgaria had held free general elections for the first time. Both of them were ex-enemy countries where fascist or semi-fascist rulers had collaborated with Hitler, and which had been occupied by the Russian armies. In Yugoslavia, voting rights were greatly extended in comparison with its pre-war system. However, Bevin continued to emphasise his hostility to what was happening in Eastern Europe. 'He has at any rate made plain where he stands' commented Walter Holmes in the *Daily Worker* 'and that is behind the Tories. He does not even lead them. He is their echo, their vulgariser, the amplifier of their more blatant imperialism. What the Tories might find it indiscreet to say, Mr Bevin will say for them.'[7]

ACTIONS TO RETAIN COLONIAL TERRITORIES

Events in the Far East were equally dismaying. Here, British and American forces were supposed to be disarming and evacuating Japanese forces from occupied territories and releasing their own prisoners-of-war. At Potsdam it had been agreed that British troops should not only reoccupy the former British colonies – Burma, Singapore, Malaya – but also the former Dutch colony, Indonesia, and the former French colony, Indo-China (later known as Vietnam). In both these countries resistance movements against the Japanese had developed among the local peoples who had set up their own provisional governments. However it soon transpired that the object of the Labour Government was not to liberate the countries concerned, but to restore them to their former French and Dutch colonial rulers.

Thus British troops arrived in Saigon, Vietnam, on 12 September, ostensibly to disarm the Japanese. But the real object was to suppress the liberation movement known as the 'Viet Minh' (which had taken over Hanoi and Saigon) and to restore the country to the French. For this purpose, martial law was imposed and Japanese troops were used to enforce it. By 9 October, Bevin had signed an agreement with France recognising her right to administer South Vietnam; soon after, French troops replaced the British in the fight to reconquer North Vietnam.[8]

The British also began using Japanese troops to fight the Indonesians while awaiting the arrival of Dutch troops. The attempts to restore Dutch sovereignty over Indonesia met with much opposition, particularly in Australia which was being used as a staging post for Dutch ships carrying troops and munitions. In Sydney, dockers refused to load these munitions, and received wide support from the Australian labour movement. Then, on 11 November when a British merchant ship *Moreton Bay*, which was taking Dutch soldiers to Indonesia, stopped off at Sydney, most of its British crew went ashore and refused to sail any further. There were huge demonstrations at which these British seamen were carried shoulder high. They returned to the ship to pack up their belongings, whereupon the officers and Dutch soldiers on board cast off without notice, heaving up the gangway. However, ten of the crew escaped back to Sydney. Some were arrested and charged with desertion, but later released.

'We owe a duty to those British seamen of the *Moreton Bay* who have helped to save the honour of the British Labour movement by opposing the transport of troops and war materials to Indonesia'. These words formed part of a resolution adopted at the Communist Party's 18th Congress. It was moved by Arthur Clegg, who had long been a leading figure in the China Campaign Committee and was a specialist on Far Eastern affairs. The congress called for a reversal of the Labour Government's policy towards both Indonesia and Vietnam. A 'Hands off Indonesia Campaign' was launched in which R. Palme Dutt and Arthur Clegg were active along with several Labour MPs; a lobby of Parliament was organised. In March 1946, the party received a letter from the Prime Minister of the Indonesian Republic expressing thanks 'to the workers who, at the instigation of your Party, have supported our struggle for freedom and democracy.'[9] However, the British continued to transport Dutch troops to Indonesia using routes other than the one via Australia.

Equally unsettling was the Labour Government's attitudes to British colonial territories. On 7 November, Gallacher asked the Secretary for War why the Malayan Communist Party, which had led the resistance to the Japanese occupation forces, was still an illegal organisation and its members subject to arrest and persecution for their political views. He got no real answer.

On 19 September Attlee outlined a plan for India's future. It signalled a continuation of the policies of the previous government – in particular, a renewal of the 'Cripps' proposals made in 1942 for a highly undemocratic constitution. 'This is not the declaration of independence that India has been awaiting' commented the *Daily Worker*.[10] The Party's Executive Committee issued a statement urging that the Labour Government break entirely with the policies inherited from the previous government and calling instead for a democratically elected Constituent Assembly.

It was soon realised that the government's colonial policies were the main reasons for the slow rate of demobilisation which was already causing discontent both in the armed services and at home. At the 18th Congress it was pointed out that 'by agreeing to the just demands of self-government of the peoples of India, Indonesia, Burma, Malaya and Indo-China, where British troops are being used against the interests of the people ... the rate of repatriation and demobilisation could be immeasurably speeded up'. The government's plan for 2½ million men to be still under arms in June 1946 was 'indefensible'.[11]

At this Congress, Bill Rust, editor of the *Daily Worker*, argued that it was time to campaign for the removal of Bevin from his job as Foreign Secretary. However, the executive made clear that the slogan 'Bevin must go' (which received much publicity) did not express their view because the main aim was to win support for changes in the government's policies.[12] In the 'Bevin must go' controversy the Party was facing an ongoing problem: the tendency of the media to concentrate on personalities among politicians rather than the policies for which they stood.

Hopes of maintaining good relations with the Soviet Union were further undermined when, on 5 March 1946, at Fulton in the USA,

Churchill launched his most outspoken attack yet. Using the outdated rhetoric to which he was prone, he spoke of the need to be shielded from the 'gaunt marauders – war and tyranny' and of the 'police governments', in the Russian-occupied territories of Eastern Europe. He said that in front of the 'iron curtain', 'Communist Fifth Columns' offered a 'growing challenge and peril to Christian civilisation'. He called for a military alliance between Britain and America, otherwise 'The Dark Ages may return, the Stone Age'.[13]

In the House of Commons, 105 MPs put their names to a motion stating that the Fulton proposals for a military alliance would injure good relations between Britain, the USA and the USSR and were 'inimical to the cause of world peace.'[14] But Prime Minister Attlee refused to allocate time for a debate. Indeed, according to his biographer, he was privately delighted with the Fulton speech.[15]

'The real trouble is that the policy of the Labour Government has made it possible for Churchill's ranting to be taken seriously' commented Emile Burns.[16] By July 1946, Pollitt was writing of the 'widespread distrust, confusion and bewilderment' over the Labour Government's foreign policy.'[17]

That autumn it was announced that demobilisation would be further slowed down and, moreover, that because of the shortage of new recruits a Bill for peace-time conscription was being planned. In response the Party Executive declared on 19 November that the maintenance of armed forces numbering 1½ million was not justified; it was a consequence of the government's foreign policies. However, the proposal to continue with conscription caused some controversy within the party. In 1945 it had set up a 'commission on army reform.' Chaired by John Gollan, and with the participation of many ex-service men and women, it had issued in June 1946 a discussion pamphlet entitled 'Towards a People's Army' which advocated universal military service provided it was accompanied by democratisation of the army. This was already a matter of debate among readers of the Young Communist League's magazine *Challenge* which had published some letters from those still in the armed forces urging abolition of conscription while others argued in favour of conscription.[18] This debate was to continue in both YCL and party branches right up to the 19th Congress of the party in February 1947[19] at which a resolution was carried advocating reductions in the size of the armed forces and 'far-reaching democratic reforms as a basis for compulsory military service.' An amendment for the abolition of conscription was defeated.[20]

SUPPRESSION OF DEMOCRACY IN GREECE

One important reason for the slow rate of demobilisation was the situation in Greece where, at enormous expense, British troops remained in occupation throughout 1946. Here, where the anti-Nazi resistance movements had been suppressed, the right-wing government installed by the British continued with its denial of democratic rights to all on the left.

In Britain, party members participated in the work of an organisation known as the League for Democracy in Greece. Many of the organisation's members were Greek Cypriots who had temporarily settled in Britain. Its Honorary Secretary was a party member, Diana Pym. In the Spring of 1946 she was one of four delegates to visit Greece on behalf of the League; the other three were Labour MPs. The League published a 2d monthly journal *Greek News*, and in October 1946 it called a conference at the London Beaver Hall with the support of the London Trades Council and the National Council for Civil Liberties. It was chaired by the General Secretary of the Civil Service Clerical Association, L.C. White (who was on the editorial board of the *Daily Worker*). The conference was addressed by two Labour MPs – Norman Dodds and L.J. Solley. The latter declared that British policy had led directly to the formation in Greece of the only fascist government in Europe outside Franco Spain.[21] There were 212 organisations represented at the conference, among them 13 local Labour parties.

The League for Democracy in Greece was to continue its activities for many years much to the irritation of the Labour leaders. Inevitably in 1950 it was declared a 'proscribed organisation' with which no member of the Labour Party could be associated.

The League's 1946 conference took place some three weeks before the Trades Union Congress at which Greece was to be a major subject of debate. Early on, the British TUC had tried to make sure that, once German troops were withdrawn from that country, a free trade union movement would be reestablished. So, with the consent of the Churchill coalition government, the TUC General Council had, in 1945, sent representatives to Greece to help in this process. Communist Bert Papworth, who was on the TUC General Council, had been one of them together with H.V. Tewson, the TUC's Assistant General Secretary, and another full-time TUC official, Victor Feather. Their job was to participate in complicated negotiations leading up to trade union elections. When the war ended, the international organisation which the British had helped to form, the World Federation of Trade Unions (WFTU) took over responsibility for overseeing the Greek trade union position. Under its auspices, a further delegation consisting of British, French and Russian trade union representatives went to Greece to supervise a trade union congress at which an executive committee was elected by ballot vote. But, a few months later, in July 1946, the reactionary Greek Government declared this election illegal, ordered the dismissal of all the elected trade unionists, and replaced them with its own chosen nominees, many of whom had collaborated with the Nazis during the German occupation. From then on, elected trade union representatives were persecuted; many of them were imprisoned.

A report on these events was issued by the TUC General Council to its congress in October 1946, and the debate on it was opened by Bert Papworth. The report was factual and made clear the General Council's concern at the events. But what it did not do was to attribute any blame to the British Labour Government for what had happened, and this was one of the criticisms levelled at it by a number of party members who participated in the debate, including Dick Seabrook of USDAW who thought the report reflected pressure from the Foreign Office, Joe Scott of the AEU, who described how members of the dismissed trade union executive had been arrested and imprisoned and Bob McLennan of the Electrical Trades Union (ETU) who said: 'British troops are in Greece, and we have been told that these troops are there in order to maintain law and order. Whose law, and whose order? It is fascist law and fascist order against the working class and the democratic people of Greece'. Among the non-party members who spoke, Jack Stanley, General Secretary of the Constructional Engineering Union, alleged that men who had been sentenced for collaboration with the Nazis had been released and appointed to trade union positions while L.C. White told how 'members of the civil service trade unions in Greece have lost their jobs because collaborators have given verdicts against them'.[22]

Later, Frank Foulkes of the ETU moved a resolution criticising the Labour Government's foreign policies; another party member, Hymie Kanter of the Tailor and Garment Workers Union, made clear the disillusionment over these policies 'As a result of the last war, we have seen in certain parts of Europe the emergence of working class forces – in Yugoslavia, Greece and Rumania'.... 'we, under the leadership of a

Labour Government, should be holding out a friendly hand of encouragement towards those people to help them achieve the very aims we are fighting for, instead of which we are aligned with the most reactionary forces of the world.'[23]

Attending as a visitor, Prime Minister Attlee went out of his way to criticise this resolution which, he said, was 'filled with the kind of misrepresentation to which we have become accustomed from the members of the Communist Party, their dupes and fellow travellers'.[24] Presumably these 'fellow-travellers' included L.C. White and Jack Stanley. In the event, although the resolution was defeated, the vote against being 3,557,000, the vote in favour reached 2,444,000, despite the efforts of the right wing.

A similar pattern was to emerge at the 1947 TUC when, on the request of the leadership, a resolution asking the British Government to put pressure on the Greek government to change course was remitted by a vote of 3,351,000 to 2,984,000. Such votes served to illustrate the fact that, although only a minority had been persuaded to oppose the Labour government's attitude to foreign affairs, this minority was big enough to offer a challenge to the right wing which could not be disregarded.

11

THE PARTY'S NEW STRUCTURE AND AREAS OF WORK; RELATIONS WITH THE LABOUR PARTY

In 1945, the party altered its organisational structure. Since 1936 its basic unit had been the 'branch', consisting of members either living or working in the area concerned. The members were divided into 'groups'; 'street' or 'area' groups and 'factory' or 'workplace' groups. The Branch Committee, on which it was intended that all groups should be represented, was elected by the branch members at annual general meetings.

Under the new form of organisation, the 'branch' remained the basic unit, but was to consist solely of members living in the area concerned. Members who had previously been in factory groups were to belong to the branch where they lived. They would, however, be called together to elect a 'factory committee' which would organise political work in the factory concerned.

INNER-PARTY DISCUSSION

A major reason for this change in structure was the extremely successful recruiting campaigns during 1943 and 1944, but the subsequent difficulties in retaining the new recruits and involving them in party activity. Most recruiting was done either at well-attended public meetings or in special drives at workplaces. Thus, in the last three months of 1943, over 7,000 new recruits were made, bringing the total number issued with party cards during that year to over 55,000. However, when the 1944 re-registration took place, it was found that not more than 47,513 people had been issued with cards by the end of

March.[1] Some of those who had held cards in 1943 had since been called up; others had moved, and their branch was no longer in touch with them; some who had been recruited at factories had been sent to other jobs and lost contact with their former colleagues; others had failed to turn up at meetings or pay their dues and their membership had lapsed.

Throughout 1944 the same thing happened. Recruiting campaigns continued, so that the total membership was estimated at over 50,000 by the end of the year. But the number re-registered in the Spring of 1945 was back to 45,435.[2]

Even so, this was 2½ times the pre-war membership, and as branches formerly composed of about 30 members expanded to over 100, the need to keep contact with new recruits faced local branch committees with many problems.

R.W. Robson, who worked full time at the party centre, was arguing in 1944 that part of the difficulty was the attitude of many of the existing members. 'One can find everywhere comrades who express the opinion that their group or branch is already "big enough" ' he wrote. 'Some argue that we ought to go in for "selective" recruiting, that recruiting large numbers together from public meetings or by special efforts in factories is wrong ... we can't hope to keep such newcomers in our ranks.' He suggested that one organisational problem was the very high standard of activity expected of members. 'When some new members are disappointed and don't respond, they are too frequently dismissed as being "no good" and allowed to drift out of the party.' He thought that 'we cannot expect, and must not demand of the average new member the same standard of activity as we get from the older comrades.'[3]

Robson's article provoked much argument. Frank Haskell from Fulham in West London suggested that the issue was not whether lower standards of activity should be accepted; it was the *form* of activity which should be considered. He thought that branches should be prepared to develop organisation as and when it was needed 'whether it be of mothers attending a clinic, parents and teachers of a school, or groups in housing estates, blocks of flats, or neighbourhoods, with a common shopping centre, transport problems, social life etc.'[4]

In March 1944, the Executive Committee sent out a circular recognising the difficulties confronting members in factory groups. 'Objective conditions, transport hours, getting home to meals, inability of wife to be member of the same group and so on, have all contributed to a very low level of factory group life.' It advocated a regular factory group meeting 'conducted in a lively and interesting manner' but also suggested that, where group members were unable or unwilling to attend their factory group meetings, they should be encouraged to go to branch meetings in the area where they lived.[5]

Poor attendance at factory group meetings was particularly marked in London where people were often obliged to travel long distances to work. Many of these factory groups were very large, but few, other than shop stewards, attended their meetings; most of the members would be on their way home by the time the meeting started.

At the Party's 17th Congress in October 1944 it was agreed that an Organisation Commission should be set up to examine these problems. After receiving its report, the Executive Committee, on 17th December, circulated a new proposal for discussion: that the basic unit of the party, the 'branch', should be composed of all members *resident* in the branch area; that work in factories should be led by 'Factory Committees' elected by the members working in the factory concerned.[6] After much argument, the proposed amendments to rule were agreed to at the 18th Congress in November 1945.

THE NEW STRUCTURE AND ITS IMPACT

The new practice of basing all members in branches where they lived may well have helped many to stay in the party who would otherwise have drifted out. For it came at a time when vast industrial changes were taking place; many factories were closing down, others were changing over from war to peace production, while firms whose products had been severely limited were suddenly encouraged to expand. So thousands of people left their wartime jobs and took on new ones. If they belonged to the branch where they lived, they could remain in touch even if their former links with a factory group had melted away.

However, despite some positive results, the new organisation caused problems. It had usually been fairly easy to keep factory group members' cards stamped up so long as the dues could be collected at the place of work. But when this responsibility was transferred to branch committees in the area where their members lived, and committee members found themselves involved in the time-consuming practice of calling round at their homes to collect the money, there was much grumbling by activists. Such problems – and others resulting from the icy weather spell in early 1947 – were to lead to a fall in membership to below 40,000.

In September 1947 the Executive admitted that, owing to difficulties in the collection of dues, hundreds of members were to be lapsed at the end of each year. 'The changeover from war to peace, and the conflict between the need to be organised for communist work in places where our members live and where they work (the factories) has resulted in organisational confusion and, in practice, in the weakening of party organisation in the factories' it said in a statement issued on 14 September. It therefore proposed that, wherever such a basis existed, party branches should be established in the factories.

The London District responded quickly to this proposal; seventeen new factory branches with a combined membership of 677 were set up within a few months.[7] The new move was endorsed by another change of rule agreed to at the 20th Congress in February 1948, under which branches were to consist of 'members living, or in some cases, working, within a defined area.' From then on, members could belong to either a local branch or a workplace branch. Within a few months, the membership was to rise once more to 43,000.[8]

Changes were also taking place in the methods of electing the Party's Executive Committee. From 1929 to 1943, the Party's Central Committee had been elected through a 'panels' system, under which a commission consisting largely of nominees from districts was appointed by congress; this commission went through all nominations made by branches and districts for the Central Committee and drew up a recommended list of names. Delegates had the right to propose additions to the list and to move that any individual should be excluded from it; after votes had been taken on each of these proposals, the recommended list was put to congress as a whole which voted for or against on a show of hands. But, after 1943 and the dissolution of the Comintern, the panel system was dropped. At its 17th Congress in 1944, it was decided that the Executive should be elected by a ballot taken on all those nominated, without any recommended list. This was the method used on that occasion and again at the 18th Congress in November 1945.

However, the results of ballots without a recommended list caused some dissatisfaction, mainly because those who got elected tended to be well-known speakers or writers, while those active in industrial work, or who came from regions outside London, were much under-represented. Indeed, after the 1945 Congress, the Executive Committee, which numbered 30, coopted another six to make up for these deficiencies. So it was decided at this congress to set up a commission to examine the question. Comprised of one member from each district and five from the Executive, this commission, by a majority vote, advocated the revival of a 'recommended list' but continuation of voting by ballot, which meant that delegates could vote for nominees not on the list if they wanted to. This proposal was submitted to every party branch for discussion; only one branch opposed it, and it was implemented at the 19th Congress in 1947. A later congress was to dispense with the ballot paper method which was, however, to be reintroduced in 1954.

THE PARTY AND THE INTELLECTUALS

The vast majority of the 769 delegates at the 18th Congress in 1945 were engaged in industrial work such as engineering, mining, building and transport. However, 80 of the delegates were professional workers. At one time, the party had been somewhat suspicious of 'intellectuals', but from the mid-thirties onwards, this attitude had totally changed; building up contacts and membership within the professions and among university students was seen to be important. As Pollitt said in his closing speech to the 18th Congress; 'May I say how glad we are to note so many comrades present as delegates from the professions. They can play a great role in strengthening the alliance between the working class and sections of the middle and professional classes. We have noted their great vigour and critical approach and we welcome it.'[9] In a debate on Marxist education, the need for professional people to develop a Marxist approach to their own subjects was stressed.[10]

The ensuing years were to see a vast proliferation of specialist party groups: historians, economists, scientists, doctors, psychologists, philosophers, writers, artists, musicians, film workers, and so on. An educational advisory committee, composed largely of teachers, was already holding discussions and meetings on the implementation of the 1944 Education Act and the need for comprehensive schools, and during 1946 many other groups started holding conferences on what became known as the 'battle of ideas'.

Meanwhile, December 1945 saw the relaunch of the *Modern Quarterly* a journal in which Marxists could exchange views, and which was edited by the philosopher John Lewis. As he put it in his first postwar editorial: 'Social and political conflicts are reaching a new intensity, and this is reflected in the conflict of ideas. We do not always remember that it is on the plane of philosophy as well as politics that the struggles of our time must be fought out.' Pointing out that the *Modern Quarterly* had first appeared in 1938, but had become 'an early casualty of the war', he said: 'The time has come to take up again and do better, if we can, the task then begun'.

The December 1945 issue included contributions from two scientists. One was the geneticist J.B.S. Haldane, who had always worked closely with the party and, in 1942, had joined it; the other was the well-known physicist, J.D. Bernal. Among those who contributed to the *Modern Quarterly* over the next three years were the mathematician Hyman Levy; the economist Maurice Dobb; the historians Christopher Hill, Leslie Morton and Rodney Hilton; the composers Rutland Boughton and Alan Bush, and writers such as Randall Swingler and Alick West.

LOCAL GOVERNMENT ACTIVITIES

In all the discussions concerning changes of rule within the party, much stress had been laid on the need for members to stimulate the democratic activities of people in the areas where they lived. This turn to community activity was to show results in the local government elections after the war, and in the great squatters' movement of 1946.

In the borough council elections held in November 1945, the party put forward 137 candidates, 43 of whom were elected. 18 of them won seats in London (10 in the East London borough of Stepney); 14 were elected in Scotland, two in Wales, two in Blyth (Northumberland) and one each in Portsmouth; Andover (Hampshire); Hemel Hempstead (Hertfordshire); Maidstone (Kent); Surbiton (Surrey); Sudbury (Suffolk); Wolverhampton (Midlands).

In the county council elections which took place in March 1946, the party put forward 86 candidates, eight of whom were elected. They were Ted Bramley and Jack Gaster for the London County Council; Lee Chadwick for East Suffolk; W. Breadin (Northumberland); Fanny Deakin for Staffordshire (she was unopposed); Dick Cornelius and Alun Thomas for Glamorgan and W. Jones for Monmouthshire.

In the urban and rural district council elections, and those for the parish councils, held in April 1946, the party put forward 352 candidates of whom 95 were elected. Twenty-one of them were in Wales, 24 in East Anglia. Since, on many councils, only one third of the seats came up for re-election, quite a number of those newly-elected joined other communist councillors who had been serving since before the war. Thus, Paxton Chadwick, a long-standing communist councillor on Leiston Urban District Council in East Suffolk, was joined by two other communist councillors.

By the end of the 1945–6 election round, the number of communist councillors had risen from its previous 81, to 215. In these local elections, over half a million people voted communist.[11]

The elections, as usual, demonstrated the difficulties facing any minority party in a first-past-the-post electoral system. Having failed to persuade parliament to adopt proportional representation, the party was forced to take certain tactical decisions. Hymie Fagan, who was in charge of the Communist Party's local government department, emphasised that the aim was to defeat the Tories by combining with the Labour Party so that the reactionaries would face a united left. 'The party did all that was within its power to avoid splitting the working class vote, and in many cases withdrew candidates, selected unfavourable areas, accepted the most difficult terms (which even then were often broken by the right wing labourites) and worked wholeheartedly for the Labour candidates where there was no communist standing.'[12]

It was against this background that a campaign had once more been launched by the party for affiliation to the Labour Party.

THE CAMPAIGN FOR AFFILIATION

The need to become affiliated to the Labour Party as one of its 'socialist societies' and so play a part in its deliberations had been one of the subjects raised in the discussion leading up to the November 1945 Congress[13] at which it was agreed that another attempt should be made to gain support for the aim within the wider labour movement.[14]

So, on 21 January 1946, Harry Pollitt sent a letter to the secretary of the Labour Party, Morgan Phillips, asking that the application for affiliation be placed before the next Labour Party Annual Conference.

In making this request, Pollitt again stressed that the party would 'accept all obligations under the constitution, rules and standing orders of the Labour Party.' He said that 'the arduous tasks which now lie before the Labour Government require the backing of a united labour movement in order to ensure the fullest success against the attempts of Toryism to stage a come-back, and against the resistance of reactionary vested interests.'

He pointed out that the constitution of the Labour Party was designed to unite all types of working class organisations, whether trade unions, cooperative societies or socialist organisations and parties and that affiliation 'would afford the opportunity for the special contribution of our party, with the devotion and campaigning enthusiasm of its membership, to be made in a constructive and helpful fashion to the common tasks of the Labour movement in the coming period.'[15]

The Labour Party NEC, not surprisingly, refused the application. At the time when the affiliation campaign started, party members were full of hope that this time they would win. As Ted Bramley observed, organisations entitled to approximately 800,000 votes at the Labour Party conference were already pledged to support affiliation; others responsible for 800,000 votes were against it, while organisations with command of another 800,000 votes were as yet uncommitted.[16]

However, an unprecedented campaign to defeat the affiliation drive was launched by the Labour leaders in the *Daily Herald*. All the old accusations were dredged up again: that communists did not believe in civil liberty, that communists believed in dictatorship, not democracy, and so on. The campaign was taken up with enthusiasm by the Tory press, while rightwing bodies, such as the Economic League, sent letters to newspapers warning against the terrible consequences to the Labour Party of any union with communists. One of the most telling arguments used by the Labour leaders was that affiliation would embarrass the Labour Government, would cause divisions and defections, and was anyhow unnecessary, as Labour had achieved power unaided, and was capable of doing its job.[17]

Unfortunately, this campaign succeeded in procuring a reversal in the attitude of some organisations which had previously been in support. One of these was the distributive workers union NUDAW. The most serious turn-around was that of the National Union of Mineworkers which was persuaded to hold district conferences on the issue. The South Wales, Yorkshire and Durham district conferences all voted against affiliation. In South Wales, the vote against was narrowly won, despite the fact that the South Wales miners had given overwhelming support for communist Arthur Horner to become general secretary of the NUM. As a result of these district conferences, the NUM withdrew its support for communist affiliation to the Labour Party.

The upshot was that, when the matter was debated at the Labour Party annual conference in June, the resolution in favour, moved by Jack Tanner of the Amalgamated Engineering Union, seconded by S.J. Merrells of the Fire Brigades Union and supported by the National Union of Railwaymen, received only 468,000 votes with 2,678,000 against – not nearly such a favourable result as that in 1943.

Most significant of all, an amendment to rule, tabled by the NEC and carried by a very big majority, laid down that political organisations with their own programme, principles and policy, which were not already affiliated on 1 January 1946, were ineligible for affiliation in the future. So it was that the original structure of the Labour Party, set up to unite trade unions, cooperative societies, and socialist bodies in one organisation, began to wither away. For the Communist Party, the fight for affiliation was finally over.

12
—
THE SQUATTERS MOVEMENT 1946

July 1946 saw the start of a squatters movement in which Communist Party members were to play an outstanding part. It was to prove a great embarrassment to right-wing Labour leaders, particularly because of its communist links.

It began as a spontaneous reaction to the appalling housing situation, and communists were quickly involved – as they always were in movements from below – participating, helping, organising. It showed how utterly untrue were allegations previously made by Herbert Morrison that the communist rank and file played no part in shaping policies but were subject to orders from above.[1]

Background to the movement was the demobilisation of some 3½ million men and women, many of whom found themselves rejoining their families in intolerable conditions. Even before the war, millions had lived in homes which were damp and lacking sanitary facilities. Since then, bombing had destroyed half a million houses and damaged many more. The Labour Government's response was to give priority to the repair of war damage; control the use of building materials by a system of licensing; introduce a programme of temporary, pre-fabricated dwellings, and to concentrate new building in the hands of local authorities. The wartime power of local councils to requisition empty houses and flats for the use of bombed-out families was extended to cover requisitioning for *all* those inadequately housed.

In practice, these good intentions were not producing the results expected. The new council house building programme was failing to get going; there was an acute shortage of building materials and many of those available were being siphoned off into the black market. And, though there were many vacant properties in London, Tory-controlled authorities were refusing to requisition them to accommodate those on their waiting lists. As Bill Wainwright put it 'good regulations are one thing, but to get them carried out is another.'[2]

OCCUPATION OF ARMY CAMPS

By the summer of 1946 there was a growing number of empty army camps, and in July came the first reported occupation by squatters when 48 families moved into two such camps at Scunthorpe in Lincolnshire. A third camp in the neighbourhood was taken over in the following week, while families in Sheffield began to move into huts on vacated 'Ack-Ack' sites. The Scunthorpe squatters were given support by their local MP who announced that the War Office did not intend to evict them, provided that the local authority took over responsibility for the camp, and that the Minister of Health authorised the supply of gas, water and electricity. This was the signal for a country-wide movement in August during which 45,000 people occupied vacated camps.

Government bodies were initially reluctant to allow the use of the camps for such a purpose, but were overtaken by events. On 18 August, Minister of Health Aneurin Bevan announced that he had authorised local authorities to supply services to those camps which were occupied; by the end of August it had been agreed that local councils would manage the camps, provide essential services and collect maintenance charges ranging from 7s 6d to 10s a week.

'While the government proceeds laboriously with its housing programme, British democracy in action has scored a tremendous success with the squatters' seizure of camps and gun sites' commented Emile Burns. 'The movement has literally swept the country ... The government has bowed to the storm and in general, the squatters are staying put.' He added: 'The Communist Party has always stressed the need for the people to take things into their own hands, and not to sit passively waiting for the government to do things for them'.[3]

The standard offered by the Army and RAF camps was low. In many cases, the huts were dirty and damp and had no cooking facilities, while the sanitary arrangements were primitive. Yet thousands were prepared to face such conditions because of the far worse ones from which they had come.

Thus many returning soldiers who wanted, above all, to be reunited with their families, had found themselves sharing a single room with their wives and children, or even sleeping in passages. Life in the camps could be less cramped, and in most of them, extensive repairs and improvements were carried out, nearly always by the squatters themselves, among whom there were often men with building skills. The local authorities were persuaded to lay on water supplies and electricity; cooking facilities were gradually installed, sanitary arrangements improved. Many of the squatters involved found it an exciting and inspiring event. For example, Joseph and Marjorie Siddall who, together with their son, were the first to occupy a camp near Doncaster, later looked back on the experience as the happiest time of their lives.[4]

In many localities, it was the local Communist Party which took the initiative. For example, in Birmingham, the party announced publicly that it was looking for suitable camps; everyone knew that if they wanted to join a squat they should contact the party. By the end of August, 257 families had been installed in 12 camps in or around the town. On 25 August a meeting representing families from all the camps concerned eestablished the 'Birmingham and District Squatters Association.' Its secretary was a communist, Harry Chapman, while Sam Blackwell, the party's Midland District organiser, was elected chairman. Chapman himself later recalled what happened in the camp where he and his wife were squatting from 1946–48.

> We set up a camp committee and drew up a set of rules covering such things as sanitation, security, social behaviour etc. This was necessary because of course the usual charges were made of filthy, unruly mobs, queue jumpers, vandals etc. We made representations to the city council and MPs and made appeals to the trade unions and trades council, wrote letters, held meetings etc. I was delegate from my trade union branch, Yardley No 1 AEU to the Birmingham Trades Council ... We used every opportunity to develop solidarity between the squatters and the unions and the political parties.[5]

Bert Ward, from Middlesbrough, was among those who squatted; together with his wife and others, they occupied a group of Nissen huts surrounding a former anti-aircraft battery. Ward, who joined the Communist Party in 1948, later recalled that the movement was led by a communist, Pat Durkin. 'On his advice, a camp committee was set up ... There were negotiations with the town council, and subsequently they accepted responsibility for collecting rents and services were switched on.'[6]

Another example of communist initiative was demonstrated over

Daws Hill camp near High Wycombe in Buckinghamshire, an area which was still full of wartime evacuees and others who could not find accommodation. The local Communist Party had a large and active membership, one of whom, Jack Spector, had stood successfully against Conservative and Labour opposition and had won a seat on the West Wycombe Parish Council.

During the summer of 1946, plans were worked out for the occupation of the Daws Hill camp which, during the war, had been the headquarters of the American Eighth Army's bomber command. Word was passed round to prospective squatters in the locality and, on a specified day, with coordinated timing, party members with such Labour Party supporters as they could muster, went to the main gate, and cut the wires that had been attached to them. Within a short time the first squatters arrived with their bedding, belongings and families. Before long, there was a dense stream ascending Daws Hill; soon the camp was accommodating 150 families – over 500 men, women and children.

Initially they faced some acute problems. For example, the water was turned off. But the authorities eventually accepted the squatters' presence, and services were laid on. The camp's internal affairs were conducted by an elected squatters' committee representing the 'Daws Hill Community Association.' At first the main concentration was on painting and renovating the huts, but soon it became a neat village with gardens surrounding the huts, its own social centre, its children's nursery, its children's bathing pool. An editorial committee produced a monthly stencilled bulletin 'Daws Hill Despatch'.[7]

THE LONDON SQUATTERS

From the beginning, the party looked on the army camps as no more than a temporary short-term solution. The most urgent aim was to get new council houses built, concentrate repair work on making damaged houses habitable, and meanwhile, step up the requisitioning by local authorities of high-grade empty properties, most of which were in private hands while the owners waited for suitable buyers.

This was a cause of growing indignation in London. Here there was a considerable number of empty blocks of flats, most of which had been used by government departments for various purposes during the war. Local authorities had the right to requisition such flats for people in need of a home and, in practice, most Labour-controlled councils were anxious to do so. However, the Tory-controlled councils – in particular Kensington, Marylebone and Westminster – in which boroughs the most spacious and luxurious flats were situated – were refusing to use their requisitioning powers. They even turned down offers from government departments which were abandoning them, so that most of such flats were about to be returned to their private owners who expected to let them out at rents which only the well-to-do could afford.

On 6 September 1946, Ted Bramley, the London district secretary of the party and a communist councillor on the London County Council, discussed the matter with the London organiser, Dennis Goodwin.[8] That evening they called in members from various parts of London and asked them, as a matter of urgency, to identify suitable empty dwellings – blocks of flats in Tory-controlled boroughs for preference. These were then pared down to a few and, the next day, party members got in touch with local people who they knew were living in bad conditions and told them, in confidence, that if they would like to join in a squat, they should turn up at an agreed spot in Kensington High Street on Sunday afternoon at 2 o'clock, bringing with them bedding and other possessions, and see what happened. It was stressed that nobody could be certain of the outcome or whether they would be able to stay in the place for any length of time.

In the event, far more people turned up than expected. Hundreds came carrying suitcases; some arrived in vans loaded with possessions including furniture. The initial target was a block of one hundred luxury flats known as the 'Duchess of Bedford House' which had been commandeered by the government during the war to house refugees, and had then been offered to the Tory-controlled Kensington Borough Council for rehousing the homeless. But the council, which had a waiting list of nearly 4,000 families, had refused this offer, so the flats were about to be returned to the owners, the Prudential Assurance Company, for re-letting at high rents.

The occupation was carefully organised. Someone slipped through a back window and opened the tradesman's entrance from inside. As people arrived outside, their names were checked by Tubby Rosen, a communist councillor in Stepney, and they were directed into the building. Those in charge of the operation included Dennis Goodwin, Bill Carritt – a communist councillor in Westminster – and Stan Henderson, a party member from Hammersmith. Henderson had been a prisoner of war in the Far East and had returned to find himself sleeping on the floor in a house infested with bugs. He participated in the squat, and was soon to be elected as secretary to the Duchess of Bedford Squatters Committee.

After a hundred families had filled the block, those who came next were taken to neighbouring houses. Thus nine families (with sixteen children) took over Moray Lodge, a 25-room mansion which, before the war, had been the home of Lord Ilchester. Others were sent on to Melcombe Regis Court at 59 Weymouth Street, Marylebone, where Joyce Alergant, another Westminster communist councillor, was waiting to receive them. Initially 20 families arrived there, but soon the number rose to 54. This block of flats had been used to accommodate US Army personnel during the war. It had been offered to the Marylebone Borough Council which, like Kensington, had turned down the offer, after which it had stood empty for eight months. Marylebone had a waiting list of over 3,300 homeless families, but had refused to requisition the empty flats and houses in the borough though these ran into hundreds.

News of these occupations was broadcast on the evening of September 8 and helped to spark off further moves. On September 9, communists Lou Kenton and Maud Rogerson organised the occupation of Abbey Lodge, near Regents Park, by 20 families from Willesden. Among them was Tom Durkin, who had earlier participated in the occupation of huts used by an 'Ack-Ack' battery in a local park. Abbey Lodge had been empty for several months, having been previously used for RAF personnel; now it was to be let out at high rents. Also on September 9, squatters took over Fountain Court in Westminster, where another communist councillor, Dr Joan McMichael (who had served on the party's executive since 1943) helped to plan the operation. Another building occupied by squatters on that day was the Ivanhoe Hotel in Bloomsbury, which had been used as a hostel for evacuees from Gibraltar. Holborn Borough Council had wanted to use it to accommodate homeless families, but had been refused permission to do so on the grounds that there was an acute hotel shortage in London.

GOVERNMENT ACTION TO CRUSH THE MOVEMENT

All over London, Communist Party branches were being approached by people seeking to take part in any further squats. Branch members were busy identifying suitable premises which could be taken over in boroughs which were refusing to use their requisitioning powers. And the London district of the party sent a letter to Aneurin Bevan, Minister of Health, asking him to receive a deputation to discuss further occupation of empty luxury flats.

But, on the day this letter was despatched, 9 September, the Cabinet met and within 24 hours it was made clear that the government was determined to crush the movement. A statement was issued from 10 Downing Street announcing that 'His Majesty's Government take a very serious view of the forcible seizure and occupation by unauthorised persons of private premises in London.' It went on: 'This action has been instigated and organised by the Communist Party and must result in hindering rather than in helping the arrangements made for the orderly rehousing of those in need of accommodation ... Unless steps are taken to check lawless measures of this sort, the rights of the ordinary law-abiding citizens are endangered and anarchy may result'.[9]

It went on to say that the police had been instructed to prevent further forcible entries, that writs had been issued against the 'trespassers' in Duchess of Bedford House and Fountain Court, and that the Director of Public Prosecutions was considering bringing proceedings against the organisers for 'criminal conspiracy'. It was obvious that, whatever the concessions made somewhat reluctantly by the Labour Government over the empty army camps, it was not prepared to tolerate any action to take over private property – even though it had given powers to local councils to do just that. A docile and inactive electorate had always been a prime objective; any kind of direct action was anathema.

Initially, most of the press had taken a sympathetic view of the squatters' campaign. But after the Cabinet decision, the atmosphere changed. This was particularly marked in Labour's *Daily Herald* which had reported in detail without criticism how the Duchess of Bedford flats had been occupied. But by the next day it had obediently changed course, arguing that unless such squatting was checked, the entire housing programme would be 'thrown into chaos' and that the weekend occupations were 'attempts to bring the law into disrepute'. This was followed on 11 September with a lengthy leading article backing the government's decision to 'uphold the law'.

This attitude was challenged by Harry Pollitt at a London demonstration on 12 September in support of the squatters. He said that 'all the talk about the sacred rights of private property, about the forces of anarchy which have been let loose, is done to help preserve the system of rich and poor.' It was not true, he said, that the squatters action would delay the provision of accommodation for priority cases. The squatters had deliberately refrained from entering empty council property. The Communist Party was urging that local authorities should use their power to requisition empty premises in their areas.[10]

On 11 September, writs had been issued against Stan Henderson and four other Duchess of Bedford squatters, and against some of the squatters in Fountain Court. But, on 14 September, came a much more ominous event: four communist councillors – Ted Bramley, Joyce Alergant, Bill Carritt, Tubby Rosen – together with Stan Henderson, were arrested and charged with 'conspiracy to incite and direct trespass'. They were released on bail for a hearing later in the month.

Meanwhile, on 16 September, a circular was sent by the Ministry of Health to local authorities requesting them to withold all facilities from squatters in premises under their control, not to supply gas or electricity, to cut off any such services, and to take action to secure the eviction of the squatters.[11]

These instructions were not carried out in every instance. When the electricity was cut off at Fountain Court, in Westminster, the squatters went out and appealed to the crowd outside for candles. These arrived in great numbers, and, after a poster parade in Trafalgar Square, the electricity was restored. Westminster Council then refused to empty the dustbins. But, when the squatters began tipping refuse out into Buckingham Palace Road, collection was resumed.

The withdrawal of services was accompanied by much police harassment, particularly at Abbey Lodge. Here, both water and electricity were cut off, and the building surrounded by police. There were big demonstrations outside, hundreds of people sat down in the road, mounted police were brought in to disperse them, but the demonstrations persisted, and finally the police agreed to allow pails of water to be taken in by supporters once a day. However, there was no gas or electricity so the squatters could not boil a kettle, let alone cook. Ivor Segal, a Young Communist League member, who was one of those helping the squatters from outside, obtained a primus stove and a bottle of paraffin which he padded with corrugated cardboard; these were then thrown through the window while a policeman's attention was diverted elsewhere; both arrived safely. A pulley was fixed up between the flats and the house next door where cooking was done for the squatters and, at night, boxes of food were surreptitiously pulled across. As Segal later recalled: 'The police were puzzled how the squatters were receiving food until, one night, the pulley broke and the 'cargo' nearly hit a copper down below'.[12]

On 17 September, 9 days after the occupation had started, a judge issued possession orders against the squatters in the Duchess of Bedford and in Weymouth Street. Simultaneously, Aneurin Bevan announced that no legal action would be taken against those squatters who left voluntarily and promised that they would not lose their places in the housing queue.

A meeting at Communist Party headquarters discussed what should be done. The leading party squatters were all present, and there was some argument about what the response should be. Some wanted to make a forcible stand against eviction. Others thought that this would put hundreds of people in an impossible position; in particular, it would lead to violence, putting the children at risk. In the end, it was agreed that the squatters should be urged to leave peacefully.

Stan Henderson returned to Duchess of Bedford House, and recommended withdrawal. He met with a certain degree of opposition; some of the squatters wanted to fight it out, but the majority agreed they should leave, and eventually a public statement was adopted and issued. It said:

> We came in together, and we have decided to go out together, confident that we have achieved our purpose. Those who were ignorant of our plight now know, and those who knew and ignored are shamed into a sense of urgency that London's homeless shall be rehoused ... We will continue to fight with other homeless Londoners for housing to be treated as a military operation and for all local authorities to bring a fresh urgency to the problem, never resting until property interests and the black market have been completely prevented from standing in the way of decent homes for London's people.[13]

Agreement was reached with the London County Council for the squatters to be accommodated in a Rest Centre in East London; buses were laid on to take them there. In the event, they found the Rest Centre full of building workers, and had to sleep on the floor. The next day, after lengthy negotiations conducted by Stan Henderson and Councillor Jack Gaster, who threatened that a committee room in county hall would be occupied unless accommodation was provided, the squatters from the Duchess of Bedford House were taken into

Alexandra House in Hampstead (formerly an old people's home). Two hundred men, women and children went there from the Duchess of Bedford, and another 80 from other squats. By 8 October, five of the families had been found homes by their local authorities; gradually others were rehoused, those with children being given priority. By Easter 1947, those who were left were moved to a half-way house at Lancaster Gate and were all eventually offered accommodation.

At the end of October, the case of the five 'conspirators' came up at the Old Bailey. Bill Sedley, a party member who was also a solicitor, was in charge of the defence, and Jack Gaster was also involved in preparing the case. They managed to secure the services of Sir Walter Monckton, KC, an eminent Conservative, to act for the defence; he developed a legal argument against the concept that there could be such a crime as 'conspiracy to trespass' or to incite others to trespass.

Ted Bramley conducted his own defence, and made a moving speech about the 500,000 families in London waiting for homes and how, among the squatters, there were men and women who had stood up heroically in the blitz and had earned the admiration of the world for their courage; there were soldiers, sailors, airmen and merchant seamen 'the people to whom we owe our present freedom'. 'Yes, it is true that we communists have helped these people' he said. 'And those among you who know what it is to be without a home of your own or to live in sordid and overcrowded conditions, will understand that we find it impossible to be unmoved or passive in the face of such human suffering.'[14]

The five were found guilty but, to everyone's surprise, the judge, who clearly felt doubtful about imposing a sentence which might inspire an appeal, merely bound them over to keep the peace for the next two years.

Communists were later to claim that the squatting campaign had gone a long way towards achieving its object: much increased requisitioning by local councils of empty property to house the homeless. By 16 September some councils – including Bristol and Chelsea – were inviting families on their waiting lists to move into requisitioned premises before repairs had been completed. Acton, Wandsworth, Chiswick and Brentford took similar steps. On 23 September, the *Daily Herald* reported that all requisitioned property, no longer essential for official purposes, was to be made available for housing. The upshot was that the number of requisitioned properties held by local councils in the London region for housing purposes went up from 54,147 in March 1946 to 60,277 in March 1947. Many of these 'properties' were blocks of flats, so the number of families accommodated was far larger.

The party continued to be the target of attack and misrepresentation in the press. But none of the families who participated in the squatting ever complained or attacked the party for organising it. Indeed, many of them joined it as a result.

13

INDUSTRIAL WORK AND ATTITUDES TO NATIONALISATION 1945–7

Despite the expansion of political work in local communities, and the change in rule intended to help this forward, the workplace was still regarded by party members as the chief focal point – the place where the ideas and values instilled by a capitalist society could be most effectively countered and the socialist message spread.

Workplace activity involved building up trade union organisation and many party members were elected as union representatives or shop stewards and found themselves negotiating with the management on issues such as pay, hours, working conditions, canteens and washing facilities, safeguards against accidents and so on. But they also discussed political issues with their workmates; distributed leaflets, sold the *Daily Worker* and tried to recruit people into the party.

Following the election of the Labour Government in 1945, the rebuilding of Britain was seen as the priority. The party argued that this required 'a positive economic programme for planned productive development'. Nationalisation of key industries should be speeded up, price control should be extended together with government control over investment as part of a plan for reorganisation and reequipment of the main industries. These aims were debated at the party's 18th Congress in November 1945, and formed the basis of a pamphlet by J.R. Campbell 'Over to Peace'.

ENGINEERING

When the war ended, Len Powell remained full-time general secretary of the Engineering and Allied Trades Shop Stewards National Council. The organisation's monthly journal *New Propellor* (soon to change its name to *The Metal Worker*) had reached a circulation of 94,000. In June 1945, when the General Election was announced, it reprinted a call from the Vickers Shop Stewards Combine Committee to 'clear out the Tories' and shop stewards committees all over the country set up election committees and invited Labour candidates to speak at workplace meetings.

The Labour victory induced feelings of enormous optimism. In August 1945, under the triumphant heading 'End of Tory domination' the *New Propellor* set out views on the way forward. 'Democracy does not only mean the struggle to gain an electoral majority' it said. 'There is an immense field of day-to-day activity which must be energetically carried out.... as engineers, we must retain and extend our wartime gains in the workshops and shipyards. This means strengthening our Shop Stewards movement and working through the JPC machinery to supervise the controllers and make full use of workers' initiative on the job.'

It was precisely these wartime gains that the engineering employers were bent upon destroying. They were determined to reestablish the 'managerial functions' which had been eroded during the war when the industry had been subjected, not only to state control from above, but increasing interference from below, particularly from union representatives on Joint Production Committees. Formation of the JPCs had been agreed to most reluctantly by the employers who now aimed to be rid of them.

Shop stewards were to face many new problems during the switch-over from war to peace production. In 1946 came the end of the Essential Work Order, a wartime regulation which enabled workers to be directed into essential industries. Though nobody wanted such an Order to remain in force, it had brought with it certain compensations – for example, it prohibited arbitrary dismissals. As expected, when the EWO ended, some employers seized the opportunity to sack leading shop stewards. From June 1946 onwards, many attempts at victimisation and the walk-outs that ensued were being reported in the *Metal Worker*. An early example was at Shardlow's in Sheffield where 1,100 workers stopped work following the dismissal of the convenor, Bill Longden. The Sheffield AEU District Committee pledged financial support, as did 11 AEU branches and shop stewards committees in five other factories, after which the Shardlow management backed down and Longden was unconditionally reinstated. In the ensuing weeks, there were many other such attempts made by employers and it was one of the problems discussed at a special conference called by the SSNC in the autumn of 1946.

At this conference it was decided to start a campaign for a 40-hour (five day) week in place of the prevailing 47-hour week. By this time, party member Dave Michaelson, convenor of shop stewards at the Lagonda motor works in Staines, Middlesex, had become editor of the *Metal Worker*. He described how, in many shops, 'feeling is ready to boil over' on the issue of working hours. 'Production does not depend on long hours' he wrote, insisting that increased output could be achieved if workers were given a real voice through Joint Production Committees, with consultative machinery at every level.[1] That autumn the Engineering Employers Federation agreed to replace the 47-hour week with a 44-hour week. However, some firms conceded an even shorter week. Thus Bill Warman, chair of the Standard Motors shop stewards' committee in Coventry, described how an agreement for a 42½-hour week had come into force at his firm, but how, as a result of better planning, production had gone up by 30%.[2] At De Haviland's aircraft factory, where the stewards were pressing for a 42½-hour week, a coffin was carried ceremoniously through the factory. The headstone was inscribed: 'Here lie the remains of the 47-hour week, born in 1919, died in 1946. His son, 44-hour week, is sinking fast'.[3]

Meanwhile, over 50,000 Clyde shipyard workers whose employers were refusing to agree to a 5-day week stayed away from Saturday work for six successive weeks, after which the Shipbuilding Employers Federation agreed to make concessions.

The engineering industry remained an important recruiting ground for communists. An outstanding achievement was that of a young Irish shop steward, Sean McKeown. Employed at a Coventry motor works, he made 50 new recruits within a few months. Writing of his experiences he said: 'Every recruit is another blow struck at the destroyers, another voice raised in protest, another dissentient from the stifling, life-blighting policies of the money-changers ... Recruits will be gained on the basis of our emerging as the only Party with a real socialist policy'. He went on: 'Party comrades ... must be informed that it is not sufficient merely to seek wage increases and improvements in conditions, but that all their work must be directed towards showing the workers the class character of our society.[4]

BUILDING

Another industry where the party was making an impact was building on which the 'homes for all' aim depended. At its 1945 Congress, the party welcomed the Labour Government's intention that local authorities should be the main house-building agency, but regretted that it had failed to take the sweeping measures needed to overcome the critical housing shortage. A whole list of proposals were made, including the setting up of a Ministry of Housing (something which was not to happen until the Labour Government left office). The party also urged the establishment of Joint Production Committees on every building site.

The building industry presented the trade union movement with special problems. Not only was most of the work undertaken by small contractors, but their employees belonged to many different unions. There were separate unions for bricklayers, for woodworkers, for woodcutting machinists, for painters, for plumbers, for plasterers, for slaters and tilers, and so forth. Most of the unions had separate Scottish equivalents. Building labourers were not eligible to join the craft unions; they were covered in turn by three different unions. Seventeen of the unions catering for building workers were affiliated to the National Federation of Building Trade Operatives, a co-ordinating body with little power to take decisions.

In 1935, a group of party members in the building trade had met and launched a monthly paper the *New Builders Leader*. The initiator had been Frank Jackson, a former member of the woodworkers union. By 1946 Jackson was employed full-time in the industrial department of the Communist Party head office. He was still acting as secretary to the *New Builders Leader* editorial board, which consisted of 19 people, all of whom were working in the building trade and writing for the paper in their spare time. The chief editor was a member of the Plumbers Union, Frank Stone, and among other party members regularly contributing were Bill Smart and Joe Alabaster of the bricklayers' union (AUBTW) Joe Krooshkoff of the woodworkers union (ASW), Alf Silverstein of the painters society (NSP), Stan Bonham and Tom Sullivan of the plumbers union (PTU), Colin Penn and Ann Wheeler of the building technicians association (ABT). Gwylyn John of the general workers union (T&GWU) wrote about the problems of building labourers.

The *New Builders Leader*'s stated aim was one union for the building industry. It sought to strengthen trade union organisation on all jobs and to win improvements in wages and conditions. And it emphasised the importance of narrowing the differentials between the wages of craftsmen and labourers.

But it also campaigned for the introduction of direct labour schemes by public bodies – particularly local authorities – in place of private contractors. It advocated better planning so as to eliminate the drift into the black market and concentrate work on essentials such as homes for the people. And it tried to involve its readers in campaigns for an adequate housebuilding programme. Unfortunately, the Labour Government was, by 1947, to announce severe cuts in the housebuilding programme – something which the *New Builders Leader* strongly opposed.

EQUAL PAY FOR WOMEN

The party still saw the fight for equal pay for women as one of its priorities. But this fight became much harder after the war ended for a number of reasons. One was the drift of women out of industry – a tendency which was, ironically, fuelled by the low pay offered to women. Between June 1945 and May 1946 the number of females in the working population fell by one million to 5.7 million.[5] Some of these women, admittedly, wanted to leave industry, particularly those who were married and whose husbands had returned from abroad, or whose children, previously evacuated, had come home. But there were other reasons, the main one being that the only jobs on offer tended to be those at very low pay.

This development was being highlighted as early as August 1945 in the *New Propeller* by an anonymous woman correspondent who described what was happening in those engineering factories where women had (at least nominally) won the right to the male rate for jobs formerly done by men. 'With war contracts drawing to a close in many sections of engineering, more and more women workers are becoming redundant' she wrote. 'One thing which is emerging clearly now is the employers' determination to continue two classes of work in engineering – men's work and women's work – at two distinct rates.' And she told how employment exchange officials arrived with lists of vacancies saying that there was plenty of work for everyone. But, while all the men were given jobs at similar rates to the ones they were already getting, women were being offered jobs only at the women's rate. In January 1946, the average weekly earnings for men were £5.14s; for women, under £3.

For married women with children, the pay was not worth the trouble. By the time they had paid for fares to work, meals out, laundry, school dinners and child minders, they had little left out of what they had earned.

In February 1946, again in the *New Propellor*, Dorothy Coulthard, a shop steward at CAV, described how employers were sacking women on men's rates, and then trying to get them back at women's rates. 'Of course it doesn't work' she wrote. In April 1946, Coulthard chaired a meeting of leading women shop stewards, at which she pointed out that during the war she had earned £6.10s a week; now she was lucky if she took home £2.10s.[6]

Women shop stewards regarded it as a great step forward when the engineering unions jointly decided to aim for the male labourer's rate – currently £4.4s a week – as the minimum for women engineers. But the employers rejected this claim, instead offering women an increase which would bring some of them up to just over £3. The unions asked the Minister of Labour, George Isaacs, to intervene; he decided to refer the matter to the National Arbitration Tribunal.

While these discussions were going on, 500 women from 22 factories assembled outside the Ministry of Labour building on 5 June; two and a half weeks later, women from 40 factories marched through London with banners. The demonstration was led by two large contingents from CAV and Cossors.[7] However, the National Arbitration Tribunal turned down the claim, and backed the employers' offer of a 4s 6d increase a week, which was far below the agreed rise for men. In other words, the gap between women's and men's pay was to widen. It was by this time clear that the Labour Government was not going to use its powers in any way to support demands for equal pay for women.

The outflow of women from employment was not confined to engineering; it was evident in other areas, particularly transport. The situation was confused by the fact that men returning from the forces were entitled to claim back their original jobs, in some of which, women had replaced them. However, employers did not confine their dismissals to such women. On 12 January, 1946, came the news that the London Passenger Transport Board had discharged 15 women bus conductors; their jobs were being taken over by men, most of whom had never been bus conductors before. 'We do not want to take the jobs of men who have been in the forces, but we bitterly resent having to make way for those we have to train to do our work' commented one woman bus conductor to the *Daily Worker*.[8]

Bert Papworth pointed out that these sacked women conductors were being offered canteen work, laundry work and other low paid jobs commonly regarded as 'women's work'. Papworth, former leader of the busmen's rank and file movement and the only communist on the TUC General Council wrote a special article on the issue in the *Labour Monthly* emphasising that 'women are being sacked who have become skilled and used to the work, and men who have never been in these industries taken on.' And he asserted that 'a trade union principle is at stake. And if a narrow and shortsighted outlook on this matter is found among certain sections of the trade unions, it only shows there has been a failure to realise the broader trade union principle that is involved'.[9]

At the Trades Union Congress in October 1946, party member Muriel Rayment, a shop steward at EMI, was one of four women on the delegation representing the Transport and General Workers Union (the rest of the T&GWU delegation consisted of 70 men). Rayment criticised the TUC General Council's report on the manpower shortage because it failed to deal with the reasons why women had left industry, and what should be done to bring them back again. Stating that the key question was the issue of equal pay, she also complained that many day nurseries were being closed because the government had reduced the grants available for them during the war.[10] Equal pay and equal opportunities were also the issues raised by another party member, Ann George from the Civil Service Clerical Association, who said that if a man was doing her job, he would get 20 per cent more money than she did. It was a 'deplorable feature' of the congress that so few women were represented – only 26 out of 793.[11]

The following month the report of the Royal Commission on Equal Pay came out. It dashed any hope of support from that quarter. For although it advocated equal pay for teachers and civil servants (a recommendation which was not to be implemented for another ten years or so) it rejected any claim that women in industry should also have that right.

Despite continual complaints from government spokesmen about the manpower shortage and pleas for women to return to industry, no steps were taken to treat women on terms of equality with men.

TUC REPRESENTATION

Because communists were tireless activists at the workplace, many were getting elected to union positions, either as full-time officers or, in some cases, as Executive members of their union. This trend became visible at trades union congresses where a growing number of the delegates who participated in the debates were known communists. For example, at the 1946 Congress, 23 out of 123 speakers were communists, while quite a number of others, though not members, shared the party's views on most political questions and co-operated with party members in their efforts to persuade the Labour leaders to adopt more progressive policies. These developments were watched with alarm by the Labour leadership, and it was frequently suggested that communists obtained elected positions only by dishonest methods. This was implied by Prime Minister Attlee when he addressed the TUC as a visitor in 1946. 'Democracy is becoming a much abused word' he said. 'It is often used by those who have never understood or practised democratic principles, to mean the achievement of power by hook – or more often by crook – by the Communist Party.'

Almost immediately after this speech, he was answered by Bert Papworth, who was making a report on behalf of the general council on the trade union situation in Greece. He said:

> The Prime Minister made reference to 'hook or by crook.' By political conviction I am a Communist, and, in spite of all the allegations of Mr Attlee against the communists, I take it that the general council, with whom I operate as part of a team, found the necessary confidence in me to present this report for them (Applause). I am sure, knowing my colleagues of the general council, that they did not get me here by hook or by crook in order to put me on the spot.[12]

Though many of the communist delegates who took part in the debates at this 1946 TUC were concerned with foreign affairs, most of those who spoke dealt with the immediate issues facing their members. The two who spoke on equal pay have already been mentioned, but, in addition, Arthur Horner – by this time General Secretary of the National Union of Mineworkers – talked about production problems in the coal mines, while Abe Moffat, also of the NUM, urged the establishment of alternative industries in the former distressed areas;

Jim Gardner, General Secretary of the Foundry Workers union, raised the question of pneumoconiosis; Walter Stevens of the Electrical Trades Union moved a resolution urging the repeal of 'Order 1305' (a wartime measure which made strikes illegal); Betty Jones of the Civil Servants Clerical Association (CSCA) wanted greater participation of young people in trade union affairs; Les Gregory (ETU) and Leo McGree of the woodworkers union (ASW) spoke of the need for price controls; Bill Zak of the Furnishing Trades Association (FTA) talked about utility furniture; Bill Smart of the bricklayers (AUBTW) spoke on housing. Roy Innes of the Association of Scientific Workers (ASW) dealt with the need for technical advances.

At the 1947 TUC again most of the Communists who spoke were concerned with the practical issues facing their members. Thus Arthur Horner described the manpower shortage in the mines; R. Elsemere (AUBTW) expressed concern about such shortages in the building industry; Jack Hendy (ETU) dealt with trade union education; Frank Foulkes (ETU) and W.A.G. Roberts (Vehicle Builders Union) spoke on production problems; A. Allan (NUM) and Wally Stevens (ETU) on the need for better control of prices and profits. Ann George (CSCA) spoke once again on equal pay for women. Kenneth Campbell of the Association of Building Technicians moved a resolution urging a public enquiry into the needs of the building industry. He was supported by Leo McGree (ASW) and, despite efforts by the general council to get it remitted, it was carried. The most contentious issues discussed at both the 1946 and 1947 Congresses were, of course, to do with foreign policy.

COAL MINING AND NATIONALISATION

One industry in which the party had always had considerable influence was coal mining. At the time the electricity power stations, on which all factories depended, were fuelled entirely by coal as were gas stations and railway engines.

Legislation to nationalise the coal industry went through in 1946, and 1 January 1947 was 'Vesting Day'. On that day, some 1,500 collieries, belonging to 800 separate companies, passed into the ownership and control of a National Coal Board appointed by the Labour Government. The event was greeted with mass demonstrations of rejoicing in all mining areas. The President of the National Union of Mineworkers, Wil Lawther, gave expression to these feelings of joy. 'It marks the end of an epoch – the reign of private ownership over the lives and destinies of those who supply the coal' he said. It meant, he thought, that the 'turmoil, strife and suffering' was over.[13]

The party did not entirely share this rosy view. While believing that coal nationalisation was a major step forward, it was regarded as a *first* step only.[14] But Arthur Horner, the NUM general secretary, stressed the possibility that nationalisation would open up for the the future. 'Everything now depends upon an adequate supply of coal to keep present industry active' he said. 'Production is the key, not only to a prosperous mining industry, but to an expanding and vigorous British economy ... The future is in our hands. Wages can be higher, conditions safer, work less arduous. The main fight of the future will not be between management and men, it will be a struggle against Mother Nature.'[15]

Ironically, just after nationalisation, Britain was beset by the coldest winter in recorded British history, and a fuel crisis such as had never been experienced before or since. It brought the rest of industry to a virtual standstill.

A fuel shortage had earlier been foreseen, owing to the wartime loss of manpower in the mines. By the end of November 1946, coal stocks were dangerously low, particularly those for the electricity companies and railways, on which all other industries depended. Deliveries of coal to individual firms were less than two-thirds of what was ordered. In the middle of January 1947, an emergency plan was announced; electricity and gas companies would get their full requirements, but allocations of coal to other users would be cut by half.

But the real emergency was yet to come. On 23 January snow began to fall and went on falling so that, within a week, large parts of the country were cut off by snow-drifts; roads and railways were blocked, coal stocks at the pitheads could not be moved. Several power stations closed down for lack of fuel as did some important factories, while others went on short time. By the end of the first week in February, two million workers had been laid off, while domestic use of electricity and gas was forbidden during hours of daylight. A slight thaw at the end of February was followed by more snow. Later, in March, rain accompanying another thaw led to widespread floods, causing enormous damage to houses in towns, and to fields and livestock in the countryside.

The response of party members in the coalfields was a determined effort to raise output. Thus on 15 February the Party Executive sent a letter of appreciation to two members in South Wales – Bill Whitehead and George Lodge – for 'their magnificent work in getting the 9 pits in the Rhondda working emergency shifts on Sunday'.[16]

However, a major subject of controversy was to be the form of nationalisation adopted by the Labour Government. In *Britain for the People*, produced in 1944, the party had urged nationalisation of the coal industry 'with adequate representation of the workers in management and control'. But the party also believed, in common with the TUC, that it was essential that the trade unions should retain their independence and their freedom to negotiate with those in charge of the industry, and should *not* therefore be directly represented on boards of management on which they would have a minority voice. It believed that, for the time being, workers' participation could best be implemented by Joint Production Committees. The party also believed that their original aim of 'confiscation without compensation' was not possible in the prevailing circumstances, because one small section of the capitalist class could not be deprived of their possessions if all other such sections were to keep theirs intact.

Arthur Horner, who had served in 1944 on a joint committee of the Labour Party, the TUC, and the Miners Federation which was preparing nationalisation proposals for a future Labour Government later recalled: 'It was made quite clear to us from the outset that the members representing the Labour Party would not agree to confiscation and that any Bill brought in by a Labour Government would provide for compensation to the former owners. Much as this went against the grain … I did not fight very hard against it because I knew it was unreal to expect nationalisation without compensation for one particular industry. We did not ask for workers' control, because we accepted that a nationalised industry in a capitalist society had to fit to that pattern. We asked for consultation on policy matters.... from top to bottom of the industry. Workers' control under socialism is one thing, but under capitalism it is another and I had to recognise that nationalisation in a capitalist society is not a complete victory. It is only the beginning of a transfer of economic power.'[17]

The 1946 Coal Industry Nationalisation Act provided for a National Coal Board consisting of nine members appointed by the Minister of Fuel and Power. Two of these members were, in fact, nominated by the TUC in agreement with the NUM. They were Citrine, former TUC secretary, and Ebby Edwards, the first secretary of the NUM who relinquished that post and therefore no longer acted as the union's representative. Each of the eight divisional boards also had one or two trade union nominees.

Later, when Citrine left the Coal Board, some pressure was put on Horner to take his place, but he refused.[18] Another communist, Abe Moffat, President of the Scottish Miners, also refused a board position.[19] This did not mean that communists who went on a board were regarded by the party as having 'gone over to the other side'; indeed some communists did accept office – for example, Jock Kane, the Yorkshire miner, who had suffered from an illness which prevented him from continuing to work down the pit. But most communists refused such positions because they believed they could make a greater contribution to the movement if they continued in their NUM positions.

There were two matters which caused concern on the left and which the party was, in subsequent years, to raise again and again. The first was that the Labour Government had appointed so many former directors of colliery companies to the national and divisional boards. They greatly outnumbered the union nominees.[20] The second issue was the huge amount of compensation provided, which was considered totally unjustifiable. The party argued that it could have been much less and should in any case be paid by the government, and not become a burden on the coal industry itself.

In 1948, after the nationalisation of railways and electricity, the party changed its attitude to union representation in nationalised industries. There was growing disillusionment on the left about the benefits of nationalisation and much discontent with the way the industries were run. In August 1948, Harry Pollitt issued a discussion document proposing that the trade unions should be directly represented on all national and regional boards of nationalised industries 'by men who keep their connection with the union and the members instead of being artificially cut off from democratic discussion and decision inside the unions as soon as they take on the new responsibilities'.[21] As time went on, disillusionment with the style of management and role in the economy of the nationalised industries grew; by 1949, Dutt was using the phrase 'capitalist pseudo-nationalisation'.[22] But at the beginning of 1947 hopes for the new system were still widespread.

THE PARTY'S 19TH CONGRESS

The fuel crisis was still acute when the Communist Party held its 19th Congress. Opening on 22 February 1947, at the Seymour Hall in Marylebone, London, there were 665 delegates present, some of whom

– particularly those coming from the north – had much difficulty in getting there. They represented 367 branches, 94 boroughs and 17 districts; their average age was 34.

At this congress, the fight to persuade the Labour Government to change course was seen as the chief aim. The main political resolution accused the government of compromising with big business at home and carrying on with imperialist policies abroad. There was an acute economic crisis, but no adequate economic plan, or direction of industry; luxury goods were being produced at the expense of necessities; obsolescent plant had not been replaced; food production was being obstructed by marketing rings; there were hold-ups in house construction while licences were granted for luxury building, and so on. There was a severe manpower shortage particularly in the most important industries; to solve this problem, it was argued that men should be withdrawn from the armed services, and there should be equal pay for women to encourage their return to industry.

The resolution accused the government of 'seeking to apply its programme without inroads into capitalism … thus transforming it into a programme to reorganise capitalism at the cost of the working class.' The Labour Government, it said, had presented its policies as the democratic and peaceful way of achieving socialism. But in fact such policies had nowhere led to the achievement of socialism. So, 'while defending the government against all attacks by the Tories and monopolists' the Communist Party demanded changes in policy and the reorganisation of the government.

It urged immediate nationalisation of steel, railways, privately-owned transport services, electricity, gas and the land; compensation to be scaled down for big owners; effective trade union participation at all levels in the running of the nationalised industries; the strengthening of workshop organisation and shop stewards; legal recognition of shop stewards committees and the extension of joint production committees, 'workers participation in solving production difficulties and in improving working conditions and the technique and methods of production.'[23]

Thus, while criticising the Labour Government, the party made clear that the aim must be to persuade it to change direction and to support any measures to help overcome the economic crisis, not to withdraw support from the government.

A high proportion of the delegates were from engineering, mining, building or transport and the debate was largely concentrated on production problems facing these basic industries, particularly coal, and how to defeat the tendency among the engineering employers to dismiss shop stewards. Harry Pollitt in his reply to the discussion told everyone to go back, whether to factory, pit, mill or farm and fight for joint production committees. 'This isn't class collaboration' he said. 'The bosses hate the JPCs and the more we fight for them, the more we are increasing working class control'.[24]

A handful of delegates did not agree with the general strategy mapped out in the main political resolution. One of these was Eric Heffer from Hertford who had argued in the pre-congress discussion that it glossed over vital theoretical problems.[25] He proposed an amendment which was seconded by a delegate from Welwyn Garden City branch. Heffer accused the executive committee of taking a reformist and opportunist path. 'The perspective of proletarian revolution has been abandoned' he declared. 'Our executive committee is committing us to the support of a Government of social traitors who are leading this country to economic disaster and the victory of reaction. We must endeavour to use the economic crisis for the overthrow of the capitalist system.'[26] Betty Matthews, the South East Midlands district secretary, opposed the amendment. She referred to it as a 'symptom of an infantile disorder' and said: 'there isn't a single word in the amendment about the Tories. We are invited to join hands with Churchill and the big industrialists to weaken the Labour Government.' The amendment was overwhelmingly defeated.

One year later, at its 20th Congress held in February 1948, the party was obliged to face the fact that the campaign to persuade the Labour Government to change course had failed. By that time the 'cold war' was under way.

14

POST WAR STRUGGLES FOR COLONIAL FREEDOM

It did not come as any great surprise that, after the Labour Government was installed, there was little change in the colonial policies previously operated by Tory governments. Strong support for colonial rule was expressed by Labour's deputy leader, Herbert Morrison who, while on tour in America early in 1946, said: 'We are friends of the jolly old empire ... we are going to stick to it'.[1] And Foreign Secretary Ernest Bevin told the House of Commons on 21 February that 'I am not prepared to sacrifice the British Empire' ... 'I know that if the British Empire fell ... it would mean the standard of life of our constituents would fall considerably.'

As already recorded, Attlee's renewal of the Cripps proposals for a highly undemocratic constitution for India had been attacked at the party's congress in November 1945, at which it was urged that a constituent assembly be established based on adult franchise for the whole of India. Thus it was communists – always accused of being against democracy – who were demanding free democratic elections, and a Labour Government which was trying to continue rule from above.[2]

By 1946 had come a huge strike wave in India, met with indiscriminate shooting by the police, and followed by strikes in the Indian navy and airforce. 'The whole of India is in open revolt against the continuation of British rule' wrote Dutt.[3] Commenting on the growing conflicts within India between the Congress Party and the Moslem League, he said: 'The internal questions of the Indian people and of the future state forms they wish to adopt, whether Pakistan or other, are questions for the Indian people to settle. They are not questions for the British people to settle or impose a settlement, any more than it would be suitable for the Indian people to determine the solution for the Scottish nationalist demand for Scottish self-government. Our task is to see that, on the basis of a democratically elected Constituent Assembly, the Indian people have the opportunity to determine their own future with complete freedom.'[4]

In March 1946, Dutt was at last able to visit India himself – his passport had been marked 'not valid for the British Empire' for over 30 years. 'On descending from the plane at the airport, I found I was faced by an array of red flags' he recorded in his diary. 'Some 100 Delhi comrades had trudged the ten miles to the airport to meet me and, according to the traditional fashion, I was garlanded with the most beautiful, many-coloured, sweet-smelling flowers'.[5]

As forecast, the new constitutional plan produced by a Cabinet mission that summer did not give Indian people the right to decide their future, and, in the autumn of 1946 came an outbreak of communal riots, which were seen by the party as the 'inevitable result of the cabinet policy to divide Hindus and Muslims'.[6] By January 1947, there were again widespread strikes – particularly in the textile areas; there were also peasant uprisings against the landowners. The police were once more sent in; there were shootings and arrests of trade unionists, including leading members of the All-India TUC. Communist Party premises were raided, documents seized, and leading Indian Party members arrested and detained without trial.

Pollitt wrote to the Secretary of State for India, Pethwick-Lawrence, protesting at the action taken against the Indian Communist Party,[7] and the matter was discussed at the 19th Party Congress in February at which the need to involve the wider Labour movement in demands for the release of the arrested leaders was stressed.

Events in the other colonial countries were equally dismaying. Ben Bradley was secretary of the party's colonial committee which issued a monthly bulletin *Inside the Empire*. In the January 1946 issue, he pointed out that the measures being taken in relation to India, Burma, Ceylon, Nigeria and elsewhere bore 'all the hallmarks of Tory imperialism.' The bulletin reported that the proposed constitution for Ceylon (later known as Sri Lanka) had been received with 'protests and dismay' in that country; the elected ministers were to have very limited powers and the Governor-General appointed by the British Government would 'continue to hold the purse-strings'.

Some of the most alarming signals of what was in store came from territories formerly occupied by the Japanese. In May 1946, Michael Carritt described in the *Labour Monthly* what was happening in Malaya. Here, where a 'Malayan People's Army' had fought a guerilla war against the Japanese, the 'People's Councils' set up by the resistance movement had initially been welcomed in the British Army. But the Councils were treated as 'the enemy'; the premises of left-wing organisations, including not only the Malayan Communist Party but those of trade unions, were raided and searched; and their leaders arrested, with the object of bringing back British rule and reestablishing the British tin and rubber companies which had formerly dominated the economy. By the end of that year, a new constitution was proposed which, apart from being completely undemocratic, advocated the separation of Singapore from the rest of Malaya with the obvious intention of retaining it as a naval base.[8]

In Burma an anti-fascist guerilla army had also been established. But Bill Carritt – who had served in the British army there – remarked soon after his return to Britain that 'the strong wind of colonial liberation' was 'not to the liking of the imperialists'. He thought that they were still under the impression that the war was fought to make colonial plantations and mines safe for the *pukha sahib*.'[9]

Civil liberties remained a crucial issue in all colonial countries. Although in many of them trade unions had become legal during the war for the first time, their rights were in practice much restricted, as was pointed out at the 1946 Trades Union Congress by, among others, party member Mary Williams of the Clerical and Administrative Workers Union. Another party member, Jack Grahl of the Fire Brigades Union, urged that a free and independent India should have unfettered use of her stirling balances.[10]

EMPIRE CONFERENCE

On 26 February 1947, a unique event took place: the opening in London of a six-day Empire Communist Conference at which representatives from communist parties in various parts of the British Empire were present. There were 28 delegates from parties in eleven countries, together with observers from parties in 15 other countries.

The fact that the conference could take place at all showed that, despite the reluctance of the Labour leaders to abandon British rule, times were changing. For, in many of the countries represented, communist parties had formerly been banned, but were now at least semi-legal.

The conference was opened with a report by R. Palme Dutt. Stressing that a basic principle of communist policy was the right of self-determination for all peoples, he said: 'We repudiate all racial theories which seek to separate mankind into 'higher' and 'lower' races, into those peoples born to rule, and those born to be ruled'. He said that although there was widespread recognition that the old basis of the Empire must come to an end, the realities of colonial domination could not be so easily got rid of. There had been an enormous growth in national liberation movements, with the colonial working class and peasantry in the forefront and communist parties playing a leading role, but the colonial bourgeoisie, the traders and industrialists and landowners, were seeking compromise with imperialism, while imperialist policy tried to take advantage of this.

'The present policy of British imperialism is characterised by its alliance with American imperialism' he said, showing how British strategic and military bases were being installed in many of the colonial territories. The offers of conditional independence being made by the Labour Government were extremely limited and, despite all talk of withdrawal from the empire, the number of British troops in empire countries was much greater than in 1939.[11]

In the debate that followed, John C Henry from the Australian Communist Party told how his government was lining up his country with the foreign policies of British and American imperialism; military bases were being established aimed at independence movements in Indonesia, Malaya, Burma, Ceylon, India and China. Tim Buck, secretary of the Labour Progressive Party in Canada, spoke of the drive to subordinate the interests of the Canadian people to the war plans of the United States.

Among those who managed to attend the conference was G. Adhikari of the Indian Communist Party; he had recently been arrested, but was out on bail. He told how his party had tried to persuade the Indian National Congress and the Muslim League to resolve their differences and launch a united struggle for Indian independence so as to defeat the imperialist plan to divide the forces committed to it.

Dr S.A. Wickremasinghe, president of the Ceylon Communist Party, explained how, under the new proposed constitution, defence and foreign affairs, external trade and currency were to remain in British hands.

Ba Thein Tin from the Communist Party of Burma described how the Burma resistance movement (APPFL) against the Japanese had been built up, but how, after the war ended, the government had returned and was reestablishing British companies.

Wu Tian Wang from the Malayan Communist Party recalled how his party had organised the resistance movement against the Japanese. But the reward to the Malayan people had been the reimposition of colonial rule. All the oppressive laws that existed before the war, denying the mass of the people elementary democratic rights, had been revived and reintroduced.

N. Ioannou, secretary of AKEL in Cyprus – then a British Crown Colony – told the conference why the majority of Cyprus people wanted union with Greece. William McCullough from Northern Ireland stressed the need to win over the protestant industrial workers from their support for the Tory unionists.

Daniel Du Plessis who represented the Communist Party of South Africa described the oppression of black Africans by whites and the vicious system of pass laws and segregation. Since there were as yet no communist parties in other parts of Africa – or indeed in the West Indies – there could be no delegates from those parts of the Empire; however, Desmond Buckle, who came from Ghana in West Africa – he had been resident in Britain for some time, and was a member of the British Party's Colonial Committee – provided a special report on what was happening in these territories, emphasizing the need for free trade union organisations.

Two delegates represented Palestine which had been a 'mandated' British territory since just after the first world war. S. Mikunis was one of the Jewish communist leaders; Emile Touma was on the central committee of the Arab National Liberation League. 'Palestine is ruled by Great Britain on the lines of a crown colony' said Mikunis. 'All the power is vested in the High Commissioner. The executive is composed entirely of colonial officials.' 'The most dangerous weapon in the hands of imperialism is the policy of 'divide and rule' dividing Jews and Arabs' he said. This sinister work was aided by 'Zionist chauvinist circles' who wanted Palestine to become a Jewish state and, on the other hand, by certain Arab chauvinists who demanded a 'pure' Arab state. The main aim should be an independent Palestine with a democratic regime and full equality of civic rights for both Arabs and Jews. Emile Touma said that both British and American imperialism had an interest in maintaining Palestine 'not only for the oil terminals and concessions which are numerous, but as a military reserve which could be used against the rising tide of the Arab national movement and against the Soviet Union'. The Zionist leaders, he said, were attempting 'to withdraw the Jewish masses from Europe, and make of them a reserve for Imperialism in the Middle East'. Certain visitors from outside the Empire – ie Syria and Lebanon – participated in the discussion on Palestine.

At the end of the conference, a joint declaration setting out common aims was adopted; it asserted that 'the democratic right of self-determination of all peoples is the cardinal principle of communist policy'. Before this, as Dutt pointed out, certain controversial matters had been debated, the main one being that although immediate, unqualified independence was demanded for some – such as India, Burma and Ceylon – for others the fight for democratic rights had taken precedence. This was particularly the case in certain parts of Africa. Dutt argued that the issue was a tactical one on the next step forward. An abstract political formula for the general right of self-determination was not enough; it was necessary to grapple with the actual problems, recognising the steps forward needed in each particular territory, particularly in those where no political movements yet existed. On the other hand, in South Africa where there was already an independent state, but where 8 million out of 10 million were disenfranchised, the fight must be for equal rights for Africans.

In addition to the joint declaration, emergency resolutions were passed demanding the withdrawal of the proposed reactionary constitution for Malaya, protesting against arrests of communists in India, calling for withdrawal of troops from Cyprus, condemning the policies of the South African Government.

A special declaration on Palestine urged 'immediate withdrawal of British troops' the abrogation of the mandate and 'the creation of a free, independent and democratic Palestine state, which will guarantee equal rights of citizenship with full religious freedom and full opportunities to develop their culture to all its inhabitants, Arab and Jewish.'

THE AFTERMATH

Within a few months, hopes for a united independent India disappeared. On 3 June 1947, Attlee announced the 'Mountbatten plan': proposals for the partition of India. Although the main political leaders in India declared reluctant acceptance of the plan, they were sharply criticised by both Indian socialists and communists. P.C. Joshi of the Indian Communist Party said: 'Mountbatten's Plan is not a genuine "quit India" plan, but rather one which seeks to keep in British hands as many economic and military controls as possible'.[12]

The plan was condemned by the British Communist Party Executive who said that partition was the legacy of 200 years of 'divide and rule';[13] it was supported by the Conservatives and, when Attlee made his initial announcement, Gallacher's was the only voice raised in criticism. Later in the debate on the 'Indian Independence Bill' on 10 July, Gallacher again spoke saying that the partitioning of India was a very dangerous development. As a result of it 'there are hopes among the ruling classes of this country that they can make a deal with the Princes of India, with big business in India and with reaction generally in India, so that they can still hold power in India, not directly as before, but indirectly through capital investments and financial connections.'

The Bill was passed and, by mid-August, was being implemented. It resulted in an explosion of communal riots and atrocities on a scale never seen before, with mass migration of minorities across the borders. It also caused economic chaos as a result of new boundaries which cut in half not only railways and canals but whole industries.

The Labour Government's colonial policies continued to be supported by the Tories, but were received with growing disillusion on the left. Its approach to problems in Africa were dominated by two main objectives: the establishment of military bases and the launch of so-called 'development schemes' which, as the Communist Party Executive emphasised, 'bring benefits neither to British nor African peoples, but only mean increased and guaranteed profits for the great monopolies.'[14] One such 'development scheme' was for the cultivation of groundnuts in Tanganyika. It had been advocated by the United Africa Company, a subsidiary of the Unilever Combine. Over the next few years, millions of government money was squandered on this scheme which turned out to be a fiasco and, in the end, was abandoned. Tanganyika was not to find its way to independence until another fifteen years had passed.

In most of the colonies minimal constitutional 'reforms' were accompanied by oppressive measures against popular movements. The saddest case was that of Malaya. Here a Legislative Assembly was established consisting of members nominated from above with no elected representatives; it gave protection to the British-owned tin and rubber companies which were once more operating there, exporting their products to America and earning millions of dollars for Britain's foreign exchange.

The sham constitution was rejected by the mass of the Malayan people and in 1948, when it became clear that British rule was to be continued and all Malayan people deprived of democratic rights, a new liberation army was formed and resorted to armed struggle. Initially this struggle was portrayed in the British press as a 'communist uprising to seize power', though later it was presented as a campaign of 'bandits' and 'terrorists' which must be suppressed. The truth was that the British were faced with large-scale guerilla warfare, well organised and receiving support from the mass of the Malayan people.

British people were, for the most part, kept in ignorance of what was happening. The only newspaper which tried to publish the truth was the *Daily Worker*. The party built up an organisation to support the struggle. It helped issue a monthly bulletin, *The Malayan Monitor* edited by H.B. Lim who was a member of the Party's Malayan Committee. Also on this committee was Jack Woddis who was working full time for the Party's London District Committee – later he was elected to the Party's Executive and became head of its International Department. Others who served on the Malayan Committee included Pat Devine, J. Dowling, Sid Kaufman and the Secretary of the Fire Brigades Union, John Horner. The committee issued speakers' notes and in June 1950 organised a 'Malayan Week' calling for demonstrations all over the country. And it published a pamphlet written by Jack Woddis entitled *Stop the War in Malaya*. In the event, it was not until seven years later, under a Tory Government, that Malaya was at last granted independence.

Another continuing problem was that of Palestine. Following enormous pressure from both the USA and Britain for an independent Israeli state, the United Nations Assembly decided on 30 November 1947 to recommend the partition of Palestine into separate Jewish and Arab states. By the summer of 1948 the State of Israel had come into being. Thereafter it was obvious that the policy advocated at the Party's Empire Conference for a united democratic Palestine was no longer a feasible possibility. So by 1949 the Communist Party in Britain was urging the Labour Government to implement the decision of the United Nations to set up *both* Jewish and Arab states in Palestine. But the proposed Arab state did not come into being and Arab-Jewish conflicts were to continue for many decades.

15
1947: ECONOMIC CRISIS: THE START OF THE COLD WAR: THE COMINFORM

The summer of 1947 saw a serious deterioration in the economic situation. There was a huge balance of payments deficit, followed by a 'convertibility crisis.' This arose because when, at the end of the war, the Americans terminated their 'lease-lend' arrangements for financial aid to Britain, they had only agreed to a further loan on condition that sterling would be made 'convertible' into other currencies by mid-July 1947. So, that month, countries holding sterling balances in Britain began to exchange them for dollars and by mid-August Britain's dollar deficit had risen astronomically. Convertibility was then suspended. However, to reduce the dollar gap, the government introduced much more stringent rationing of food and petrol; imports were cut and a new period of austerity was ushered in.

Moreover, the government was apparently dithering over its promise to nationalise the steel industry, though this was regarded as fundamental to the recovery of Britain's manufacturing base. At the 1947 TUC, Jim Gardner, of the Foundry Workers, urged that a Bill for the nationalisation of iron and steel be introduced in the next session, while Les Gregory of the ETU pointed out that, unless this was done, the House of Lords could use delaying tactics. The Foundry Workers resolution was rejected by 4,457,000 votes to 2,360,000.[1] But it turned out that Gregory's apprehensions were justified; the House of Lords was to force postponement of steel nationalisation until July 1950.

In communist eyes the basic reason for the Labour Government's austerity measures was its refusal to cut defence expenditure. This arose from its foreign and colonial policies. There were still over a million men and women in the armed services. As Communist MP Phil Piratin asserted in the Budget debate in November 1947, the government had no right to call upon the people to make sacrifices to meet the economic crisis when it was lavishing £900 million on military expenditure which was not in their interests.[2]

The party's misgivings were reinforced by what was happening in America.

THE 'TRUMAN DOCTRINE'

On 6 March 1947, in a speech on foreign economic policy, President Truman made clear his belief that communism – and indeed socialism – must be regarded as the chief enemy. He asserted that freedom was more important than peace, and that freedom of worship and freedom of speech were dependent on freedom of enterprise. On 12 March he made a further speech denouncing what was happening in the Eastern European countries and saying that the United States must be willing 'to help free people maintain their free institutions and their national integrity against aggressive movements that seek to impose upon them totalitarian regimes.' As Palme Dutt put it, Truman's speech 'stakes the claim of the Wall Street millionaires and the high-power generals ... to dominate the political system of every country in the world and lay down for them their 'way of life.''[3]

What Truman meant by 'freedom' became clear on 23 March when a sweeping order was made requiring a check on the 'loyalty' of 2 million government employees, thus starting a witch-hunt against communists and 'fellow-travellers' in government service. It was accompanied by an Act which severely restricted trade union rights. Meanwhile, an official 'Committee on Un-American Activities' launched an unprecedented campaign of political persecution under which leading American communists were brought to trial, while many actors, writers, journalists, artists and others thought to be on the left were deprived of their jobs, and victimised. The avowed object was to eliminate 'communist influence' in films, on the radio, in books, and in the theatre. 'The process of intimidation has gone much further in America than in any country since the defeat of fascism' observed one writer in *World News and Views*.[4]

Outside America, the Truman doctrine had serious repercussions. In France, where communists had won 145 seats in the 1946 general election, and were participating in a coalition government, the Prime Minister dismissed all four communist ministers and thereafter excluded communists from the Cabinet. This happened in May 1947;

by June, the Italian Prime Minister who was desperately seeking American financial aid, had also expelled all communists from his Cabinet.

THE MARSHALL PLAN

On 5 June came a statement from US Secretary of State George Marshall on America's plans for economic aid to European countries. But, as a member of the Party's Political Committee, John Gollan, pointed out 'dollar assistance would be made available only to countries willing to toe the American, anti-Communist line'.[5] From the start indeed, British party leaders were sceptical about the Marshall Plan (which became known officially as the 'European Recovery Plan' or ERP). Palme Dutt said it was a plan which the advocates of the Truman doctrine 'hope to use for promoting a dollar-dominated Western European Bloc against democracy in Europe with Western Germany as its main base and Britain as the American agent to put it through.'[6]

As later historians have revealed, the Americans never intended that the Soviet Union and its allies should benefit from the Marshall Plan. By attaching conditions to it they hoped to manoeuvre the USSR into rejecting what seemed like a generous offer of assistance, and thus make it appear that the Soviet Union was to blame for the intensification of the cold war.[7]

And that is what happened. At a meeting of Foreign Ministers from Britain, France and the Soviet Union held to discuss the Marshall Plan, the Soviet representatives raised objections to proposals that spelt interference in the rights of countries to manage their own affairs. Moreover they put pressure on the countries of Eastern Europe to refuse any offers of Marshall aid.

The background to this was the resolve of the Russian leaders, headed by Stalin, that all countries on the USSR's borders should retain friendly relations with the Soviet Union. During the war most of them had served as bases for the Nazi invasion of Russia, and Stalin was determined that none of them should again be used to accommodate a hostile power, a possibility opened up if they became economically dependent on America. But unfortunately protection of Soviet borders was not the only consideration. By this time, Stalin had become determined to dominate Eastern European countries, and to impose his decisions upon them.

In Britain, the attitude of the Soviet Union to the Marshall Plan helped to confirm the belief of Communist Party members that it was a device to enable the Americans to dominate Europe, and should therefore be opposed. At the Trades Union Congress in September 1947 Foreign Secretary Ernest Bevin, as a guest speaker, made a long and rambling statement justifying acceptance of the Marshall Plan and attacking those who spoke of 'dollar diplomacy'. He was followed by Leo McGree of the woodworkers' union. 'I know what it means when you talk about "the importance of being Ernest",' he said. Asserting that every dollar that came from America was 'accompanied by an impudent note informing us how we were to conduct our internal affairs', he said: 'I listened to Mr Bevin explaining the Marshall Plan. I am going to explain to Mr Bevin that there is no Marshall Plan; it is a Marshall Plot'.[8]

At this same congress a resolution supporting Bevin's foreign policy was opposed by some unions. An amendment urging the government to 'resist the pressure of dollar diplomacy' was moved by John Horner of the Fire Brigades Union; it was seconded by another party member, Jeff Mildwater of the Civil Service Union, and supported by Ralph Bond of the Cine-Technicians Union who said 'dependence on the dollar will mean death for British socialism.'[9] But the amendment was defeated.

SPLITS OVER GERMANY'S FUTURE

It was on the issue of Germany that hostility between East and West came to a head. Under the agreement signed at Potsdam by Attlee, Truman and Stalin, Germany had been split into four zones each of which was occupied by the troops of Britain, France, the USA or the Soviet Union. Authority was allocated to the commanders of each of these four countries, and coordinated through an Allied Control Council with headquarters in Berlin, the former capital, which was situated in the Soviet-occupied zone.

The principles under which the ACC was to work were laid down in the Potsdam agreement. They included total disarmament and demilitarisation, the elimination of industries which could be used for war purposes, and the prohibition of all arms production. Nazi organisations were to be destroyed, Nazi propaganda prohibited, and discrimination on the grounds of race or religion forbidden. All officials who had been active members of the Nazi Party were to be removed from office. These steps were to be taken in preparation for the eventual reconstruction of political life on a democratic basis. The economy was to be decentralised to eliminate the concentration of economic power in cartels, and monopolies. Special arrangements were made for the payment of reparations to the allied powers. Since Russia had suffered the greatest devastation, it was agreed that her reparations should not be confined to the Soviet zone, but that she would be entitled to 10 per cent of surplus capital equipment from the Western zones. As the major part of German industry was concentrated in these zones, this was an agreement of great importance to the USSR.

From the start, the programme went ahead at very different speeds. In the Soviet zone, the huge estates which had belonged to the Prussian landowners – most of whom had supported Hitler – were broken up and redistributed to the peasants, a process overseen by committees of the peasants themselves. Much industry was taken into public ownership, while de-Nazification committees were set up to make sure that key jobs in administration were held by people with an anti-Nazi background. In the British and American zones, by contrast, the implementation of the Potsdam agreement was delayed and in some cases avoided. 'In the Western zones of Germany, Nazis are still at large' observed Bill Wainwright in June 1946 'They occupy important positions in industry and administration. Police are being recruited from Nazi officers and NCOs.'[10] He drew attention to the sustained campaign in the British press to discredit the Potsdam agreement. Indeed, the agreement for the economic unity of Germany was soon to be abandoned; instead, British and American governments went ahead with plans for the economic unity of the Western zones alone. The USSR did not receive the reparations to which she was entitled. By mid-1947, many West German war plants had still not been dismantled. As a writer in *World News and Views*, Chris Freeman, pointed out, the ruling circles in Britain and America had not fought the war with the aim of destroying fascism; now the dominant aim was 'reconstruction of an anti-Communist West German state'.[11] This process went ahead. By the end of 1947 it was revealed that the US Treasury had printed new currency notes for a West German economy. By June 1948 the plan to partition Germany was to be completed, and a separate currency introduced into the Western zones. Shortly afterwards the Western powers announced that this new currency would be introduced into their sector of the city of Berlin which was, of course, situated some 125 miles inside the Soviet zone.

Faced with the prospect of economic chaos resulting from this, the Soviet Government announced that transport between the Western zones and Berlin would be cut off. The response from the Western powers was what became known as the 'Berlin airlift'.

Shortly afterwards the Russians introduced their own separate currency, but the Berlin blockade was to continue until May 1949.

FORMATION OF THE COMINFORM

The foreign policies of the British and American governments and the reaction from the Soviet Union paved the way for the formation of the Cominform (Communist Information Bureau). Initiated by Stalin as a means of unifying the leading Communist Parties in Europe behind his policies, it was inaugurated in September 1947 at a meeting in Poland, consisting of representatives from the Communist Parties of the Soviet Union and of the six countries of Eastern Europe – Bulgaria, Czechoslovakia, Hungary, Poland, Romania, Yugoslavia – and of two countries in Western Europe: France and Italy. These nine parties issued a joint declaration saying that, since the war, two camps had come into existence. One was the 'imperialist, anti-democratic camp with the basic aim of establishing world domination of American imperialism and routing democracy.' The other was the 'anti-imperialist, democratic camp with the basic aim of disrupting imperialism, strengthening democracy and eliminating the remnants of fascism.' The imperialists, it said, were using the treacherous policies of 'right-wing socialists of the type of Blum in France, Attlee and Bevin in England, Schumacher in Germany, Renner and Schaerf in Austria, Saragat in Italy' who were 'loyal accomplices of the imperialists, bringing disintegration into the ranks of the working class and poisoning their outlook.' 'It is not accidental' the statement said 'that the foreign policy of British imperialism found in the person of Bevin its most consistent and zealous executor.' And it went on to say that the French socialists and British 'labourites' were 'facilitating by their grovelling and servility the task of American capital'.[12]

Thus the Cominform came into existence 'with the task of organising the exchange of experience' and coordinating the activities of the Communist Parties concerned. The Bureau was composed of two representatives of each of the nine parties with its headquarters in Belgrade. Its formation undoubtedly played into the hands of Truman and his European allies who wanted the Soviet Union and communists to be seen as 'the enemy', while its abrasive language and denunciation of British 'labourites' such as Attlee and Bevin helped to boost support for the Labour leaders' anti-communist drive in Britain.

THE BRITISH PARTY'S CHANGE OF ATTITUDE

Unlike the Comintern which had provided opportunity for contact and discussion on policies between Communist Parties all over the world, the Cominform consisted only of those parties which were involved in their countries' governments or, as in France and Italy, had previously been so though, in both these cases, they had been expelled from their country's cabinets in the spring of 1947. The British party was not represented in the Cominform, nor did it play any part in its deliberations though, as some party members were later to recall, Pollitt was privately somewhat annoyed that it had not been asked to participate. However, there was no doubt that its policies would be influenced by the attitudes taken up by such a body, and at its meeting in October 1947, the party's executive committee welcomed the nine parties' declaration and its 'call for the strengthening of the forces of peace and democracy in the struggle against the plans of American imperialism for the political and economic enslavement of Europe',[13] saying that it would intensify its campaign for a reorganisation of the government and the removal of 'those Ministers responsible for the present disastrous position.' Ironically, the executive was adopting the very tactic it had repudiated two years earlier when the 'Bevin must go' policy suggested by Bill Rust was rejected.

Later, in preparation for the Party's 20th Congress (which was to be held in February 1948) Pollitt took a self-critical stand. 'We correctly worked for the victory of the Labour Government in the General Election, and quite rightly gave constructive support to (it) for the fulfilment of its election programme' he said in a report to the executive. 'But we were late in appreciating the full scale of the drift to the right of the Labour Government, and clung to old formulas and approaches after it had revealed itself.'[14]

The new attitude to the Labour Government was agreed to unanimously at the 20th Congress which called for the dismissal of the government's right-wing leaders and the formation of a 'Labour Government of the left',[15] though Johnny Gollan was among those who pointed out that the demand for a new 'government of the left' would remain an empty phrase unless mass movements were developed in all industrial localities on issues such as wages and prices and the need to cut profits.[16] Unlike previous congresses, the drive to increase production was no longer seen as a priority.

This change in the party's attitude did not go far enough in the opinion of the Australian Communist Party which, in April 1948, continued with some of the criticisms it had already been making before the congress on the policies of the British party. In a letter to the British leadership, the Australians accused them of forgetting 'Lenin's evaluation of the right-wing social democrats as the bourgeois enemies of socialism within the labour movement' and said that this attitude had led to the exaggerated hopes 'reinforcing social democratic illusions among the masses.' The British party replied to these criticisms and the correspondence was published in *World News and Views* in August 1948. Ironically, the Australians used some quotations from Marshall Tito of Yugoslavia to bolster their case. It was, however, the Yugoslav Party which was soon to be expelled from the Cominform for departing from 'Marxism-Leninism'.

LABOUR LEADERS LAUNCH A WITCH-HUNT

The formation of the Cominform and its denunciation of right wing 'Labourites' were much used by the Labour leaders in their attacks on the British Party and their determination to rid the Labour Party of members who associated with communists. This was to be shown in the Spring of 1948 in a row over relationships with the Italian Socialist Party. In Italy, a minority government in the hands of the Christian Democrats had held office for some years. With another election about to take place, the Italian Socialist Party, led by Pietro Nenni, had come to an agreement with the Italian Communist Party and other groups on the Left, to run a joint electoral campaign. But a right wing splinter group in the Socialist Party, led by Saragat, broke away to join forces with the Christian Democrats, a move supported by the Americans. Some 38 Labour MPs in Britain sent a telegram to Nenni expressing good wishes for the coming election. The Labour leaders immediately declared their support for the Saragat splinter group and, on 28 April, they expelled Labour MP John Platts Mills from the Labour Party and warned the other signatories to the Nenni telegram that they too would be expelled unless they undertook to desist from 'such conduct' in the future. By this time, the anti-communist purge in the civil service was about to begin.

Meanwhile, Bevin had initiated a plan for 'western union' and on 17 March representatives of five countries – Britain, France, Belgium, the Netherlands and Luxemburg – met in Brussels and signed an agreement for 'collective self-defence' thereby establishing what *World News and Views* described as a 'Western War Bloc': an open military alliance directed against the Soviet Union and the new democracies of Eastern Europe.[17]

Within a year came the birth of NATO.

16

THE CIVIL SERVICE PURGE

On 15 March 1948, Prime Minister Attlee announced that the government had decided 'to ensure that no one who is known to be a member of the Communist Party, or to be associated with it in such a way as to raise legitimate doubts about his or her reliability, is employed in connection with work, the nature of which is vital to the security of the state.' He added, almost as an afterthought, that the same rule would apply to those associated with fascist organisations, thus indulging in the right-wing's favourite ploy of lumping fascists and communists together.

The announcement heralded a quite new stage in the attack on the left. For the first time, government employees were to be victimised, not for anything they had done, but for their alleged political beliefs or those of their friends or relations. They did not have to be engaged in leaking classified information or revealing confidential matters to outside bodies; they did not even have to be accused of such conduct. All that was required was an allegation of friendship or association with a member of a perfectly lawful political party. As the *Daily Worker* remarked the following day: 'The Labour Government is now daring to do what no Tory Government has ever attempted, namely to begin a witch-hunt in the civil service.' However, as could be expected, the proposed purge was approved of by the Tories and was to be built on by succeeding Tory governments, resulting in an enormous expansion of the political activities of MI5 and the secret police. The background to the purge was, of course, pressure from the United States – already conducting its own anti-Communist witch-hunt on a massive scale – and the desire to establish the idea in the minds of all that the Soviet Union was now the enemy.

Encouragement to Attlee to take such action had been delivered ten days earlier by W.J. Brown, former general secretary of the Civil Service Clerical Association (CSCA) which, with 150,000 members, was much the largest union in the civil service. W.J. Brown was by this time an 'Independent' MP, but he still acted as the CSCA's parliamentary secretary. Addressing the Commons on 4 March during a debate on the air estimates, he remarked that if we were to prepare for war, it was Russia who must be regarded as the potential enemy, so he demanded a purge of communists in the civil service. 'How many members of the Communist Party are there serving in the headquarters of the Air Ministry today?' he asked. 'I know at least one communist serving there because he is president of my union.' There was, he said, 'at least one cabinet minister who had a communist as his private secretary. Whether he knows it or not, I do not know, but I know of it.'

The President of the CSCA, to whom Brown referred, was E.J. Hicks, employed at the Air Ministry. He was also secretary of the staff side of the department's Whitley Council (the negotiating body on which all unions with members working for the Air Ministry were represented). Hicks had never hidden his communist views. The other communist Brown was talking about was Ann George, secretary to George Tomlinson, at that time Minister of Education. Ann George was also one of those who had made her political opinions perfectly clear. She was an elected member of the CSCA Executive.

W.J. Brown's speech was received with what the *Daily Worker* described as 'thunderous Tory cheers' and the next day was acclaimed in the Conservative press, particularly the *Daily Mail*. It was the start of a right-wing campaign within the civil service unions and outside, launched by a body calling itself the Conference Campaign Committee, which was led by Brown and sponsored by the Conservative Party and the Catholic Church, with the object of getting communists removed from office both within the civil service and within their unions.

Following Attlee's statement on 15 March, 43 Labour MPs put down a motion regretting his decision. Pointing out that the Official Secrets Act and other measures had 'always provided adequate protection against subversive activities by any person in the public service', they believed that the decision was a 'departure from the principles of democracy and civil liberty.'[1] Their motion was countered by another resolution signed by 31 Labour members congratulating the Prime Minister on his action. But when MPs pressed for a debate on the subject, it was refused.

It was not until 25 March that a short discussion was forced on the government in an adjournment debate, during which Gallacher attacked the whole purge policy. The Communist Party was fighting for the independence of this country, he said, while Tories and Labour leaders were selling it to the big dollar boys of America. This was why the Party was under attack. 'I ask the Prime Minister,' he said, 'Is this attack on the communists, backed by a State Department, connected with a demand from Marshall that wages in this country must come down?' He also thought that the anti-communist attack could not be dissociated from talk of war. 'America wants to make war against the Sovet Union and to use Britain as a forward base,' he said. 'By the time such war finished, this country would be a mass of radioactive mud.' But, he alleged, the Labour leaders dared not tell the truth about their policies; instead, they talked about 'democracy'.

The points made by Gallacher were emphasised by Harry Pollitt at an Albert Hall meeting commemorating the centenary of the publication of the Communist Manifesto on 30 March. 'Today there is a purge against communists in the civil service' he said. 'It is time to put the issues quite clearly. Who are the patriots of Britain? Who are the real traitors in Britain?' He went on: 'Those are patriots in the best sense of the word who defend the interests of the working-class and fight for socialism, for this alone can lead to the best defence of our country. Those are the traitors who are selling Britain to the United States, who are encouraging it in its war plans against the socialist world ... To be a communist means to be faithful to the traditions of those workers who, throughout the ages, in fair weather and foul, have had no other aim than service to the cause of the common people'.[2]

Until then, communists in the civil service had been engaged in the same kind of workplace activity as other party members. They made no secret of their political views. They met in groups which were based on the government departments where they worked or, where there were too few members, those from several departments would come together. They discussed political activities, held political education classes – for example, at the time the attack was launched, one of the groups was organising a course on Engels' 'Anti-Duhring'. Each group sent a representative to a secretariat which met monthly. These meetings usually opened with a political discussion, and then moved on to report on political activities, progress in mobilising support among colleagues, and on suggestions for trade union involvement in progressive moves. Aggregate meetings would be held from time to time and weekend schools. At these meetings, trade union policies would be formulated, and nominations for union positions discussed.[3]

The general secretary of the biggest union, the CSCA, was a left-winger, L.C. White, who was not a member of the Communist Party, but was on the editorial board of the *Daily Worker*. The union's deputy general secretary was another left-winger, Bill Ellerby, who was an active supporter of the National Council for Civil Liberties, denounced as a 'communist front' organisation by W.J. Brown.[4] Party members on the CSCA Executive – apart from E.J. Hicks and Ann George – included Betty Jones and Doris Lancaster. There were also some other party members working at the union's headquarters.

Immediately after Attlee's statement, representatives of the civil service unions involved – including the CSCA, the Institution of Professional Civil Servants (IPCS) the Civil Service Union (CSU) and the Post Office Workers union – summoned a special meeting and adopted a resolution reaffirming the principle that civil servants should be free to join any lawful party and should not be penalised for any such association. It urged that, where a charge was made against an individual, the grounds should be stated and the individual concerned given an adequate opportunity to appeal, and should be accompanied by a staff representative if he so wished. It noted with satisfaction that the government intended to safeguard state secrets 'the unauthorized release of which might endanger the security of the state'.[5]

On 25 March, Attlee conceded that individuals under suspicion would be given 'chapter and verse' for the accusation; that the evidence would go before the minister concerned who would be assisted by a special advisory committee before which the accused person would appear. However, the government refused to agree that such individuals could be represented by their union when coming before this advisory committee. Attlee's stated reason for this was the 'need to safeguard sources of information'.[6] The truth was that information about members of the Communist Party, wherever they worked, was regularly collected by MI5 which had always planted (or recruited) 'informers' where thought necessary. Any close examination of the evidence against members of the civil service appearing before the advisory committee might well have revealed the identities of the 'informers' concerned, or at least raised supsicions about them. Protecting MI5 and its sources had become a priority; it transpired, bit by bit, that the individuals under suspicion were not to be allowed to see or cross-examine the witnesses who had provided the evidence against them, nor to have such evidence set down in written form. This did not affect those who openly claimed to be members of the

Communist Party, but was crucial for others who were alleged to be related to, or in some vague way 'associated' with members of the party.

Among the first to be subjected to the purge was Ann George, private secretary to George Tomlinson, Minister of Education. Tomlinson had originally been Minister of Works; when, in February 1947, he was made Minister of Education and elevated to the cabinet, he made sure that Ann George – whom he had described as the 'perfect secretary' – moved with him. However, in April 1948 she received a letter from the head of the Department of Education informing her that 'the Minister had decided there was a prima facie case for considering that she was a person whose reliability for employment on secret work was open to suspicion.' The charge against her, the letter said, was that she was known as a member of the Communist Party. To this Ann George replied: 'I refuse either to deny or admit the charge, and I say quite emphatically that no employer has any right to ask such a question.' She pointed out that no information which cast doubts on her loyalty and integrity had been placed before the Minister, though it was true that in 'certain official quarters' efforts had been made to persuade her to give up her trade union work. 'I found no difficulty at all in never allowing my TU loyalties to interfere with my official loyalties' she wrote. 'My political convictions are my own concern.' This correspondence, together with a photograph of Ann George, appeared on the front page of the *Daily Worker* on 24 April. Ann George was suspended on leave pending enquiries into her political activities. She was re-elected to the executive committee of the CSCA at its annual conference the following month. Soon after, the Ministry of Education transferred her to exceedingly mundane work where she spent most of her time operating a Gestetner machine.[7]

The president of the union, E.J. Hicks, was less fortunate. His renomination as president by several branches was not supported by his own Air Ministry Branch and a resolution at the union's annual conference in May to allow him to stand for re-election was narrowly lost by 3,091 votes to 2,909.[8] The Air Ministry had delayed taking action against him until the conference was over, but a few days later he was suspended from his post as higher clerical officer in the contracts department. The staff side of the department's Whitley Council unanimously deplored Hicks's suspension, and expressed their 'confidence in his loyalty and integrity in the service of the state'. Following this protest, Hicks continued his work as secretary of the staff side for some weeks, despite his suspension. In a letter to the Secretary of State for Air he replied to the allegations made against him.

'At different times, ministers speaking on behalf of the government have stated that Civil Servants are free to join any political party, including the Communist Party. With these pronouncements in mind, I have sought neither to advertise nor conceal my political views. I affirm that I am a member of the Communist Party of Great Britain. The form of your minute ... makes clear that the decision to remove me from the Air Ministry is based on apprehension that I am likely to betray official secrets to a foreign power to the injury of my country and my fellow citizens. Since I am neither charged with any dereliction of duty nor given any opportunity to establish my integrity, it appears I have no redress on what can only be described as a monstrous slander.'

Shortly after, it was announced that Hicks would be moved to the Ministry of Health.[9]

Despite the defeat of Hicks, it became clear at the CSCA annual conference that W.J. Brown's campaign, in cooperation with his Conservative and Catholic sponsors, had not achieved all he had hoped. He had thought it likely that there would be no communists left on the union's Executive Committee[10] but, in the event, the *Daily Worker* was able to report on 28 May that, though 14 anti-communists had been voted on to the new EC, so had 12 'Communists and progressives'. Moreover, the conference adopted a statement deploring the activities of Brown's campaign committee, and it was decided to terminate his own appointment as the union's parliamentary secretary, thus officially distancing itself from him. And though the union decided to cancel its affiliation to the British Soviet Society (which was on the Labour Party's proscribed list) it decided to continue its affiliation to the National Council for Civil Liberties which Brown had attacked as a 'communist front'.

L.C. White, the union's general secretary, continued to emphasise his opposition to the purge. 'I shall go on associating myself with the *Daily Worker*' he told the conference. 'I believe in political freedom'. A week earlier, in a special *Daily Worker* article, White had ridiculed the idea that Moscow secret agents would draw attention to themselves by joining the Communist Party; he thought that any spy who really wanted to cover his tracks would join the Conservative Party.[11]

The MI5 informers made their usual series of blunders. One of those suspended, on the grounds that he was a member of the Communist

Party, was a clerical worker at the Ministry of Supply, Albert Prince. He had, in fact been a member of the Communist Party, but had left it two years earlier and was, by this time, treasurer of his local ward Labour Party. After pointing this out to those in charge, the accusation was changed to an alleged 'association with the Communist Party in such a way as to raise legitimate doubts as to your reliability'. However, by the end of July, after much publicity, an embarrassed Ministry was obliged to withdraw the charge and Prince was reinstated in his former job.[12]

In June, the smaller but highly influential union, the Institution of Professional Civil Servants, held its annual conference and by an overwhelming majority declared its opposition to the government's purge. And it appointed Stanley Maine, who had always worked closely with the Communist Party, as its new general secretary.

Despite the stand made against the purge from within the civil service, the reaction from those outside was less encouraging. The party's effort to mobilise opposition to it from other trade unions was not very successful. At their Easter Conference, the Clerical and Administrative Workers Union supported the purge, and resolutions against it were defeated at both the USDAW, (shop assistants) conference and the Co-op Party conference.

The TUC leaders were not prepared to object to the purge. They simply agreed to take up one issue only: the right of individuals to be accompanied by a union official when called before the advisory committee. However, they refused to take a stand even on this side issue, as became clear at the 1948 Congress held in September. Here the Association of Civil Service Designers and Draughtsmen had tabled a resolution expressing concern that individuals were being denied this right. But Vincent Tewson, TUC general secretary, asked for the resolution to be withdrawn on the pretext that the matter was 'still under negotiation.'[13] The movers refused to withdrew, but the resolution was defeated by 3,841,000 votes to 3,467,000.

The truth was that, behind the scenes, the TUC leaders had bowed to Attlee's ruling that no individual facing such a charge would be allowed union representation, and Tewson was already, therefore, suggesting an 'alternative': the appointment of a trade unionist acceptable to the general council to the advisory committee before which individuals would appear. In view of the general council's open hostility to communists, some of the unions involved argued that such a nominee would diminish rather than enhance the advisory committee's prestige as an impartial body. However, Attlee agreed to the proposal, and a retired general secretary of the Union of Post Office Workers was appointed to the advisory committee, after which the general council let the matter drop.[14]

There was no sign that the general council's nominee made any difference to what was happening. According to Bob Anderson, who represented the Civil Service Union at the 1949 TUC held in September of that year, there had by that time been 42 purge cases, but only one of them concerned a fascist. The people involved had been either dismissed or transferred to other work. He said: 'When the purge was first introduced, the Prime Minister gave a pledge that it would be limited entirely to persons engaged on secret work.' But, he said, 'we find in practice that ministers are ignoring the pledge'. He stressed that at the Air Ministry the entire department was regarded as on secret work despite the fact that the bulk of it was routine. He said:

> One civil servant whose only work was the examination of expired contracts (work on matters long since dead) has been purged. He was not engaged in secret work of any kind. We have a case of a scientist engaged in research on penicillin. The results of the research, the formula for the chemical, have been published in the scientific press. He was not engaged in any kind of secret defence work, or indeed secret work of any description. He has nevertheless been purged ... It is clear that the purge is being applied in a manner quite unrelated to the needs of state security.'[15]

Another case mentioned by Anderson related to the War Office where there was a messenger who had lost an arm in Spain fighting with the International Brigade. He was not engaged on secret work of any kind but was, nevertheless, transferred. At this congress Anderson moved a resolution calling on the government to abandon the purge. He was supported by L.C. White on behalf of the CSCA, but the resolution was lost on a show of hands.

Although most of the victims of the purge were not dismissed but transferred, the process had a demoralising effect on many non-party members within the civil service. If they associated with others on the left their opportunities for promotion could be blocked, their careers damaged. Suspicion as to who were and were not 'informers' was rife, while the political rights of those in lower grades became far more restricted than ever before. At the same time, quite a number of those formerly in the party drifted out of it, though decisions on this were not purely the result of pressure from within the service but were also fuelled by the vast growth in anti-communist propaganda which was becoming widespread in newspapers and on the radio during the late forties. After the Labour Government lost office in 1951, the Conservative Government which succeeded it continued the process, and by 1956, 135 civil servants had been affected. Of these, 24 had resigned, 25 had been dismissed outright and 86 had been transferred.[16]

17

ATTITUDES TO PROFESSIONAL WORKERS AND INTELLECTUALS

Civil servants were not the only victims of the government's anti-communist drive. Among those who lost their jobs were 17 scientists. In April 1948, Conservative MP Sir Waldron Smithers asked Attlee what action was to be taken against J.B.S. Haldane, who was working on two government scientific committees. In reply, Attlee claimed that Haldane was involved purely in medical research. However, by 1950, Haldane was to be removed from any government work.[1]

It was at a time when communists in professional work of all kinds were facing discrimination. Though this never rose to anything like the level of that in the USA, it had a noticeable impact. This was particularly the case among school teachers when it was realised that some local councils were attempting to introduce 'political tests'. Thus Middlesex County Council was to reject the appointment of Max Morris as a headteacher solely on the grounds that he was a communist. In universities it was well known that many failed to get promoted because of their communist views.

Ever since the war ended, communists in the various professional and specialist groups – scientists, historians, writers, musicians, and so on – had been actively engaged in debates about the way forward. In the autumn of 1946, a series of lectures had been organised by the London District of the Party on 'The Communist Answer to the Challenge of Our Time'. These were held on Sundays at the Beaver Hall which was packed out – indeed, some of the lectures had to be relayed to overflow meetings in adjoining halls.

Among those who participated was the scientist J.D. Bernal who showed how new scientific discoveries and developments offered great opportunities for control of the human environment with much increased welfare for all, but how, unfortunately, both Britain and America were still spending far more on science for war than on science for peace. Others who gave lectures included the writer, Randall Swingler, who discussed what was meant by the 'freedom of the individual'; B. Farrington, Professor of Classics, who argued that Marxism was the 'supreme defender of the moral values revealed in history'; John Lewis, who described the 'last desperate huddle of frightened philosophers wondering what they can do to stave off the intellectual menace of Marxism.'

The content of the lectures demonstrated the optimism for the future felt by those on the left who believed, in 1946, that capitalism was in its final stage. They formed the basis of a booklet published in 1947 under the title of *The Communist Answer to the Challenge of our Time* for which George Thomson, Professor of Classics, provided the introduction. 'The time is not far hence' he wrote, 'when the exploitation of man by man will be a thing of the past. Then, free to devote all his energies to the enrichment of cultural and spiritual life, the individual will be really free.'

Among the resolutions adopted at the Party's 19th Congress held in February 1947 was one on 'Music and the Arts' which called for support and encouragement for the 'great cultural awakening of the mass of the people at this time, when bourgeois writers, painters and composers are escaping almost wholesale into attitudes of mysticism, other-worldliness and cynicism.'

Another subject raised was the film industry. Regular visits to the cinema were part of the way of life for most people – television had not yet arrived. A resolution deplored the dominating position of the big American film monopolies on British screens. 'Not only does the present extent of film importation from America involve a high dollar expenditure which Britain can ill afford, but the bulk of the imported productions, with their glorification of cynicism, self-interest and immorality, exercise a harmful influence advantageous to the reactionary and aggressive purposes of monopoly capitalism.'

At this congress, much stress was laid on the need to develop work in the ideological fields. So, at its first meeting following the congress, the party executive decided to set up a 'Cultural Committee.' It was to be chaired by Emile Burns who, during the war, had been editor of *World News and Views*. Others appointed from the executive to serve on it were John Gollan (full-time party worker, later to become the party's General Secretary); G.T.C. Giles, a teacher who was by this time President of the National Union of Teachers and who had served on the party's executive since 1943; Professor George Thomson, who had just been elected to the executive for the first time. The function of the Cultural Committee was to plan and coordinate the activities of party members who worked in the cultural sphere – such as actors, musicians, writers, film producers – and, at the same time, to link up with other specialist groups which included a Science Advisory Committee, a Historians Group, an Architects Group (of which Graham Shankland was secretary) and committees of doctors, economists, philosophers and so forth.

Soon after the formation of the Cultural Committee, Emile Burns was to cause some resentment among writers – in particular Edgell Rickword, Jack Lindsay and Randall Swingler – over his criticisms of the contents of *Our Time*. This was a 6d monthly bulletin which had been founded by Swingler in 1941. It provided commentaries on contemporary theatre, ballet, books, films, music and painting. By 1945 its circulation had risen to 18,000, but after the war ended its readership began to fall and by 1947 its publisher, Fore Publications, was in serious financial difficulties. There were divisions of opinion in the writers' group as to whether the bulletin should aim to broaden its appeal by drawing more widely from all shades of progressive opinion – Rickword's view – or whether it should adopt a more polemical and aggressive tone. But Emile Burns sharply attacked the way in which *Our Time* was compiled, insisting that its aim must be to promote the party's political line. The circulation continued to fall and after several changes in the editorship, it came to an end in 1949.[2]

THE BATTLE OF IDEAS

In contrast to what happened to *Our Time* most of the initial actions taken under the auspices of the Cultural Committee were positive. Throughout 1947, specialist groups were growing and flourishing, and more and more people were involved in what was termed the 'battle of ideas'. The circulation of *Modern Quarterly* was rising and that year 'Modern Quarterly Discussion Groups' started up in various parts of the country – for example in Liverpool, where monthly meetings were held, and in Glasgow. By 1948 discussion groups were going ahead in Manchester, Birmingham and Bristol.[3] At the same time work among students expanded. Students who were members of the party were organised in separate branches and, by autumn 1947, reached a membership of some 600. Their work was coordinated under a National Student Committee elected by an annual party student conference. They not only took part in campaigns to provide wider numbers of people with opportunities for higher education, but aimed at introducing Marxist ideas into their own fields of study, seeking to undermine existing reactionary ideologies within the universities.

As Burns put it to the 1948 Congress: 'In the present period, the battle of ideas is of exceptional importance for the future of humanity ... It is the task of communists to defeat the imperialist propaganda, to expose its class character, whether it finds expression in open politics or in concealed forms in ethical, philosophical, historical or sociological ideas, or in the field of science, literature or art. To do this is a job for professors and workers at the bench, for lecturers and teachers as well as for dockworkers and labourers'.[4]

In April 1948 a conference on the 'Battle of Ideas' was held. Over 600 people attended; the introductory statement was made by Sam Aaronovich (joint author of a book *Crisis in Kenya* – later he became a lecturer in economics) who was the cultural committee's secretary. He said that the battle must be fought out not only where the class fight was open, but where it was concealed in academic institutions, in the fields of education, literature, science, over the radio, in the films and in the press. Those who participated in this event included the scientist, Sam Lilley, from Cambridge, who said that reactionary scientists were forging weapons out of mysticism and obscurantism; the teacher, Max Morris, who told how 'bourgeois propaganda was being disseminated through school text books'; the historian, Leslie Morton, who, in discussing how the centenery of 1649 must be celebrated, said that the bourgeoisie had become ashamed of its progressive past.[5]

THE WROCLAW PEACE CONGRESS

That summer of 1948 saw an international event: a Cultural World Congress for Peace, held in Wroclaw in Poland from 25-28 August. Initially intended as a joint meeting between French and Polish intellectuals, it was, at short notice, broadened out, with invitations being sent to leading scientists, writers and artists all over the world. 500 from 45 countries responded and took part. As J.D. Bernal put it, the Congress marked a first attempt by intelligent and responsible people to arrest the drift towards yet another war.[6] 42 people attended it from Britain, including the scientists Bernal and J.B.S. Haldane, the mathematician Hyman Levy, John Lewis, the philosopher, the historian Christopher Hill and the writer Jack Lindsay. But the majority who came from Britain were not communists; among them were such famous names as John Boyd Orr, Ritchie Calder and Julian Huxley, while some of the British participants were far from left wing. Indeed, one of the Russian speakers, Fadeyev – who was secretary of the Soviet writers union and a central committee member of the CPSU – aroused fury among some of the British and Americans who attended. Fadeyev stated that three years after the end of the war, people now faced the danger of another, and he laid the blame for this on the USA which, he asserted, wished to make a world safe for capitalism even if it meant the rebuilding of fascism which the war had overthrown.[7]

After four days of discussion in which representatives from many countries participated, the congress adopted a manifesto which incorporated many of Fadeyev's points. It said that 'contrary to the will and aspirations of the people of all countries, a handful of selfish men in America and Europe, who inherited from fascism its ideas of racial superiority and the negation of progress, who took over its tendency to settle all problems by force of arms, are again making an attempt against the spiritual wealth of the nations of the world.' Drawing attention to the new 'hotbeds of fascism' being created in countries like Greece, Spain and Latin America, it also stated that the 'oppression of human beings and of whole nations which the oppressors style as coloured continues and even increases.' It stressed the need for mutual understanding among cultures and peoples: it protested against the use of science for purposes of destruction and called for it to be directed towards reducing poverty and disease. It said: 'We raise our voices for peace, for the free cultural progress of the nations, for their national independence and close cooperation.' It called for national congresses of intellectuals in defence of peace to be held in all countries; for national committees in defence of peace to be set up everywhere, and for international connections between intellectuals in all countries to be strengthened.[8]

35 of the 42 British participants signed this manifesto. But four of them voted against it and three abstained. Among those who refused to support it was Julian Huxley. However, by the following year, many of those who had attended the congress were to be involved in the launch of a World Peace Movement.

SCIENTIFIC AND MUSICAL CONTROVERSIES IN THE SOVIET UNION

Despite the positive results of the Wroclaw Congress, it came at a time when the post-war mood of optimism on the left had begun to fade. And, although communists remained convinced that solidarity with the Soviet Union was essential for the future of the world, some of the actions taken within the Soviet Union were causing unease. One of these actions concerned what became known as the 'Lysenko controversy.'

Lysenko, President of the Soviet Academy of Agricultural Science, had for many years argued that inheritable changes could be produced by modification of the environment. His views were not accepted by most geneticists in this country. One of those who disagreed with him was J.B.S. Haldane and, indeed, in 1947 two articles by geneticists who were critical of his theory appeared in the *Modern Quarterly*.[9]

However, in August 1948, Lysenko's theories received official backing in the Soviet Union, and he became director of the Soviet Academy's Institute of Genetics. As a recent historian has suggested, Lysenko's victory was the result of his ability to convince Stalin and other Soviet officials that his methods could lead to a rapid improvement in the productivity of Soviet agriculture. In practice, his methods were not successful, and by the late 1950s this was to be recognised in the Soviet Union and 'Lysenkoism' was discarded.[10]

In Britain, despite the objections of the leading party scientist J.B.S. Haldane, Communist Party leaders endeavoured to build up support for Lysenko's views. Though no official statement on the matter was ever issued by the executive, several articles promoting Lysenko's theory appeared in the *Labour Monthly* in 1949 (including one by Bernard Shaw) and, in 1950, a booklet entitled *Lysenko was Right* was published. It was written by a botanist, James Fyfe, who had originally expressed doubts about the Lysenko theory.[11]

The main object was, of course, to counteract allegations being made in the press that in the Soviet Union all criticisms of the Lysenko view were being suppressed and his critics persecuted and done to death. In fact, some of these allegations were true. Thus Nikolai Vavilov, the chief critic of Lysenko's theories before the war, had been one of the victims of Stalin's purges and had died in a Siberian prison camp in 1943.[12] Accustomed as they were to trying to counteract anti-communist propaganda, most party members failed to accept that some of the allegations of injustice in the Soviet Union could be true.

The issue helped to cause divisions among left-wing scientists, and disillusionment with the way things were run in the Soviet Union which began to spread during the late forties.[13]

Another controversy of which much use was to be made in the British press concerned music. On 19 February 1948, the Central Committee of the Communist Party of the Soviet Union issued a document which was highly critical of an opera produced by a Russian composer, Muradele, and which went on to state that 'many Soviet composers have, in their mistaken pursuit of novelty, divorced their music from the needs and artistic taste of the Soviet people, formed an esoteric circle of connoiseurs and musical gourmands, lowered the high social role of music and restricted its significance, confining it to satisfaction of the spoiled tastes of individual would-be aesthetes.' The document named a number of composers 'whose work most strikingly illustrates the formalistic distortions and anti-democratic tendencies in music which are alien to the Soviet people and their artistic tastes.' Among these were Shostakovitch, Prokofiev and Khachaturian. The Central Committee's chief spokesman on this question was Zhdanov who stressed the need to protect Soviet music from the penetration of 'elements of bourgeois decay.'

The denunciation of certain composers came as a shock to some music-lovers on the left, many of whom remembered being deeply impressed by Shostakovitch's 'Leningrad Symphony' which had been received with acclaim during the war when the beleaguered people of Leningrad were resisting the Nazi onslaught.

The criticisms in the document were, of course, widely attacked in the British press. But they received support from the British composer, Alan Bush, a member of the party, who wrote a detailed examination of what the document implied, arguing among other things that the organisation of Soviet music, the award of Stalin prizes, the chances of publication and performance in the Soviet Union, had got into the hands of a small group of composers, while the public had shown increasing indifference, and indeed hostility, to contemporary music.[14]

Indeed, even before the Soviet Party's criticisms were made public, one British composer, Rutland Boughton, had written an article in the *Modern Quarterly* objecting to the trends in modern music in Britain and saying that 'it is more and more clear that a new and growing public has no use for modern stuff'.[15]

Despite the stand taken by such composers as Bush and Rutland

Boughton, the new developments in the Soviet musical world caused worry and uneasiness among many musicians on the left. It was not so much the question as to whether the views proclaimed by Zhdanov were justified; it was the rumours about how those who disagreed with him were being victimised and persecuted.

For three years, the British press had been engaged in campaigns aimed at undermining the widespread public support for the Soviet Union which had arisen during the war, denouncing it as a dictatorial system under which individuals were denied democratic rights. Communists and others on the left had spent much time repudiating these allegations, arguing that under a capitalist society 'freedom' meant freedom for capitalists to exploit the mass of working people, whereas in a socialist society, such as that prevailing in the Soviet Union, working people had the right to participate in governing the country. But now, at last, uncertainty was showing itself evident not only among scientists and musicians in the party but among other professional workers who had been engaged in the 'battle of ideas'. They began to wonder whether some of the allegations which they had branded as lies could in fact be true.

Such doubts were exacerbated by events taking place in eastern Europe, beginning with the split between the Soviet Union and Yugoslavia.

18

TRADE UNION ACTIVITIES: ATTACKS FROM THE RIGHT 1948–9

The growing influence of party members in the trade unions was a matter of much concern to the right-wing Labour leaders. On 21 December 1947 they launched a campaign to undermine this influence. A circular from Morgan Phillips, Secretary of the Labour Party, was sent out to every affiliated organisation. 'Now is the time' it said 'to go out on a great campaign against communist intrigue and infiltration inside the Labour movement'. 'It would be a tragedy' it continued 'If the communists, who have been rejected time and time again by a free vote of the electors, were to win political power and influence through the back door of trade union branch meetings.'

The circular accused communists of 'slavishly following the Cominform doctrine, which has described Attlee and Bevin as "traitors" and "lackeys" '. Alleging that communists 'blatantly exploit legitimate grievances for political purposes', it suggested that 'in recent years the communists have gained an influence inside certain trade unions out of all proportion to their real strength.' The explanation for this, according to Phillips, was that communists 'thrive on apathy.' 'When large numbers of trade unionists stay away from their meetings, the communists begin to take charge.' The circular exhorted Labour Party members to play a more active part inside their trade unions. 'An aroused and active trade union movement is our best safeguard.'

Phillips' circular was received with delight in the Conservative Press. For once the Labour Party, the subject of constant attacks in the newspapers, had gained Conservative approval.

One of the most absurd suggestions in the circular was that communists had 'infiltrated' the trade unions. 'I "infiltrated" the miners' union when I was 16 years old,' declared communist William

Pearson, Scottish area secretary of the National Union of Mineworkers (NUM) addressing his organisation's annual conference.[1]

Most of the party's male members had, indeed, been keen trade unionists *before* they joined the Communist Party. And, because they were not passive people, but were rapidly involved in union activities, this soon led on to responsibilities for negotiations with management. 'Communist strength in the unions depends upon their ability to give leadership to the members' asserted Bill Jones, who had just been re-elected to the Central Bus Committee of the Transport and General Workers Union. No communist had 'infiltrated' his union; they had joined it like any other member, he said.[2]

The suggestion that communists reached trade union positions by the 'back door' was equally untrue, as was shown by the number of votes received by some well-known communists in trade union ballots. Thus Arthur Horner, general secretary of the NUM, had won 226,205 votes, compared with 167,074 for the other chief contender. Abe Moffat, president of the Scottish area of the NUM, had got over 33,000 votes compared with less than 11,000 for his main opponent. Wal Hannington, in a ballot for National Organiser of the Amalgamated Engineering Union (AEU) had received 41,825 votes; far more than any other candidate.

The idea that communists 'thrived on apathy' was equally far from the truth. Indeed, they had always tried to persuade all trade unionists to play an active part in their unions. It was those who joined in such activities, and therefore associated with communists, who became their chief supporters. It was those who stayed at home who fell victim to the anti-communist diatribes in the press.

The immediate response to Morgan Phillips' call was not particularly encouraging to the right wing. In Birmingham where the annual election of the Trades Council's executive was about to take place, the Borough Labour Party sent a letter to all ward Labour Parties calling on those members who were delegates to the trades council to turn up at its ensuing meetings in order to oust the communists, and putting forward a list of Labour members to be supported for executive positions. This campaign back-fired; there was an all-time record attendance of 257 delegates who elected *more* communists on to their executive committee than ever before.[3] Communists continued to win executive seats on other local trades councils. Thus, Julius Jacobs, full time secretary of the London Trades Council was, in February 1948, returned unopposed, while five other well-known communists were elected to its executive.

Meanwhile, in January 1948, all five communist members of the executive committee of the South Wales Area NUM were re-elected after a secret pithead ballot; a communist, Walter Stevens, was elected General Secretary of the Electrical Trades Union; two communists were voted on to the London Regional Council of the National Federation of Building Trades Operatives; three well-known communists were elected to London positions in the Amalgamated Union of Building Trade Workers; communist Les Ambrose topped the poll at 49,690 in an election for AEU organiser, while Wal Hannington was returned once again, this time with 48,176 votes.

The greatest setback for Morgan Phillips occurred in the Transport and General Workers Union, where right-wing Arthur Deakin, the union's general secretary, was making frantic efforts to undermine communist influence. But, in the ballots for the union's General Executive Council (whose members were chosen partly on a territorial basis and partly to represent trade groups) eight communists were re-elected, several with much higher votes than before. They were the busworkers, Bill Jones and Bert Papworth, representing London; Jim Sloan (Northern Ireland); Charles McKerrow (Scotland); Bert Slack (road haulage), Alex Grant (passenger transport) John Trotter (building) and Muriel Rayment (metal and engineering).[4] A shop stewards convenor, Rayment had, a year earlier, been one of the few women ever elected to the union's executive; she was a member of the Communist Party's Executive Committee.

During January 1948, 2,247 new members joined the party. This was 'not the kind of response Mr Morgan Phillips anticipated when he launched his attack in December' was the comment in *World News & Views* on 21 February. In the event, the registered membership that spring was over 43,000 – the highest for two years. And in Stepney, at a local council by-election, voters in Spitalfields West, a former Labour ward, gave a majority to the communist candidate A.C. Steinberg, so that the number of communist councillors there rose from 11 to 12.

That summer, a number of annual conferences of trade unions rejected Phillips' anti-communist call. They included the Foundry Workers, the Fire Brigades Union and ASSET (supervisory staffs and technicians) while the Printing, Bookbinding and Paper Workers union turned down a suggestion to ban 'communists and fascists' from holding office by 122 votes to 78.

179

THE FIGHT ON WAGES

The Party always assumed that the issue which triggered off Morgan Phillips' campaign was the Labour Government's desire to impose wage restraint. Ever since the 'convertibility crisis' in 1947, the threat to wages had been on the agenda. On 6 August that year, Attlee had made a public appeal to workers in all industries not to press for wage increases. After meetings held between TUC leaders and ministers, the TUC General Council began urging trade union executives to 'exercise even greater moderation and restraint than hitherto' in the formulation of wage claims.[5] On 4 February 1948, the government's views were set out in a White Paper (Cmnd 7321). 'The Tories are delighted' said Phil Piratin in a Commons debate on this White Paper. 'The Tories are having their policy carried out by a Labour Chancellor of the Exchequer'.[6]

At the Communist Party's 20th Congress held in February 1948, the economic crisis and the aims of the Labour leaders to undermine wage standards were major topics for discussion. It was argued that a satisfactory level of exports could not be achieved by lowering real wages; what was needed was the modernisation of industries which had been jeopardised by cuts in capital expenditure; changes in foreign policy, and the release of men from the armed forces. The congress called for the pegging of prices, the restriction of profits, and higher taxes on the rich. Moreover, the party no longer saw drives to increase production as the way forward. As Pollitt observed, the government had advocated increased production as their principal method for solving the crisis in order to cover up their anti-working class policy as a whole.[7]

Jim Gardner, general secretary of the Foundry Workers union, opened the debate on the wage freeze saying 'it cannot be expected that dissatisfied work people will respond to the need for more production, and dissatisfaction there is with wages, as everyone knows'. Many of those who spoke on wages did so from personal experience. They included Ethel Denton, a cotton worker; Sally Jerome, a Yorkshire textile weaver; Bill Jones, the London busman; Syd Abbot from Lancashire who described the Merseyside ship repairers' wages struggle; Joe Matthews who highlighted the attempts to freeze agricultural workers' wages.[8]

At this congress, 762 delegates were present, and the average age was 33. As the Party's National Organiser, Petter Kerrigan, said: 'the enemies of the workers employ hired hacks to peddle in the capitalist press the lie that the Communist Party is controlled from Moscow and that communism has no roots in Britain. This congress is the answer to them … We challenge any other organisation to hold a gathering so widely representative of Britain's mines, factories, shops, offices, professions and homes.'[9]

Throughout the congress, the link between the economic crisis and Britain's foreign policy was stressed.

However, the TUC General Council had already accepted the government's wage restraint proposals and, on 24 March 1948, it called a special conference of trade union executives to ask for endorsement of its stand. Party members on union executives tried hard to dissuade their colleagues from supporting wage restraint. Thus Arthur Horner and Abe Moffat took a stand against it on the NUM Executive, but were defeated by a 2-1 majority. At the TUC conference, Gilbert Hitchings, a party member on the AEU Executive, was the first to call for rejection of the TUC's report; he was supported by other CP members such as Joe Scott, also of the AEU, Bill Smart of the AUBTW, and John Horner of the FBU. Others on the left joined in expressing their disagreement. But the General Council's report was endorsed by a card vote of 5.4m to 2.0m.

During the following months, prices went on rising; by June 1948 they were 10% above those of a year earlier. Yet wage rates had risen by less than 6%. Rationing of both food and clothing was still in operation but, for the first time, many families were unable to afford the use of their clothing coupons. Not surprisingly, there was growing impatience at the workplace, and industrial disputes were on the increase.

One example was an unofficial dock strike which arose in June 1948 out of a dispute over terms for 'dirty cargo' money at the Regents Canal dock in London, when 11 dockworkers were suspended for two weeks and deprived of 'attendance money' for a further 13 weeks. In response to this action, 1,100 men at the Regent's Canal dock went on strike, whereupon all over London other dockworkers came out in support, following which, mass meetings at Merseyside voted to do likewise, as did others at Birkenhead and Liverpool. A tribunal reduced the 13 weeks penalty to two weeks; nevertheless, the strike continued and by the end of the month, 30,000 dockworkers were out. The government proclaimed a state of emergency, troops were brought in. At last, on 29 June, a mass meeting at the London Victoria Dock voted to return to work on the recommendation of the strike committee.

The strike committee which had led the strike was composed of over 40 dockworkers of whom 5 were Communists and 19 were Labour Party members, the rest belonged to no party.[10] Nevertheless the strike was denounced by the Conservative press as a 'Communist plot'; it had, of course, been strongly opposed by the T&GWU secretary Deakin.

George Sinfield, the *Daily Worker*'s industrial correspondent, responded to the 'communist plot' allegations on 3 July in a special article after the strike was over. 'Who are these communist plotters, conspirators and agitators?' he asked. Naming three of the communists involved – Pat Coleman, Ted Dickens and Joe Cowley – he said: 'These men and others like them do not suddenly discover dockland at the time of industrial unrest. They were born there, they work there and they struggle to improve their working conditions ... (They) are among the most active trade unionists. They have succeeded in holding the ranks together, preventing breakaways.' He said that dockers treated with scorn accusations by the Prime Minister Attlee of 'subversive activities'.

The 1948 Trades Union Congress held at Margate in September saw the sharpest conflicts between left and right since the war ended. The tone was set by the president, Florence Hancock of the T&GWU who, in her opening address, accused the party of trying to provoke industrial trouble. 'We must rid our movement of these mischief-makers' she said. Ironically, Hancock, as president, had later that day to award the Congress Gold Badge for trade union recruitment to one of these communist 'mischief-makers'. This was Rose Carr of the Tobacco Workers Union. She had worked in Carreras tobacco factory for seven years; despite hostility from the management, she had devoted herself to building up the union and was now the chief woman shop steward there. In reply to Hancock's words of praise for her 'untiring efforts', Carr said: 'I have always been inspired by the knowledge that our great trade union movement is broad and democratic enough to embrace all that is best in the ranks of the working class, regardless of politics, race or creed. I believe this great organisation ... will preserve its democratic character and resolutely set itself against all forms of discrimination.[11]

These hopes were not to be realised. The unofficial strikes which had been taking place were denounced as 'disloyal activities of small factions';[12] a proposal for emergency measures to nationalise the steel industry was rejected and one of the arguments used against it was that all three of the speakers who favoured it were communists.[13] (They were Jim Gardner of the Foundry Workers, F.W. Elms of the AEU and Les Cannon of the ETU.)

Since prices were rising, a resolution opposing the stabilisation of wages at their current levels was moved by Walter Stevens of the ETU and supported by several of the larger unions. But, after opposition from the general council, it was defeated by 5.2m to 2.2m votes. On Greece, although a statement was adopted expressing concern at the mass executions which had taken place, Congress rejected an amendment moved by John Horner of the FBU, demanding the withdrawal of British troops and the ending of British support for the reactionary fascist Greek government.

'The British workers may have to pay a heavy price for the bad decisions of Margate' commented a writer in *World News and Views* on 18 September. (She was Margot Heinemann, writing under the name of Margaret Hudson). Showing how the right wing had built on the fear of embarrassing the Labour Government in order to achieve the defeat of the left on both international and home affairs, she said: 'The vital thing now is to carry the fight from the floor of congress back to the workshops, to report fully and clearly to the workers how shamelessly the right wing leaders have thrown aside trade union principles, and rouse the rank and file to protest and action against the decisions taken in their name'.

This statement was to be seized on by the TUC leaders as an example of how communists were trying to undermine 'democratic' decisions. Meanwhile, the Margate Congress gave them the green light to launch their own anti-left campaign.

THE TUC GENERAL COUNCIL'S ANTI-COMMUNIST CAMPAIGN

The party had never made any secret of its industrial activities or the way in which they were organised. Whatever their workplace, members met up in groups to discuss not only immediate issues concerning wages and conditions, but how to spread the wider political message. The industrial work was coordinated by the District Committees covering the area concerned, and was overseen by the party's 'Industrial Department' at 16 King street. The work of this department was described in an Executive Report to the February 1948 Congress. It showed how contact was maintained with leading comrades in various industries via a number of 'Industrial Advisory Committees' – for example, a Mining Committee, a Rails Advisory Committee, a National Agricultural Committee and so on. Other advisory committees were attached to the districts concerned. Thus the Lancashire District was responsible for the cotton industry, the Yorkshire District for woollen textiles.

These advisory committees not only discussed urgent questions; they drew up plans for the future of the industries concerned, setting out what they believed to be the way forward. They also discussed union affairs, including which candidates should be supported in union elections.

However, on October 27 1948, the TUC General Council issued a 'Warning to Trade Unionists' urging union executive, district and branch committees 'to counteract every manifestation of communist influence within their unions and to open the eyes of all workpeople to the dangerous subversive activities which are being engineered in opposition to the declared policy of the Trade Union Movement.'[14]

The reasons given for this new anti-communist drive were that communists were seeking to obstruct the economic policy approved by the Margate Congress; that these 'disruptive activities' were being carried on in 'servile obedience' to the Cominform; that the dissolution of the Comintern was a pretence to enable Communist Parties to deny charges of acting on orders from Moscow; that Communist Parties had been ordered to oppose the Marshall plan, and that sabotage of the European Recovery Programme was the communists' present aim. 'Communist influences are everywhere at work to frame industrial demands for purposes of political agitation; to magnify industrial grievances; and to bring about stoppages in industry.' Communists, it was alleged, were acting as the 'slavish agents of forces working incessantly to intensify social misery'.

In reply to these allegations, the party's Political Committee said that a new attack on wages was being prepared by the employers and the Labour Government, that the TUC General Council had hastened to their assistance with its call for a heresy hunt against communists who held trade union positions; that the TUC had no evidence for its slanderous assertion that the party was out to sabotage recovery. The accusation that communists wanted to promote 'social misery' was the opposite of the truth; on the contrary, communists were supporting the fight for higher wages which the general council was opposed to. The party advocated a policy that would secure real economic recovery for Britain, would obtain independence from the USA and strengthen peace and friendship with all nations, whereas the Marshall Plan placed Britain's resources at the disposal of the USA; its aim was to make Britain the outpost for America's war preparations against the Soviet Union.[15]

Shortly afterwards Harry Pollitt outlined the aims of communists in trade unions. They stood, he said, for 100 per cent trade unionism, 'the largest possible attendance at trade union branch meetings, the democratic election of shop stewards in every department and representing every trade, and the election of shop stewards committees representing whole factories.' He went on to say: 'We stand for periodic democratic elections of all trade union officials, and we are against election of officials for life. We also oppose too great a concentration of power in the hands of trade union executive committees, for this destroys interest among the branches. No communist fears a democratic election; he welcomes it and will always support democratic procedure against those who, with the word 'democracy' on their lips, aim to make the trade unions the subordinate organs of capitalism.'[16]

On 24 November the TUC General Council issued a further statement which was published as a 2d pamphlet under the title 'Defend Democracy'. This asserted that it would be fatal to the trade union movement if it permitted its democratically determined policies to be disrupted at the behest of an outside body. Noting the party's change of line on production, it drew attention to its 'industrial committees' and suggested that unions should investigate the extent to which 'interference' had gone in their own particular industries. Describing the party's 'carefully planned arrangements' for operating inside the trade unions, it announced that the general council intended to safeguard trades councils against disruption. Commenting on this on 25 November, the *Daily Worker* observed: 'As far as can be gathered from this lengthy and involved document ... the charge against the communists is that they are critical of the Labour Government, do not agree with the decisions of the TUC and seek to change them. To these charges, the communists will naturally plead guilty. These ideas they share in common with millions of other trade unionists, as is shown by the two million vote against wage freezing at the Margate TUC'. And Johnny Campbell poured scorn on the references to the Communist Party as an 'outside body'. He argued that the wage policy which the general council supported had been injected into the trade union movement by an 'outside body' – namely, the cabinet.

The TUC pamphlet *Defend Democracy* was to be followed in March 1949 by another entitled *The Tactics of Disruption* in which it was alleged that communists did not regard the trade unions as a means of organising workers to improve their standards of living, but as instruments for the development of 'mass struggle' to be used as a means of securing political power. 'Once political power is achieved, the independence of the unions is snatched away'. The concentration by the Communist Party on activities in the workplace was characterised as 'interference' in trade union matters; meetings of building workers, engineers, ship-repair workers, bakers, etc., called by the party in various parts of the country were cited as examples of communist 'intrusion' into trade union affairs.

At the time, Conservatives, Liberals and Roman Catholics all had their own organisations within the trade unions. However, the TUC General Council had never taken action against them. This had been made clear at the 'Lynskey' tribunal event in December 1948 – an official government enquiry into allegations that a businessman, Sydney Stanley, had offered bribes to government ministers in return for favours granted to various companies. It was revealed during this enquiry that certain right wing trade union leaders had used Stanley's services to raise funds for an organisation called the 'Freedom and Democracy Trust.' The stated aim of this trust was to fight communism.[17]

In his reply to the TUC's pamphlet, Pollitt again set out the party's aims though, as he pointed out, there was nothing new in what he was saying. 'We fight to strengthen the trade union movement, not only by 100 per cent trade unionism, but by strengthening the factory organisation and shop stewards ... we urge the largest possible attendance at all trade union branch meetings and for making such meetings more attractive and more vigilant to prevent executive committees usurping powers that rightly belong to the rank and file.'

Again stressing that the party stood for the periodical democratic election for all trade union positions, both at local and at national level, he summed up: 'It is not the communists who are disrupting the trade union movement. It is the right wing trade union leaders who, despite the rank and file ... resort to the most anti-democratic methods, whereby to secure positions of authority in order that they may be used on behalf of capitalism.'[18]

Initially the TUC circular was rejected by certain unions at their annual conferences. These included the Foundry Workers, the Tobacco Workers, the Fire Brigades Union, the Engineering and Shipbuilding Draughtsmen, the Vehicle Builders and the Electrical Trades Union, while the National Union of Public Employees and the Bakers Union both turned down proposals to bar communists from holding office. However, the TUC's anti-communist campaign had considerably more impact than that initiated by Morgan Phillips. The circular was welcomed by the Tailors and Garment Workers Union, by the Clerical and Administrative Workers Union and by USDAW which catered for shop assistants.

The worst setback came with the biennial conference of the Transport and General Workers Union in July 1949 when it was decided by 426 votes to 208 to support the proposal of the general secretary, Arthur Deakin, to bar communists from holding any office in the union either as a lay member or as a paid official. The new rule (which was not reversed until 1968) came into operation in January 1950. From then on people nominated for a position in the union, from branch secretary right up to general secretary, were required to sign a declaration that they were not communists. It meant that the eight members mentioned earlier who had been elected by huge votes to the union's General Executive Council in 1948 could no longer stand. Among them was the London busman, Bert Papworth, who had also been serving as the only communist on the TUC General Council since 1944. At the same time, nine full-time officials of the union refused to sign the declaration that they were not communists and were sacked. They included Sam Henderson, national secretary of the Passenger group.[19]

The T&GWU was much the largest union, with 1.3 million members, and the decision had a demoralising effect, particularly among busworkers and dockers. But Deakin was not satisfied with his success in the fight against communists in his union. By September 1950 he was suggesting that 'legislative action should be taken by the government to ban the Communist Party.'[20]

Meanwhile, when the annual Trades Union Congress took place in September 1949, it was already clear that opposition to the anti-communist drive was crumbling. When a card vote was taken endorsing the general council's actions, the vote was 6,746,000 in favour with only 760,000 against.

THE WFTU SPLIT

On 27 October 1948, the day the TUC General Council began its witch-hunt against communists, it also decided to ask the World Federation of Trade Unions to suspend its activities, and threatened that if it refused to do so, the British would withdraw from that organisation.

Ironically, the British TUC had been the body mainly responsible for the formation of the WFTU. It originated from a decision of the 1943 TUC Congress to hold a conference of trade union representatives from other countries. So a preparatory meeting took place in London in February 1945 at which trade union representatives from nearly all except enemy countries were present. It was followed by one held in Paris in October 1945 at which the WFTU was finally established by delegates from over 50 countries.

This inaugural conference agreed that the Federation's headquarters should be in Paris, and it elected an executive committee of 26 members: 3 from USSR, 3 from the United States and Canada; 2 each from Great Britain, France, Latin America and the West Indies, and one each from China, Australia, Africa, India and Ceylon, Scandinavia, Western Europe, Eastern Europe, South East Europe, South West Europe, the Middle East, and so on. An executive bureau of nine members was elected with Walter Citrine as president (he was general secretary of the British TUC), Louis Saillant (France) as full-time secretary; the seven others represented the USSR, the USA, France, Latin America, China, Italy, and the Netherlands. In September 1946, after Citrine moved to the National Coal Board, Arthur Deakin of the T&GWU replaced him as the British representative at the WFTU, and in turn became its president.

The WFTU's stated aims were 'to organise and unite within its ranks trade unions of the whole world, irrespective of considerations of race, nationality, religion or political opinion'; to help workers in less developed countries to set up trade unions; to carry on the struggle for the extermination of fascism; to combat war and work for an enduring peace; to assist trade unions of all countries to maintain economic and social rights and democratic liberties, and to work for full employment and improvements in wages and conditions'.[21]

After three years' existence, the WFTU could claim certain achievements. For example, it had helped to re-establish trade unions in ex-enemy countries and to set up union organisations in Africa. In some other ways it had been less successful. Its endeavours to protect trade union rights in Greece had been foiled by the actions of the British and American governments; its protests at the slow rate of de-Nazification in the British and American zones of Germany were brushed aside.

Although the American trade union centre, the CIO, was participating in the WFTU's activities, the other American centre, the AFL, had from the start campaigned against it, characterising it as 'an instrument of Soviet imperialist interests and foreign policy'. The AFL aimed to set up an alternative international union centre, and sponsored the formation of breakaway unions in countries such as Japan, Italy, France, Austria and Greece. By early 1948 these activities were being financed by the American Government's intelligence agency, the CIA.[22]

In Britain, Labour's Foreign Secretary, Ernest Bevin, had long been using his influence to break up the WFTU[23] and had tried (unsuccessfully) to persuade Arthur Deakin not to become its president.

However, the TUC Congress held in September 1948 revealed that Deakin was succumbing to Bevin's pressure, when he said that the WFTU was 'rapidly becoming nothing more than another platform and instrument for the furthering of Soviet policy.' And a resolution reaffirming support for the WFTU was defeated. At this Congress, no fraternal delegate from the WFTU was present, for the first time. But two representatives from the AFL spoke, one of whom made a virulent attack on communists. 'You know even better than we do that the communists only devitalise unions, only use them for furthering the destructive purposes of their party and its masters behind the iron curtain' he said.[24]

As a result of this pressure, British representatives on the WFTU Executive proposed in January 1949 that the organisation should suspend operations for a year. The proposal was backed by representatives of USA and Holland, but was opposed by those from France, Italy, China and the USSR, who urged that the matter should be referred to a congress of all 67 affiliated national centres. But Deakin and his American and Dutch colleagues refused to accept this proposal for democratic consultation and walked out of the meeting. This was how the split came about.

At the 1949 TUC Congress, despite the efforts of left wingers (including Leo McGree of the Woodworkers, Les Gregory of the

Electrical Trades Union and Bob Anderson of the Civil Service Union), the withdrawal from the WFTU was endorsed by a card vote of 6.2 million to 1 million.

19

EASTERN EUROPE AND STALIN'S INFLUENCE

As noted in Chapter 10, in his very first speech as Foreign Secretary in August 1945, Bevin had sneered at the 'totalitarian' regimes set up in Eastern European countries after their occupation by the Red Army. In fact, in most of these countries, democratic elections had been held at the end of 1945 or the beginning of 1946, in some of them for the very first time.

Before the war, Bulgaria, Rumania and Hungary had all been subject to authoritarian regimes, and their governments had supported the Nazi invasion of Russia. The war, the defeat of Hitler, the occupation by Soviet troops, had led to the downfall of these pro-fascist governments, and their replacement by anti-fascist coalitions in which the previously illegal communist parties were at last able to participate. Thus in Hungary, where free elections were held for the very first time on 4 November 1945, 4.7 million people voted, and the result was 242 seats for the Smallholders Party, 70 seats for the Social Democrats, 69 seats for the Communists, 23 seats for the National Peasants Party. In Bulgaria, where a general election took place on 18 November 1945, a coalition of five parties which had joined together in resistance to the Nazis, calling itself the 'Fatherland Front', put forward 276 candidates, of whom 94 belonged to the Agrarian People's Union, 94 to the Communist Party (its leader was the international hero, Dimitrov), 45 to Zveno (a middle class patriotic party whose leader became Prime Minister), 31 to the Social Democrats, 11 to the Radicals. In the election, 3.4 million voters backed the 'Fatherland Front' candidates, while only 473,425 voted for the opposition candidates, none of whom were returned.

With the exception of Czechoslovakia, most of the countries neighbouring the Soviet Union were industrially backward and agriculturally primitive. The coalition governments which were elected brought in major reforms, confiscating the property belonging to former Nazi collaboraters, and introducing extensive land reforms, breaking up the old semi-feudal land estates and handing them over to the peasants.

In all these countries, the anti-communist Truman doctrine and the introduction of the Marshall Plan had a profound impact. Stalin, who had previously tended to hold aloof from their internal affairs – mainly in the hope of not antagonising the Western Powers – now began to put pressure on them, not only to refuse Marshall Aid, but to take action against alleged 'anti-communist' elements within them. A signal of what was in train came from Hungary where, in May 1947, several members of the Smallholders Party were ousted from the government, and the prime minister forced to resign, after an alleged 'fascist plot' had been uncovered.

However, it was events in Czechoslovakia in February 1948 which had the most impact in Britain, and were to be widely used in the anti-communist campaigns taking place.

CZECHOSLOVAKIA

Before the war, Czechoslovakia had been carved up and handed over to the Germans as a result of the Munich agreement engineered by the British Prime Minister, Chamberlain. During the war, a Czechoslovak 'government-in-exile' had been set up consisting of representatives of all anti-fascist parties involved in the resistance movement and, by a joint agreement of the allies, a provisional government headed by Benes (the country's pre-war president) and comprising six anti-fascist parties, had returned to Prague in May 1945.

The coalition government so instituted carried through an extensive programme of democratisation. All parties which had collaborated with the Nazis were banned, land reform was introduced, trade unions were established once more and some major industries were nationalised. In May 1946 the first election to a national assembly was held. It was conducted by universal secret ballot. The Communist Party, which received 38 per cent of the vote and won 114 seats out of 300, emerged as the strongest party; the Social Democrats won 12.1 per cent of the vote with 37 seats. This meant that the communists and socialists together had a narrow majority. The other seats went to parties of the centre, some of which were anxious to collaborate with the Western powers rather than with the Soviet Union. But President

Benes re-appointed Klement Gottwald, the communist leader, as Prime Minister, and a coalition government, consisting of representatives of all the parties concerned, was formed once more.

Throughout 1947 economic difficulties mounted – partly because of a severe summer drought – and by 1948, the Communist Party had prepared a programme aimed at restricting the activities of the private sector, and strengthening the socialist base; meanwhile, the right wing within the centre parties was trying to undermine deep-rooted support for the communists – particularly among industrial workers. On 20 February 1948, the conflict came to a head when 12 Ministers from the centre-right parties resigned from the government, on the ostensible grounds that some high police officials had been ousted and communists installed in their place. However, the Social Democrat Ministers refused to resign their seats, as did two non-party Ministers. This meant that the government still retained majority support within the Assembly and was, therefore, able to continue functioning.

There were huge demonstrations in support of the Gottwald government, more than 2 million people participated in a one-hour token strike against the right-wing and, on 25 February, President Benes agreed to accept the resignations of the 12 right-wing Ministers and to appoint a new government of 24 Ministers, of whom 12 were Communists, 4 Social Democrats, 2 non-party and the other six from the centre parties. Gottwald remained Prime Minister.

This event – described in this country as a 'communist coup' – received incredible coverage in British newspapers, most of which had been backing the demands of the Czech right wing that President Benes should set up a government which excluded communists, despite the fact that communists had received the widest popular backing. 'Never, and I mean never, has there been in history such a spate of dishonesty, hypocrisy, misrepresentation and slander' observed Ivor Montagu, examining what had appeared in the press in the April issue of the *Labour Monthly*. Dutt also commented on the 'extraordinary manic outburst of rage which has greeted the victory of the working class and popular forces in Czechoslovakia.' The establishment of a united socialist–communist government on the basis of a freely elected parliamentary majority, with the backing of the trade union movement should have received the support of the British Labour movement, he suggested. But it had been met with 'howls of despair and lamentation' not only from the press, but from Attlee and Morrison, and the entire official leadership of the Labour Party.

Unfortunately, the event was to lead to something British party members had not anticipated: a much more centralised and bureaucratic structure within Czechoslovakia. For although a multi-party system was ostensibly still in existence, the opportunity to voice political views which differed from those of the Communist Party leaders, both in and outside parliament, rapidly disappeared. As one historian put it later 'the previous talk of a Czechoslovak road to socialism was all forgotten as the kind of administration, planning and political system already existing in the USSR was introduced into the country'.[1] Like the other Eastern European countries, Czechoslovakia was subjected to pressure from Stalin, with tragic results.

YUGOSLAVIA

Though British communists were doing their best to counteract the anti-communist propaganda surrounding events in Czechoslovakia, they were deeply disturbed in the summer of 1948 by the sudden emergence of a breach between the Soviet Union and Yugoslavia. Eight of the nine parties which, in 1947, had joined together to set up the Cominform, met in Rumania in June 1948 and unanimously backed a statement attacking the leadership of the ninth party involved, the Yugoslav party headed by Tito. The meeting followed an 'exposure' by the Central Committee of the Soviet Communist Party of 'incorrect' policies of Tito and his colleagues who were denounced for their 'anti-Soviet' attitudes and for pursuing a line which represented a 'departure from Marxism-Leninism.'

The resolution adopted by the Cominform leaders supported this view. It alleged that the Yugoslav 'bureacracy' was spreading 'slanderous propaganda against the Communist Party of the Soviet Union.' ('borrowing from the arsenal of counter-revolutionary Trotskyism') It stated that the Yugoslav leaders were breaking with the Marxist theory of classes and the class struggle; that nationalist elements had come to the top; that the Communist Party was no longer seen as the principal leading force. It criticised the Yugoslav leadership for offering the prospect of a smooth and peaceful transition to socialism, for its refusal to recognise class differentiations among the peasantry and for its rejection of Lenin's teaching that the working class is the only consistently revolutionary class, and that only under its leadership can the transition to socialism take place.[2]

Tito and his colleagues refused to attend this Cominform conference and were from then on to be treated as outlaws.

The background to the controversy was Stalin's determination to exercise control over the countries of Eastern Europe, particularly those bordering the Soviet Union. Stalin was not motivated only by the reasonable desire to prevent the establishment of hostile military bases in these countries. Within the Soviet Union itself, any leading communists who were suspected of disagreeing with him had long been silenced, some executed, others imprisoned. As long as the possibility of post-war collaboration with the Western powers existed, Stalin had refrained from any obvious meddling with the internal affairs of the countries on his borders, but once the cold war had started he put pressure on them to follow his path. Those party leaders who challenged his supremacy, or aimed at a socialist structure which differed from the Soviet model, would be branded as traitors.

An important element in Stalin's quarrel with Tito had been a disagreement over Russian plans for the economic integration of the socialist countries, and the Yugoslav objections to the terms of trade proposed by the Soviet Union. Moreover, a proposal mooted for a Balkan Federation, discussed by Tito and Dimitrov of Bulgaria, was regarded by Stalin as a threat to his position of power. He decided that it was time to bring about Tito's downfall. However, he did not succeed in this aim. At a Yugoslav Party Congress, held just after its expulsion from the Cominform, Tito received almost unanimous backing. One of the results of the breach was that trade relations between Yugoslavia and the Soviet Union were disrupted, while the other socialist countries of eastern Europe either terminated or greatly restricted their trade links with Yugoslavia which had no alternative but to try to establish such links with the West, an endeavour which met with eager cooperation from the British and American governments, among others.

The British Communist Party was not part of the Cominform, and the resolution attacking Tito came as a profound shock since many members had felt great admiration for him and for the resistance movement which he had led during the war. Indeed, some British members had been involved in this movement; others had gone to Yugoslavia after the war ended, to help with road building projects; there had been many enthusiastic descriptions in the party press of what was happening in that country.

However, in July 1948, the executive committee of the party adopted a resolution supporting the criticisms made of the Yugoslav

Party by the Cominform, and it then held a series of aggregate meetings to discuss the Cominform statement. 'There can be no doubt' said Harry Pollitt to the London aggregate 'that the resolution of the Communist Information Bureau ... has come as a profound surprise to the party membership of every Communist Party in the world.' He went on to claim that the 'presentation of our standpoint this evening will in no way seek to damp down the enthusiasm which all of us have felt for the constructive achievements of the Yugoslav republic; nor will it aim in any way to weaken the bond of friendship between the people of Britain and Yugoslavia.'[3]

At these meetings, only a handful of members voted against the executive's stand in support of the Cominform – for example, at the London aggregate, the vote was 1,000 in favour, two against, and 20 abstentions. But many of those who voted in favour were privately expressing doubts. And, as Pollitt pointed out, some members, though not prepared to defend the Yugoslav Party's stance on certain matters, thought that it was a pity that differences within the Cominform should have been brought into the open, since the enemies of communists always thrived on splits. Pollitt, however, argued that public controversy within the international communist movement had led to strengthening of communist parties in the past. What neither he nor other party members realised in 1948 was that the Yugoslav controversy heralded the start of a much more serious train of events.

TRIALS IN EASTERN EUROPE

Stalin, defeated in his aim of unseating Tito, adopted other tactics. The portrayal of Tito as someone who had made anti-Marxist errors developed into accusations similar to those made against Trotsky in the pre-war Moscow trials: that he was a 'traitor' acting as an agent of the imperialists.

So it was that a whole series of rigged trials began in various Eastern European countries. Thus, in Hungary in September 1949 there was the trial of Laszlo Rajk and seven others. Rajk, a long-standing member of the Hungarian Communist Party, who had fought with the International Brigade in Spain, and was Minister of Foreign Affairs in the Hungarian Government, was suddenly expelled from the party and denounced as a spy for the imperialist powers and a 'Trotskyite agent'. At the trial he was alleged to have acted as a police informer in the past, and to have been endeavouring since 1945 to carry out a plan hatched up by the American imperialists for the overthrow of the Hungarian regime, trying to replace the true democrats in state positions with agents of Tito and of the US, British and French intelligence. The 'conspirators' were all found guilty and several were executed.

Not long after, on 7 December 1949, the trial opened in Bulgaria of Traicho Kostov and his 'accomplices'. Kostov had held a leading position in the Bulgarian Communist Party and had worked closely with Dimitrov, who had died some months earlier. He was now accused of a plot to overthrow the Peoples Republic of Bulgaria and to assassinate Dimitrov; he and his gang of 'conspirators' were alleged to have taken their orders from Tito and from 'Tito's own masters, the Anglo-American imperialists'. The accused were found guilty and executed.

In 1952 a rigged trial began in Czechoslovakia, which resulted in the execution of eleven communist leaders, including Rudolph Slansky and Otto Sling, whose British-born wife had already been arrested – she was kept in prison for 2¼ years but never brought to trial[4].

In Czechoslovakia, as in the other East European countries, the trials were accompanied by the repression of many communists, especially those who had fought in Spain, or had escaped as refugees to Britain during the years of Hitler's domination.

THE ATTITUDE OF THE BRITISH PARTY

As with the notorious Moscow trials of 1936-8 in which Trotskyists had been depicted as agents of fascism, the party in Britain assumed that these post-war trials in eastern Europe were justified. In a resolution adopted at the Party's 21st Congress in November 1949 it was alleged that Tito's regime 'now stands exposed as a grouping linked up with secret intelligence services of Western Imperialism'. And it said: 'Like Trotskyism, from which it is directly derived, Titoism seeks to organise disruption in the international working class movement.'[5] Moreover, because of the use being made of the trials for the purpose of anti-Soviet propaganda, a number of publications defending them were issued – in particular, *From Trotsky to Tito* by James Klugmann which appeared in 1951.

A few years after Stalin's death in 1953, it was admitted by all the countries concerned that the trials had been rigged and those executed were posthumously 'rehabilitated'. So why was it that the British Party was so ready to accept the findings of the trials at the time?

The main factor was the long-standing commitment to solidarity with the Soviet Union. As the first country to establish a socialist system it had, ever since 1917, been seen as offering a threat to the capitalist powers which had sought in various ways to bring about its downfall. For a brief period during the war, when the Red Army was defeating the Nazis and so saving the rest of the world – including Britain – from fascism, the USSR had been treated as a friend. But that period was now over and the Soviet Union was once more targeted as 'the enemy'. Accustomed as they were to exposing the anti-communist lies and distortions which appeared regularly in the British press, party members found it hard to believe that some of the allegations made against the Soviet Union and other Eastern European countries might be true.

The background to this attitude was the basic assumption that capitalism was the main source of oppression and injustice in the world, whereas socialism meant rule by the people for the people – in other words, ordinary people would participate in the decision-making processes. In Britain those who joined the Communist Party were dedicated to the socialist cause and, in many cases, were prepared to make great personal sacrifices in working for it. People whose guiding line was self-interest, or who wanted to further their own careers, did not join the Communist Party. What party members did not fully appreciate was that, in countries like the Soviet Union and its post-war European neighbours, this was no longer the case. From the late 1920s onwards, the Communist Party of the Soviet Union had become the party which people joined if they wanted to further their careers. Here the party was closely intertwined with the state machine, a power structure which had become more and more centralised and bureaucratic; 'Soviets' were no longer a system of 'rule from below'.

Apart from these basic beliefs, the allegations made at the trials in Eastern Europe – that their Communist Parties had been infiltrated by spies and informers from the West with the object of destabilising their governments – were not at all difficult to accept. It was widely known that this was the sort of thing the secret police did in Britain, and in the colonies, so why not in Eastern Europe?

Finally, Stalin was himself regarded as a hero – the man who had led the Soviet people to victory in the anti-fascist war. On the occasion of his 70th birthday in 1949, a resolution paying tribute to him as the 'greatest living exponent of Marxist-Leninist theory' and for his 'unswerving devotion to the cause of the proletariat' was passed at the

Party's 21st Congress. 'It is the Communist Party of the Soviet Union, under your leadership, that heads the forces of the camp of peace in deterring the warmongers and in exposing the treacherous role of their Titoite agents' it said.[6]

So it was that most communists were prepared to accept the findings of the trials as valid. Sadly, the classification of Trotskyists and, in particular, 'Titoists' as 'agents of imperialism and fascism' was not only totally unjustified; it meant that urgently needed discussion and the development of theory on the way forward for socialist countries was held back, while in most of the Eastern European countries the Stalinist model was imposed.

In 1956, after the 20th Congress of the CPSU when the terrible truth about Stalin's crimes began to emerge, members of the Communist Party in Britain were forced to rethink their attitudes, and, indeed, to explore the reasons why and how such atrocities could have taken place – a process which was to continue for many years.

20

EVENTS OF 1949 AND THE 1950 ELECTION

Early in 1949 the party suffered a sudden loss when Bill Rust, editor of the *Daily Worker*, died of a heart attack. He had been the paper's first editor in 1930 and, after leaving it for other work, had returned to the post in 1939, and again in 1942 when the ban on the paper was lifted. In 1945 he had helped to set up the Peoples Press Printing Society which was to own and publish the paper and which, by 1948, had 30,000 shareholders. They included over 700 trade union and cooperative bodies, despite opposition from the TUC General Council which had 'advised' local trades councils not to invest in the PPPS and had tried to persuade national unions not to give it any support.[1]

In November 1948, the paper had moved to premises in Farringdon Road and had come out in a new form. Three months later, Rust died. He was succeeded as editor by J.R. ('Johnny') Campbell, who had worked with the paper for many years, while John Gollan became its assistant editor.

For communists, one of the few encouraging events in 1949 was the victory of the Chinese Liberation Army over the Kuomintang forces led by the nationalist Chiang Kai-shek. So came the creation of the People's Republic of China under the leadership of Mao Tse-tung. Chiang Kai-shek and his army – which had received much support from the Americans – was relegated to Formosa (later known as 'Taiwan').

The Chinese victory was preceded by a tragic episode known as the 'Amethyst affair'. In April 1949, the Peoples Liberation Army (PLA) had reached the Yangtse river. It was pursuing the Kuomintang forces which were in full retreat. Getting no reply to the announcement that it was about to cross the Yangtse, the PLA started shelling the Kuomintang troops on the opposite bank, whereupon a British warship, the *Amethyst*, sailed up the river between the two opposing armies, thus appearing to be 'intervening' in a civil war which was no affair of the British. The *Amethyst* was hit by PLA shells, and ran aground with 17 killed and 20 wounded. On the following day, as the PLA was crossing the river, another British ship, *Consort*, came under fire and a further 15 were killed and 17 wounded.

The British press used the occasion to foment anger against communists, thus diverting attention from the real issue: why British warships were there at all? One of those who suffered from this was Harry Pollitt who had been booked to speak at meetings in Dartmouth and Plymouth, both of which were major naval bases. Incited by the local Tory press, crowds attacked Pollitt, who was so savagely kicked that he had to have hospital treatment for an injury to his back which resulted in months of pain, and was to prevent him from attending the party's congress in November.

THE WORLD PEACE MOVEMENT: HOW IT BEGAN

Throughout 1949, hopes for a world free from war were fading. The National Service Act, under which men were conscripted into the armed forces, was amended so that from January 1949 the period of compulsory service went up from 12 months to 18 months. Though the party had previously agreed to peacetime conscription, it was strongly opposed to the increase in the length of service, regarding cuts in the armed forces as a priority.

On 4 April the North Atlantic Treaty was signed on behalf of the USA and Britain and ten other Western European countries. Thus NATO came into being – a military bloc providing for the maintenance of huge armies, vast expenditure on weapons and the establishment of bases for American bombers in Britain and elsewhere in Europe. Before the pact was signed, the Communist Party Executive had issued a warning of what lay ahead, saying:

> The Atlantic Pact is not a pact for peace. It is a pact for war. It is the direct continuation of the policy of Churchill's Fulton speech and the Truman doctrine – openly directed to the aim of building up a war front against the Socialist Soviet Union and the People's Democracies of Eastern Europe.[2]

It was widely assumed that, in agreeing to the formation of NATO, the British Government was succumbing to American pressure. In fact, as was later revealed, the Americans were initially reluctant to participate in a European military bloc; it was pressure from Labour's Foreign Secretary, Bevin, for their involvement which helped to tip the balance.[3]

The formation of NATO came after the rejection by Britain and America of a Soviet proposal for a reduction in armaments and the banning of the atom bomb.[4] However, in September 1949, the NATO powers were shocked to discover that the Russians had succeeded in creating an atomic explosion. It had previously been assumed that the Soviet Union would not have the capacity to produce an A-bomb for some years. The Soviet representative to the United Nations continued to urge the international banning of the atom bomb, and for atomic energy to be brought under international control. These proposals were, as usual, rejected by the Americans and the British.[5]

In the light of the NATO launch came the birth of a world peace movement. A 'World Congress of the Partisans of Peace' was held in Paris in April 1949. Though the French Government had refused visas to many of the delegates representing the USSR and other Eastern European countries, the congress was attended by 2,000 delegates from 59 countries. Some 300 came from Britain. It issued a manifesto saying: 'Four years after the last great tragedy, the people are being precipitated into a dangerous armaments race. Science, whose role is to ensure the happiness of mankind, is being diverted from its goal and is forced to serve the ends of war.' It went on: 'The atom bomb is not a defensive weapon. We refuse to play the game of those who wish to oppose one bloc of states to another bloc of states; we are against the policy of military alliances which has already been tried with terrible effect.'[6]

The congress elected a permanent committee with representatives from France, Great Britain, Italy, USSR, USA, China and Mexico. Its president was the French scientist, Professor Joliot-Curie, and one of the British representatives on the committee was the well-known physicist, Professor J.D. Bernal.

On its return the British delegation set up a British Peace Committee under the chairmanship of J.G. Crowther, a leading member of the Association of Scientific Workers and the *Guardian's* science correspondent. Since the British Peace Committee was to be constantly attacked as a 'communist front' organisation, it should perhaps be noted that Crowther was not himself a communist.

The British Peace Committee held its first Peace Congress on 22 October 1949; 1,159 delegates attended, and it adopted a programme of demands which included 'immediate reduction of armaments; the banning of the Atom Bomb and destruction of all stocks, together with control to prevent their further manufacture.'[7]

The Labour leaders had done their best to discourage the growth of such a peace movement, so it was not surprising that Labour MP K. Zilliacus was hastily expelled from the Labour Party because he had been involved in the 'communist inspired World Peace Congress ... and had accepted membership of its permanent committee'.[8] Soon after, two other MPs were also expelled because of their criticisms of the government's foreign policies: they were Leslie Solley, MP for Thurrock, and Lester Hutchinson, MP for a Manchester constituency – he was a journalist who had been one of those arrested in India in the notorious Meerut conspiracy case in 1929.

TRADE UNION RIGHTS UNDER ATTACK

It was not only on the issue of foreign policy that disillusionment on the left was growing. On the home front, democratic rights were being undermined. In May 1948, just after a huge and perfectly orderly May Day march had been held under the auspices of the London Trades Council, Home Secretary Ede had imposed a temporary ban on all political processions in London. The pretext for this was the 'depleted state of the police'. Yet, as the Communist Party Executive pointed out, hundreds of police were being used to protect meetings called by the fascist Oswald Mosley who was trying to reestablish his anti-semitic organisation.

On 21 March 1949, the ban was reimposed on the grounds that a fascist attempt to march through North London with the protection of 400 police had resulted in 'disorder'.[9] The ban meant that the London Trades Council was obliged to abandon its traditional May Day march which had been a regular event for nearly 60 years. Instead, the Trades Council called on trade unionists to gather at fixed assembly points and then to make their own way to a central rally at Trafalgar Square. Some trade unionists defied the ban and marched despite police attempts to stop them; others walked in groups along pavements carrying their banners and facing continual harrassment by mounted police; in the end Trafalgar Square was packed out; it was the largest May Day demonstration seen for many years.

The real reason for the ban seemed obvious to members of the party. Most of the London Trades Council's Executive were left-wing, and its secretary, Julius Jacobs, was a communist representing the furniture workers union, NUFTO. It had long been an object of concern to the right-wingers on the TUC General Council which, in 1950, accused it of being used as 'a platform for disruptive bodies'[10] and threatened it with dissolution. This was in fact to take place a couple of years later, when the London Trades Council was to be one of a number disbanded on orders from the TUC General Council.

One event which caused dismay in 1949 was the use of troops as strike breakers when dockworkers came out in support of some Canadian seamen who had been called on to strike by their union. In April, there were several Canadian ships berthed in British ports; their crews went on strike, whereupon some London dockworkers refused to move one of these ships, the *Beaverbrae*. They were immediately locked out by their employers, and thus prevented from working on any other ships. However, their example was followed in other ports. By May, Canadian shipowners were bringing in vessels crewed by strike-breakers. In response to an appeal from the Canadian Seamen's Union, 80 dockers at Avonmouth refused to unload a ship, the *Montreal City*; threats by employers to penalise the men brought the Avonmouth docks to a standstill and soon hundreds at the Bristol City docks came out in sympathy. Troops were then brought in to unload ships, but the crane drivers declined to work with them; meanwhile, the strike had moved on to Liverpool, where 45 men had been suspended for refusing to unload a ship sent on from Avonmouth.

Back in London, the dispute continued as troops were deployed and, by 20 July, the number on strike had reached 15,000. However, shortly afterwards, the Canadian Seamen's Union announced that it was ending the strike, so British dockers called off their action and went back to work.

Throughout these months, dockworkers in Britain had taken action to uphold a deep-rooted principle of international trade union solidarity. They were not acting out of personal interest – indeed, their behaviour was jeopardising their own job security. But to the Labour Government such international solidarity was unacceptable, and it was used to heighten the anti-communist press campaign. After the strike was over, George Allison – at that time head of the party's Economic Department – said that the press 'were all set on the job of trying to convince the London docker that he was being a stooge for the communists'. But, as he pointed out, the London dockers 'did not fall for all the scare stories about the Red Bogies and communist plots ... they set up their own elected lock-out committee which developed and organised the day-to-day activities ... In carrying out this action, the dockers remained true to the best traditions of their union.'[11]

However, the T&GWU leaders under Deakin launched their own enquiry when the strike ended, the upshot of which was a declaration that the strike 'was part of a wider plan, inspired from communist sources, the object of which was to dislocate the trade of the country and so add to our economic difficulties'. And, though the union's new rule to ban communists from holding office was not yet in operation, it disciplined six out of the seven strike leaders – those, as Jack Dash later recalled, who were thought to be communists.[12] They were Jack Dash, Vic Marney and Ted Kirby who were suspended from holding office in the union, and Harry Constable, Ted Dickens and Bert Saunders who were all expelled from the union. Dickens was one of those who joined the Stevedores Union, and was soon to be elected to its executive. Meanwhile, the Labour Government had already started its own enquiry under the supervision of the Attorney-General, Shawcross, into the extent of communist involvement in the dock strike. Such enquiries were to continue into other disputes in the 1950s.

THE 1950 ELECTION

In 1949 there were plenty of other matters of concern on the left. The wage freeze continued, but food subsidies were pegged which meant that prices of staple foods – meat, cheese, butter etc – were rising. In late summer, a balance of payments crisis and a dollar deficit led to the devaluation of the pound and was followed by further cuts in housebuilding, a proposal to introduce prescription charges in the health service, increases in the costs of school meals and so on. And it became clear that the government was back-tracking on its iron and steel nationalisation Bill; having delayed its introduction until October 1948, it now found itself under pressure from the House of Lords to postpone its vesting day. This it did.

Such was the background to the party's 21st National Congress held in Liverpool at the end of November 1949 at which a decision to put up one hundred communist candidates in the next general election was finally agreed.

The proposal had first been mooted in a political letter signed by Harry Pollitt on behalf of the executive committee and sent out on 28 December 1948. It had caused much argument among party members, some of whom were strongly opposed to the idea on the grounds that such a tactic might help the Tories to gain seats. These fears were reinforced by the results of the local government elections in the spring of 1949 which had seen big Conservative gains and a massive drop in support for Labour, while communists had also lost seats which they had previously won.

However, the argument of the party executive for taking such an unprecedented step was the need to campaign for an alternative policy to that of the Labour Government: in particular for a socialist policy. The participation of 100 candidates would provide an opportunity to spread information about this alternative policy. For though the British people had rejected the Tories in the 1945 election, the Labour Government had betrayed their trust by carrying out a Tory policy. It was asserted at the party's 21st Congress that the best way to ensure that there was not a Tory victory at the next election was to fight for the policy and candidates of the Communist Party while calling on the Labour movement to replace right wing Labour candidates with militant ones.[13]

In the event, at the general election which came less than three months afterwards – in February 1950 – the party suffered one of the worst setbacks in its history. Not only did it lose the two seats in parliament it had previously held, but, out of the 100 communist candidates, 97 got less than 12½ per cent of the poll and so lost their deposits. The aggregate number of votes received by the 100 candidates was only 91,815 – less in total than the 102,780 received in 1945 for a mere 21 candidates.

The defeat of former MP Phil Piratin was not altogether unexpected since his small Mile End constituency in Stepney had been amalgamated with two others to cover the whole of Stepney borough. In 1945 he had won the seat with 5,075 votes out of a total poll of 10,658; for the new Stepney constituency in 1950, the number who voted was 47,809; Piratin got 5,991 votes, just 12½ per cent of the poll.

On the other hand, the failure of William Gallacher to retain his seat in West Fife – which he had occupied for 15 years – came as a shock. His vote, which had been 17,630 in 1945, dropped to 9,301 and the Labour candidate got in. Another disappointment for the party was in Rhondda East. Here, in 1945, Harry Pollitt had received 15,761 votes and had narrowly missed winning the seat. But in this election his vote went down to 4,463 or 12.7 per cent of the poll.

In all the constituencies where communists had stood in the previous election there was a dramatic fall in their vote. Thus, the teacher G.J. Jones who, in 1945, had won 10,058 votes in the London marginal Tory seat of Hornsey, now got only 1,191. Howard Hill who, in 1945, had received 4,115 votes in the Sheffield Brightside constituency, got only 1,081. In the contest for the Scottish seat of Greenock, J.R. Campbell's vote went down from 5,900 to 1,228. Indeed, 78 of the 100 communist candidates had votes of less than 1,000. Of the 22 who got more than 1,000, 11 were in Scotland, four in Wales, four in London, two in Yorkshire and one in Lancashire.

The election was not only a blow to communists but also to others on the left. Thus all five of the Labour MPs who had been previously expelled from the Labour Party for their left wing stand and had stood as 'labour independents' were defeated. (They were D.N. Pritt, John Platts Mills, K. Zilliacus, Lester Hutchinson and L.J. Solley).

In this election a much bigger proportion of the electorate participated than in 1945, so Labour's vote went up by 1½ million to 13.3 million. However, its proportion of the vote went down from 47.8 per cent to 46.1 per cent and Labour-held seats fell from 393 to 315. Liberals also received more votes than before – 2.6 million – but the number of seats won fell from 12 to 9 and as many as 319 Liberal candidates lost their deposits. Thus it was not only the communist Party which suffered from this particular rule.

Only one party made gains and that was the Conservative Party whose vote went up to 12½ million compared with under 10 million in 1945 (43.9 per cent of the poll compared with the previous 39.8 per cent). Conservative seats rose from 213 to 298. The result was that Labour had an overall majority of only five seats. Governments in such a position do not usually last long, and it was obvious that another election could not be far off.

Members of the Communist Party had not really expected such a rise in the Tory vote. Indeed, despite the increase in votes at the local government elections, they still believed that widespread disillusionment with Labour would lead to a swing to the left provided a left-wing alternative was on offer. This belief was one of the factors which had led the communists to put up 100 candidates. Most of them stood in what were regarded as 'safe' Labour seats. But 13 of these former Labour seats were won by Tories.

The outcome of the election as usual highlighted the unfairness of the electoral system. Much activity had to be devoted to fund-raising, if only to provide the compulsory deposit of £150 for each candidate at a time when the average male weekly wage was around £7. A total of over £40,000 was raised, but £14,550 of this went in forfeited deposits. The Communist Party was not able to recoup such losses, unlike the Liberal Party whose massive £47,000 in lost deposits was mainly covered by an insurance scheme.

However, the main criticism of the electoral system was not the financial problems it raised, but the undemocratic structure which habitually provided parliamentary majorities for parties which got only a minority of the votes, prevented minority parties from getting seats, and deterred supporters of minority parties from voting for them on the grounds that their vote would be wasted. Indeed despite its fall in popularity, the Communist Party failed to get nearly as many votes as it would have done under a system of proportional representation. For many on the left who were critical of the Labour Government's right-wing policies knew that if they voted communist it could split the anti-Tory vote. A typical story was one from Swindon where a voter shook the party candidate by the hand, told him he had a good policy and even gave some money to the CP election fund, but then said he was going to vote Labour.[14]

But there were of course other factors which caused the Party to lose support. Gallacher, whose constituency covered a mining area, thought that the main reason for his defeat was the feeling among the miners that they owed a debt of gratitude to the Labour Government for nationalising the mines.[15] Pollitt's Rhondda constituency was also a mining area, where this feeling was no doubt widespread. Moreover, many other workers thought they were getting a better deal under the Labour Government than before, with comparatively full employment, the start of the National Health Service and so on; they wanted to show their support for Labour and to see the advances made consolidated.

The major factor in the communists' bad results was the anti-communist crusade which had been carried on by the Labour and TUC leaders ever since the end of the war. Thus, Prime Minister Attlee when addressing the 1949 Trades Union Congress had not only denounced the Communist Party for 'fomenting industrial disputes wherever they think there is favourable ground' but actually alleged that communists would 'welcome a Tory Government'.[16] Such anti-communist smears had been systematically peddled by the press and on the radio (television was not yet part of the scene). People who had been in personal contact with communists – for example, in the workplace – usually disregarded these anti-communist lies, and went on happily electing communists as their union representatives. But those who had no personal contact – the vast majority of voters – were inevitably influenced by the anti-communist propaganda which was widespread. Moreover, despite the party's dismissal of allegations about repression in Eastern Europe, concern on this matter was just beginning to develop among many on the left.

Although the party made 1,280 new recruits during the election campaign, the total membership in 1950 fell once more below 40,000 and was never again to reach above that number. In May 1950 it stood at 38,853.

It was obvious that another General Election might take place at any time, so the party's Executive Committee was that summer once more considering its electoral tactics, and a discussion document was issued based on a report from Pollitt on the 'Fight for Peace and Working Class Unity'. Here it was proposed that in the next election, only a limited number of communist candidates should be put forward. This document led to disagreements, some members suggesting that, if it would now be incorrect to put forward more than a few candidates, it should also be regarded as having been incorrect in February at the time of the election. But the Executive Committee rejected this view. Indeed, it never admitted that fielding 100 candidates had been a mistake, though it was self-critical about the style of the campaign. It argued that 100 candidates had been justified when Labour held a massive majority, but that the growth in the Tory vote, and in the number of marginal constituencies, meant that, if the Tories were to win a majority in the future, it might be attributed to the Communist Party's intervention.

Once again, the dilemma of an unfair electoral system was to be highlighted.

21

THE FIGHT TO BAN THE BOMB: WAR IN KOREA

Shortly before the 1950 election, news came through that the Americans were developing a hydrogen bomb which, it was said, had far greater destructive power than the atomic bombs dropped on Japan in 1945. In response came a huge growth in the movement against nuclear weapons.

The movement was initiated at a meeting of the Permanent Committee of the World Peace Congress in Stockholm in March 1950, which issued an appeal for the banning of all atomic weapons, with strict international control to ensure the ban was enforced. The Committee called upon 'all people of goodwill' to sign this appeal. Hundreds of millions did so in countries all over the world.

In Britain, the British Peace Committee started a campaign for signatures to the appeal which became known as the 'peace petition'. The aim was not only to persuade people to sign, but to involve them in action to ban the bomb, no matter what their political views. The response to this campaign was impressive. In many areas, local peace committees were set up; their supporters went out collecting signatures on the doorstep, and passed the petition round in workplaces. By September 1950, over a million people had signed, while the demand to ban the bomb was supported at a number of trade union annual conferences.

The Labour leaders were, of course, greatly alarmed at this development and hastily decided to add the British Peace Committee to its list of 'proscribed' organisations, which meant that no member of the Labour Party could be associated with it or participate in its campaign – indeed, those who helped collect signatures could be expelled. From August 1950, reports of such expulsions began to appear regularly in the *Daily Worker*.

The TUC General Council sent out a circular to local trades

councils, telling them that the British Peace Committee was a subsidiary of the Communist Party, and that any association with its activities was against the rules. It also tried to persuade affiliated trade unions not to support the movement. Attempts to reverse this decision failed. A resolution urging the government to take fresh initiatives for the banning of atomic weapons was defeated on a card vote of 5.6 million to 1.9 million at the September TUC Congress.[1]

GOVERNMENT ATTEMPTS TO STOP THE WORLD PEACE CONGRESS

On 23 September 1950, the British Peace Committee announced that it planned to hold the Second World Peace Congress in Sheffield City Hall on 13–19 November. The first congress had been held in Paris in 1949.

Before making this announcement, the secretary of the British Peace Committee had written to Prime Minister Attlee asking for an assurance that no obstacle would be put in the way of the congress by government departments. The letter had gone to Attlee on 3 August. Six weeks later had come a reply from the Prime Minister's secretary, dated 13 September, saying that 'in this free country, there is no power to prohibit the proposed congress provided that it is conducted in such a way as not to infringe the law regarding the holding of public meetings. Applications from foreigners to attend the congress will be dealt with on their individual merits and His Majesty's Government must reserve the right to refuse admission to any foreigner who is 'persona non grata'.[2]

The letter did contain one danger signal. It stated that the government was not prepared to allow foreigners to come to the UK for the purpose of organising the congress. This meant that the preparatory committee, set up to plan the event, would be obliged to meet in Prague.

Nevertheless, preparations for the congress went ahead. The Ministry of Civil Aviation gave consent to 18 charter flights from Prague to London to bring hundreds of delegates from Eastern Europe. Invitations from the British Peace Committee were sent to thousands of organisations in Britain – trade unions, churches, women's organisations, co-op guilds, sports clubs and cultural bodies – suggesting that they elect delegates to attend the Congress. The committee called on local peace councils to hold a 'Peace Week' from 5 to 12 November to arouse interest in the congress which was to open on 13 November.

The growth in support impelled Morgan Phillips, secretary of the Labour Party, to despatch a circular to all Labour Party organisations and affiliated unions warning them that participation in the Congress was 'incompatible with membership of the Labour Party'.[3]

Silence about the event in most of the press was suddenly broken when Attlee, speaking at a Foreign Office Press Association dinner on 1 November, denounced the British Peace Committee and alleged that the congress was 'rigged'. This speech was headlined in the newspapers. Attlee was then invited to address the Sheffield Congress himself, but refused.

Soon after, the assertion that the 'ancient tradition of freedom' would prevent the banning of the congress was to be shown up as bogus. It was admitted by Home Secretary Chuter Ede that up to 10 November, 561 applications for visas had been received, of which no less than 215 had been refused.[4] Moreover, though 300 visas had been granted, some of those arriving with them had been interviewed and *then* refused entry. As left-winger D.N. Pritt was later to recall: 'Some of the more innocent of us were quite shocked to discover that one motive of this government reticence was to provide an opportunity for the immigration officers to interview the arrivals, look at their documents, copy out the names and addresses of every British resident that they had in their notebooks or other documents, and *then* send them away on the next ship or plane.'[5]

Of the 196 delegates from non-visa countries who arrived, 65 were refused entry, though no warning whatever had been given that they would be so treated. Those not allowed entry included some who, both before and after the date of the congress, had been freely admitted to Britain, so it could hardly be claimed that they were 'persona non grata'.

Simultaneously, and without any explanation, the government cancelled its consent to the 18 charter flights from Prague.

Altogether some two thirds of the delegates from abroad were excluded. Among them were many famous names – for example, Shostakovitch, the composer, whose work had been heavily criticised by the Soviet Communist Party. Almost all the members of the World Peace Committee were refused entry. Since so many had been prevented from attending, it was obvious that the congress would have to be held elsewhere. So, after a one-day session on 13 November, –

during which the 3,000 seats in the Sheffield City Hall were packed, and there was an overflow of some 1,500 outside – it was decided that the congress must be transferred to Warsaw. Here, with 1,656 delegates from 80 different countries, the congress was resumed.[6]

J.G. Crowther, President of the British Peace Committee, expressed to the congress in Warsaw his sadness and indignation at the way the Sheffield event had been dealt with; 'We British have been injured in our patriotism and pride' he said ... 'Our ancient traditions of freedom have been damaged.' Labour MP S.O. Davies sent a message to the congress expressing his 'disgust and resentment at the action taken by certain people in sabotaging your original efforts to hold your gathering in Britain.'[7] Among the British delegates were 17 active members of the Labour Party who published a joint statement saying they had come to the congress to work with all people and organisations who thought that the question of war and peace transcended all considerations of party politics. As was to be expected, most of them faced expulsion from the Labour Party on their return.

The congress called for the unconditional prohibition of all atomic weapons, to be enforced by 'rigorous international control'. It also demanded the banning of chemical weapons, the reduction of armed forces on land, sea and sky. It proclaimed the right of all colonial peoples to self-determination, arguing that the violence employed to hold peoples in a state of colonial subjection was a menace to peace, while all forms of racial discrimination promoted hatred and were dangerous to peace.

As one of the British delegates, Elinor Burns, commented, the ban by the British Government against people coming to the congress at Sheffield had raised an important question: 'Where is the iron curtain?'[8]

WAR IN KOREA

Withdrawal of foreign troops from Korea was among the demands made at the Warsaw Congress. The war in Korea began in June 1950 when North Korean troops crossed the border into South Korea. This led the Americans to intervene on the side of the South Koreans and enlist the help of British forces, ostensibly under the flag of the United Nations. From the beginning, the *Daily Worker* sided with North Korea and was to face the possibility of legal action against it as a result.

Until 1945, Korea had been part of the Japanese empire. But during the war anti-Japanese resistance movements arose, and when in August 1945, the Russians entered North Korea and the Japanese surrendered, these movements set up 'Committees of Preparation for National Independence'. These 'peoples committees' were broadly based; they represented all political groups except those which had collaborated with the Japanese, and they came together in the Korean capital of Seoul on 6 September 1945 to form a 'People's Republican Government'.

The United States had previously reached agreement with the Soviet Union for a demarcation line between Russian and US troops at the 38th parallel, just north of Seoul. After the American forces landed in South Korea on 8 September 1945, the 'People's Republican Government' was declared 'unlawful' in the American-occupied territory. Instead, a government consisting of former exiles was installed, with the right-winger Syngman Rhee at its head. But north of the 38th parallel, the People's Republican Government was recognised by the Russians. It was headed by Kim Il-Sung, a Korean communist, and one of the resistance movement's former leaders.

From the Autumn of 1946, the American-sponsored government of Syngman Rhee set about arresting, imprisoning and even executing those who opposed his views, and the left were once again driven underground. In 1947, the Soviet Union proposed the withdrawal of all Soviet and American troops so that the future of Korea could be decided by that country's own people. The Americans refused. Despite this, in December 1948, the Russians withdrew from North Korea and that part of the country became self-governing. It was not until June 1949 that the Americans followed suit, and they left behind them some 500 'military advisers' in South Korea.[9] However, in an election held on 30 May 1950 in South Korea, the anti-Rhee groups won more than half of the seats for the National Assembly, after which Rhee only retained office because the opposition was divided.

Rhee had publicly made clear, on many occasions, that he wanted to launch a war to conquer North Korea; he was, as one American historian has put it, 'explicit about his intentions to do so sooner or later'. On the other hand, Kim Il-Sung had, earlier in 1950, visited Moscow to discuss plans to send troops into South Korea in order to reunify the country.[10] On 25 June, after allegations that Syngman Rhee had started his attack, Kim Il-Sung ordered an offensive into South Korea. The advance of the North Korean troops was rapid, while

Rhee's army's crumbled. Within 24 hours, the North Koreans had occupied Seoul, and were moving quickly south.

Under pressure from America a meeting of the UN Security Council was hastily convened and a resolution adopted demanding the immediate withdrawal of North Korean troops from South Korea, and calling on all members for assistance. The Russians were not present at this security council meeting – had they been, they could have vetoed the decision to provide help for Syngman Rhee under UN auspices. But they had been boycotting the security council because of its refusal to allow Communist China to be represented in place of the defeated Chiang Kai-shek. Following the security council's decision, the US announced that its naval and air forces would give support to South Korea; this was to be followed by an order to bomb North Korean cities.

As was to be expected, the Labour Government sided with the Americans, voting with them at the UN, and releasing naval forces from Hong Kong to go to the support of the American troops in Korea. However, this was not enough. There was American pressure on the British to send land forces as well, and this was agreed to by the Cabinet on 25 July.[11] By mid-August British troops were on their way. By 1 October the North Koreans had been forced back to the 38th parallel; by 9 October, American troops under the command of General MacArthur had crossed the border and a full-scale invasion of North Korea was under way.

From the start, the Communist Party denounced the Americans as the aggressors and the British Government as their accomplices in a war to destroy a democratic republic and reestablish imperialist rule. On 1 July Harry Pollitt was reported as saying: 'Never in history has there been such a deliberate and swift attempt to use the colonial armed forces of one aggressive nation to interfere in the internal affairs of a small nation and impose its will'.[12]

On 9 July, a statement was issued: 'The Executive Committee of the Communist Party condemns the American invasion of Korea carried out with British armed support and assistance, and sends its warm greetings to the Korean people in their heroic fight for independence.'[13]

However, the Labour Government received endorsement of its action from the National Council of Labour which, as early as 28 June, described the invasion of South Korea as 'a flagrant act of aggression'. This statement was supplemented by a lengthy and somewhat inaccurate document issued by the TUC General Council. Opposition to the general council's stand was voiced by Wally Stevens of the Electrical Trades Union at the Trades Union Congress held in September; he was supported by both Leo McGree of the Woodworkers and Ralph Bond of the Cine-Technicians. But the attempt to change the attitude of the TUC was overwhelmingly defeated.[14] At the Labour Party annual conference in October further endeavours by some of the left to reverse the policy received little support.

DAILY WORKER REPORTER UNDER THREAT

From early on in the war, the *Daily Worker* had a correspondent with the North Korean forces. This was Alan Winnington who, on the suggestion of Harry Pollitt, had gone to China in 1948 to act as adviser to the Chinese Party's information service. On 15 July 1950, the *Daily Worker* announced that Winnington was to leave for the North Korean front. Not surprisingly, this caused concern in government circles. He was to be the *only* British correspondent with the North Korean army; all others were attached to the command of the American General MacArthur, saying what they were told to say.

At a press conference held by the Foreign Office on 18 July, an *Evening Standard* reporter asked whether the government would be taking any legal steps against Winnington. The Foreign Office spokesman replied that the presence of any British subject in the North Korean theatre of war was being studied by legal experts. 'We regard the Foreign Office statement as an attempt to intimidate and silence the only newspaper giving its readers the truth about the war in Korea' declared a *Daily Worker* editorial on 19 July. 'We further consider that the action of the Foreign Office in raising the question of the legal status of our correspondent is a direct result of American pressure.' It added that it had had telephone enquiries about Winnington from a New York newspaper, and had reason to believe that the matter had been discussed in US diplomatic quarters in London. Asserting that the government had no legal right to take action against Winnington, it said: 'On the contrary, this newspaper regards the Korean invasion itself as an illegal act.'

By 1 August, Winnington had travelled down through North Korea to Seoul, and was describing the exuberant welcome given by the people in the South. He also said that Rhee's troops had no stomach for the offensive which had been ordered, and had abandoned the big gun emplacements near the frontier.

Journeying further into South Korea, Winnington gave an account on 9 August of a visit to a mass grave where, early in July, some thousands of 'political prisoners', thought to be Rhee's opponents, had been massacred with American 'military advisers' looking on. Later, he was to describe the saturation bombing by the Americans, and their use of napalm.

On 19 September, a Tory MP, Major General Beamish, expressed concern that the *Daily Worker* correspondent was sending such news, and asked the Attorney General whether he would 'take steps to forbid such contacts?' Shawcross replied: 'This question involves difficult problems both of international and municipal law to which the government have been giving urgent consideration. Meanwhile, no one should be in doubt that the law of treason is applicable in connection with the present conflict. The activities of the only individual at present known to be with the North Korean forces, as well as the newspaper he represents, are being watched.'

Undeterred by this threat, it was announced in the *Daily Worker* on 26 September that a pamphlet by Winnington entitled *I saw the Truth in Korea* was about to be published. It appeared early in October.

Behind the scenes, the Cabinet had a discussion on Winnington's activities and endorsed the allegation that his pamphlet constituted 'treason'. However, it was at a time when the only penalty for treason was death. Fearing that a jury might refuse to convict him, the Cabinet decided not to prosecute either the author or his publisher who was, at that time, Johnny Campbell, editor of the *Daily Worker*.[15]

By October the assumption in the TUC leaders' document that it was the intention of the United Nations to force the North Koreans to withdraw to the 38th parallel had proved to be unfounded. The UN forces (including British troops) under the command of the US General MacArthur had begun their invasion of North Korea and by November were advancing towards the Yalu river, on the borders of Manchuria.

The Chinese leaders had already warned that, if this happened, the Chinese people would not stand idly by. So it was that Chinese troops entered North Korea, and threw back MacArthur's forces, who soon found themselves in headlong retreat. On 30 November, President Truman suggested at a press conference the possibility of using the atom bomb. Widespread alarm resulting from this suggestion caused

Prime Minister Attlee to fly to Washington. Following an ambiguous public statement he returned on 11 December and was hailed in the press as the 'bringer of peace'. But, in fact, as George Matthews pointed out, the statement made clear that the Americans would retain the right to decide whether the weapon would be used. 'It does not even promise to "consult" Britain, as some papers have tried to pretend. All it says is that Truman will "keep the Prime Minister informed of devleopments".' Moreover, it showed that the British and Americans had no intention of abandoning their aggressive policy in Korea.[16]

By January 1951, the Chinese had pushed MacArthur's forces back over the 38th parallel, and in July of that year, the North Koreans proposed a truce. This was rejected, while the Americans stepped up their bombing activities over North Korea.

Early in 1951, Winnington was visiting British soldiers in a prisoner-of-war camp. He reported favourably on their treatment by the Chinese, and sent back photos of them to their relations, together with a list of 85 names which was published. This came as a great relief to some families who had previously been told that their relatives had 'gone missing'. However, his reports raised fury among pro-war circles, and after a question from Labour MP Raymond Blackburn, the Minister of Defence Emanuel Shinwell once again discussed with the Attorney-General the possibility of taking legal action against the *Daily Worker*. In a subsequent letter to Blackburn, reprinted in the *Daily Worker* on 13 April, Shinwell said of his consultations with the Attorney-General:

> He is well aware of the undesirable activities of the *Daily Worker* in this connection, some of which have every appearance of coming within the definition of treasonable offences. This does, of course, turn to some extent on the question of whether or not we are at war with China. On this, it seems likely that, from a legal point of view, the state of hostilities between China and ourselves is sufficient to bring the act of 'giving aid and comfort' to the Chinese within the definition of treason.
>
> The difficulty about instituting prosecution, however, is that no other charge than treason would be possible, and that the only penalty for treason is death. In these circumstances you will appreciate that it is difficult to take action, but you may rest assured that the position will continue to be closely watched.

In response to this, the *Daily Worker* published an editorial saying that it was proud of what it had done to turn people against the war in Korea. 'We do not need Mr Shinwell to tell us that the Government has been watching our activities' it said, but asserted that this would not deter it from doing its duty. 'Thousands of reservists have been torn from their families and sent to the other side of the world in order to prevent the unification of Korea on the basis of democracy and land reform, and to turn it into an American war base against China' it said.[17]

In the summer of 1951, Winnington attended the unsuccessful talks between the opposing forces at which the communists were proposing a cease-fire, but the Americans were finding endless reasons for continuing the conflict. In the event, the war dragged on until 1953, when it came to a standstill with the country still divided at the 38th parallel. Winnington continued his reports until the war ended. By this time, a Tory government was in office, and he was told that his passport could not be renewed. This meant that he could not come back to Britain, and was indeed to spend the next twenty years in exile first in China and later in Germany.[18]

THE IMPACT OF THE WAR ON THE HOME FRONT

On 30 August 1950 it was announced that the period of compulsory national service was to be increased once again – this time to two years. It meant that the number in the armed forces, which had fallen below 700,000 was to rise again, reaching 835,000 by 1951. There was a huge increase in spending on 'defence' and large sections of industry were diverted to war production.

Party members were in no doubt that it was this expenditure on 'defence' which was leading to new austerity measures such as cuts in the meat ration. The shortage of goods was persisting and prices were rising fast.

Since wages were not keeping pace with prices, living standards were going down. Yet the government persisted in its call for wage restraint, a demand which had the support of the TUC General Council until the 1950 Congress, at which a resolution urging the abandonment of wage restraint and asking the government to introduce statutory control of profits was moved by Wally Stevens of the Electrical Trades Union. It was supported by left-winger L.C. White of the Civil Service Clerical

Association and, despite opposition from the general council, was carried by a narrow majority of 3.9m to 3.7m. At this same congress, a resolution declaring that the 'time was now opportune' for the government to implement a policy of equal pay for women was moved by communist Betty Jones of the CSCA and was carried by 4.4m to 2.3m thus brushing aside efforts by the general council to get it remitted. The defeat of the right wing at this congress was a sign of the growing discontent with the government's management of the economy.

The rise in defence spending led to a drop in exports, and to another acute balance of payments crisis. In a desperate attempt to deal with this, the government introduced several extremely unpopular measures in its 1951 April budget. Purchase tax was increased on many items, while expenditure on the National Health Service – the most popular of all the government's social achievements – was to be reduced. Charges were imposed for spectacles and dentures – up till then they had been freely available to all. So came the resignation of Aneurin Bevan from the government; he was followed by Harold Wilson, President of the Board of Trade.

Commenting on the 1951 budget, Steve Boddington (a party member who wrote under the name of 'John Eaton') said:

> The government, acting on orders from Washington, has embarked on a war programme that – at present prices – will cost about £1,300 million in this year, 1951-2. The productive resources devoted to war purposes will be more than doubled. Housing and other 'social service' building will have to make way for the war machine … Production for export – for which the workers were told, when the wage freeze was imposed, all else must be sacrificed – is to be wrecked to please the warmongers.[19]

As Margot Heinemann, editor of *World News and Views* put it on 21 April, the government was 'robbing the poor for America's war'.

In February that year, the World Peace Council had launched a campaign for the signing of a Peace Pact by the 'Five Great Powers' – USA, USSR, Great Britain, France, China – and in May the British Peace Committee issued a call for the collection of signatures to a petition for such a pact. By September 1951, the number signing in Britain had reached over 700,000.

22

CAMPAIGNS FOR DEMOCRATIC RIGHTS 1950-1

The Labour leaders had always boasted of their devotion to freedom and democracy. But, during the year 1950-1, government circles were, as one historian put it, increasingly obsessed with the 'red menace'.[1] This led them to use extraordinary measures to undermine existing democratic rights. Having managed to block the Peace Congress event in Sheffield, they revived a wartime regulation enabling them to prosecute strikers, and tried – unsuccessfully – to prevent young people travelling to a World Youth Festival held in Berlin.

ORDER 1305 AND THE TRIAL OF THE SEVEN

'Order 1305' was an emergency measure brought in under the wartime Defence Regulations in 1940. It laid down that no employee could go on strike 'in furtherance of a trade dispute' unless the dispute had been reported to the Minister, who had the power to refer it to an arbitration tribunal whose award would be binding on both employer and employee. If the Minister did not do this, and took no action, the strike might become legal.

The wartime Minister of Labour, Ernest Bevin, who had been responsible for introducing this Order had promised at the time that it would be repealed when the war ended. But this had not happened. At the 1946 Trades Union Congress, Walter Stevens had moved a resolution demanding its repeal, but was defeated. At every subsequent congress, motions put forward for its repeal were lost. There were two reasons for this. Firstly, the Order could be used to enforce 'recognised terms and conditions' upon employers. Secondly, the penal provisions against those who took part in strikes had not, in practice, been invoked since the war ended. That part of the law appeared to have been put in cold storage.

However, in 1950, the government suddenly decided to use Order 1305 to bring strike leaders to trial. This decision was taken following discussions with, among others, the Attorney-General, Sir Hartley Shawcross, who had already participated in enquiries into the extent of communist involvement in the dock strikes in support of the Canadian seamen in 1949. The upshot was that, in October 1950, ten leaders of an unofficial strike over an inadequate pay award for gas workers in London and the South East were arrested and prosecuted.

The ten gasworkers appeared in court on 5 October, where they were charged with breach of Order 1305. They pleaded guilty and were sentenced to one month's imprisonment, but given leave to appeal. Following this, the employers agreed to negotiations on a new bonus scheme. On 9 October, the strikers returned to work. When the appeal was heard, the prison sentences were reduced to fines of £50, on the ostensible grounds that the men had not known they were infringing the law.

It was widely assumed that, in withdrawing the prison sentences, the Court had been influenced by the mass protests against Order 1305 which had been provoked by the gasworkers case. A demonstration in Hyde Park had been followed on 11 November by an emergency conference called at short notice in London's Beaver Hall at which were represented nine trade union district committees, 161 trade union branches, five trades councils and 21 shop stewards committees. It was decided to campaign on three issues: (1) acquittal of the ten gas workers (2) the ending of Order 1305 (3) the disbanding of police organisations set up to spy on trade unionists. This third demand arose as a result of reports in the press that police were to investigate 'communist influence' in trade unions.[2]

All this was the prelude to one of the most important events in labour movement history: the trial of the seven dockers.

On 1 February 1951, a national docks delegate conference decided by 46 votes to 23 to accept an offer from the port employers for a very small increase in pay. The offer had already been agreed to by Arthur Deakin, the anti-communist general secretary of the Transport and General Workers Union. Its acceptance was recommended by the T&GWU officials at the conference, but was much resented by dockworkers in the north of England, who regarded it as inadequate and believed that it would not have been accepted were it not for the undemocratic way in which delegates were chosen for the docks conference which was unrepresentative of the rank and file. Their anger was demonstrated by an immediate walkout of 2,000 port workers at Birkenhead, after which the strike spread to Liverpool and Manchester.

For some years, unity in the docks had been promoted via unofficial 'port workers' committees' which enabled representatives of the different unions in the docks to come together. For instance, on the London Port Workers Committee there were members of the T&GWU, the Stevedores' Union, the Lightermen's Union, and so on. Unlike shop stewards committees in the engineering industry, these committees had no official recognition – indeed Arthur Deakin was bitterly opposed to them.

After the walk-out in the North, representatives of the Merseyside Port Workers Committee contacted the London Committee and asked for support. The London Committee – which included several of those disciplined or expelled by Deakin during the Canadian seamen's strike – was in some difficulty, since a large proportion of London port workers were not affected by the national wages decision; they had independent wage agreements with their employers. However, since solidarity was an important aim, the committee called a meeting of men to enable the delegates from the northern ports to put their case. Only 500 workers turned up at this meeting out of a workforce of over 9,000. This militant few voted to join forces with the strikers on Merseyside and elsewhere, and staged a march urging those at work in London ports to walk out in support. Only 450 did so; it was clear that support from London dockworkers was at a very low level, and any action would soon fizzle out altogether.

Ironically, it was the government's Attorney-General, Sir Hartley Shawcross, who was to transform this situation. On 8 February, seven dockworkers – three from Merseyside and four from London – were arrested and charged under Order 1305 with conspiracy to incite dockworkers to strike. Unlike the call for support for the Merseyside wage campaign, this news provoked an immediate walk-out of some 6,700 London dockworkers.

The seven dockers were remanded on bail until February 20. Although they were all active trade unionists, their political views were by no means uniform. Joe Harrison, aged 39, from Birkenhead, and chairman of the Merseyside Port Workers Committee, had been a life-long member of the Liberal Party. But, as he had been active in the campaign in support of the Canadian seamen in 1949, he was obviously someone against whom Deakin, along with Shawcross, wanted to retaliate. Under arrest with him was Bill Johnson, aged 32, also from Birkenhead and a member of the Merseyside Committee. Bob Crosbie, 42, was one of the strike leaders from Liverpool. He was a Catholic and did not belong to any political party.

Of the London four, three were well-known as communists. Ted Dickens, aged 43, belonged to the Stevedores' Union, having been expelled from the T&GWU for his activities in support of the Canadian seamen. Harry Constable, aged 36, had been expelled from the T&GWU for the same reason; he was by this time holding a temporary card in the Stevedores' Union. Joe Cowley, aged 45, was still in the T&GWU having been disciplined by Deakin, but not expelled. The fourth Londoner was a Catholic and member of the Labour Party; he was Albert Timothy, aged 48, who came from East Ham and was on the Executive of the Stevedores' Union. All four of the Londoners arrested had been members of the London Port Workers Committee and had been trying to persuade London dockers to show solidarity with the Merseyside strikers.[3]

After the initial walk-out, London dockworkers met in Victoria Park, where they were addressed by Vic Marney (a young Communist docker who had been awarded the Military Medal during the war). Here it was agreed that they should all return to work, but walk out once again the next time the court hearing took place, under the slogan: 'When they're in the dock, we're out of the docks'. Thereafter, this became the accepted form of action, and was to be repeated no less than nine times. Thus, when the hearing was resumed on 20 February, four ports came virtually to a standstill – London, Glasgow, Manchester and Liverpool – as 20,000 walked out. In London, hundreds of dockworkers made their way to the court, where they stood outside singing 'Land of Hope and Glory, Mother of the Free' while balloons bearing the slogan 'End 1305' were let into the air. After a hearing which lasted all day, the seven were again remanded on bail, this time until 27 February, when thousands of dockers again came out. The case was once more adjourned, this time until 14 March. After a two-day hearing, the seven were sent for trial at the Old Bailey. As before, on 16 March, dockers from most of the Port of London marched out in protest; crowds stood all day outside the court. When the accused emerged, once more on bail, they were greeted with cheers and carried shoulder high down Bow Street.

Shawcross's efforts thus resulted in the opposite of what was intended: a massive increase in industrial unrest. It also fuelled the campaign among trade unionists for the repeal of Order 1305. Indeed, by the end of February, the TUC General Council was at last obliged to change course, and began to press the government to restore the freedom to strike.[4]

While in the dock, the accused made clear their beliefs. 'I am a trade unionist of 27 years standing' said Ted Dickens. 'I am convinced that no legal action will prevent the portworkers or trade unionists in general from striking in defence of their legal conditions or for improving the same.' Joe Cowley said: 'The dockworkers have always stood together and no action that the government may take will prevent them from doing so.'[5]

Unlike the gas maintenance men prosecuted under 1305 the previous autumn, 'the Seven' pleaded 'not guilty'. The three from Merseyside were defended by Labour MP and solicitor, Sydney Silverman; those from London were represented by the party solicitor, Jack Gaster. On behalf of the accused, they put forward an argument which the government had obviously not anticipated: that Order 1305 applied only to strikes in connection with *trade disputes*, whereas this strike was not in that category: it was a dispute between members of the T&GWU and officials of that union led by Deakin. 'The only thing the men had in mind was to induce officials of the union to do the things which the men considered should be done' said Silverman, while Gaster argued that what had set off the strike was the 'appalling manner in which the union leadership exhibited contempt for the men'. This point was emphasised by Harry Constable who said from the dock: 'It is obvious to any intelligent person that the wrong people are in the dock. The persons who should be here are Mr Arthur Deakin and many of his fellow officials' – a statement greeted with cries of 'hear, hear' from the gallery.[6]

Though this argument failed, and the Seven were, on 16 March, committed for trial by jury at the Old Bailey, Shawcross was by this time concerned that the defence's interpretation of Order 1305 might be accepted by a jury, and the Seven found 'not guilty' on the grounds that it was not a 'trade dispute'. So, two additional charges were hastily made under ordinary criminal law, accusing the men of conspiracy to cause injury to employers in the conduct of their business. This meant that if, by any chance, they were found not guilty on the grounds that it was not a trade dispute, they could be found guilty on the second and third charges made under criminal law.

The trial at the Old Bailey began on 9 April and continued for over a week but, in the event, the result was a shambles. For, though the jury found the men guilty on the second charge, they could not agree on that made under Order 1305 – in other words, they could not decide whether or not it had been a trade dispute. Since the validity of the second charge depended on the 1305 decision, the case fell through and, on 18 April, Shawcross was obliged to announce that it would be withdrawn.

For the ninth time, during the hearings of the case, the docks had been at a standstill, and huge crowds had gathered outside the Court. When the withdrawal of the charges was announced, the 'Seven' were, as usual, carried away shoulder high, but this time they were celebrating what was regarded as a glorious victory.

Victory celebrations were to continue for many days. At a May Day demonstration in London organised by the London Trades Council – the first May Day march not banned since 1948 – the dockers and their banners were greeted with deafening cheers from the 30,000 people assembled in Trafalgar Square. A black coffin labelled 'Order 1305' was ceremoniously placed in front of the plinth.

It all heralded a government retreat. In August, Order 1305 was at last repealed.

THE BERLIN YOUTH FESTIVAL

The determination of the Labour Government to preserve its own 'iron curtain' was to be demonstrated once more in August 1951 when the 3rd World Festival of Youth and Students for Peace took place in Berlin. The festival was organised jointly by two bodies: the World Federation of Democratic Youth (WFDY) and the International Union of Students. The WFDY had been founded at an international conference in London in November 1945; it had received a message of support from Prime Minister Attlee. However, by 1948 it had been declared a 'proscribed organisation' by the Labour leadership.

In Britain the party's work among youth was coordinated through a Youth Advisory Committee composed of representatives from 18 districts. It was chaired by George Matthews. It discussed the work of the Young Communist League which had just over 3,000 members and whose secretary was John Moss; its recruits came mainly from the workplace. Another responsibility of the Youth Advisory Committee was to oversee work among students. A National Student Committee met regularly to discuss activities, and student branches had grown up in most of the universities. Both students and YCL-ers had been much engaged in collecting signatures for the 'peace petition'.

When the Berlin Youth Festival was announced under the rallying call 'Youth unite against the danger of a new world war' a preparatory organisation, the 'British Youth Festival Committee' was set up to arrange travel and accommodation for those who wanted to go; its secretary was Bert Pockney, a member of the YCL, while Monty Johnstone, then an undergraduate at Oxford, who was also chair of the Party's National Student Committee, went to Berlin during the summer vacation to serve as British representative on the International Festival Committee.

The 2nd World Youth Festival held in Budapest in 1949, though attended by a large party of British youth, had been ignored by government circles, but the 1951 festival was a different matter. Herbert Morrison – who had succeeded Bevin as Labour's Foreign Secretary – said in the House of Commons on 30 May that, while he was 'reluctant to interfere' with the freedom of action of British youth, the purpose of the festival, which was 'sponsored by Communist-controlled youth organisations' was to support the 'campaign for peace on Soviet terms'. He had, therefore, agreed to 'consultations' with the three Western High Commissioners in Germany 'on ways and means of preventing this exploitation of young people to serve the aims of the Soviet Government'.

Despite Herbert Morrison's disapproval, local festival committees were set up; meetings were held at factories and Youth Clubs to elect delegates and raise money for fares and, in the end, some 1,700 young people applied to go. Most of them were young workers, but there were also 210 students and 400 young people from the colonies temporarily stationed in Britain. Also included were some members of the Labour League of Youth.[7]

The main party, numbering 960, was to travel by rail and sea to Dunkirk via Boulogne and then embark on a Polish liner. However, 41 of them were refused entry by the French and sent back to Britain. It was obvious that the 41 were on a hit list supplied by the British authorities – indeed a French official told one of them that they were complying with instructions from the British police.[8]

Another 430 young people had planned to fly to Prague in a specially chartered aircraft and go on from there by rail. For this, permission to fly over West Germany was required and had been applied for, but at the last moment it was refused, and those concerned had to find an alternative route. Some flew via Holland and Switzerland and were not interfered with, but 61 who tried to go via Brussels were forced on to trains and boats to take them back to England. A Belgian official told one of them 'Your government has given us orders to stop all British subjects from leaving for Eastern Europe, so you cannot blame our government'.[9]

Another 310 started their journey from London to Dieppe, intending to go through Paris to Linz in Austria, then on to Prague and thence to Berlin. 90 of this contingent were students and it included youth choirs, bagpipe players from Scotland and a team of dancers. Chair of the Workers Music Association, Charlie Ringrose, was in charge; its president, the composer Alan Bush, was also present. On arrival at Dieppe 13 of them were refused permission to proceed, but the rest continued their journey to Austria and were joined by several hundred young French participants.

Austria was still divided (as was Germany) into four zones occupied by the British, the French, the Russians or the Americans. When the train carrying the contingent reached Saalfelden in the American zone, it was stopped by American officers, and the three coaches on which the party was travelling were unshackled from the rest of the train. The contingent was confined to these coaches for several hours. At last Ringrose was allowed to contact the British Consul by telephone. The consul told him that people with British passports were free to travel through the American zone. However, the American colonel insisted that he had instructions from a 'higher authority' to prevent the party continuing on its journey. In the end, the coaches were driven back to Innsbruck, in the French zone, and the travellers were provided with an empty train to sleep in.[10]

Ringrose visited the British Consul who began by being helpful but, after telephoning the British authorities, changed his tune, and told Ringrose that the contingent would have to go back to England via Calais. That night, the contingent agreed unanimously not to go back, and the following day, 4 August, they marched through Innsbruck to the British Consulate carrying flags and singing freedom songs. They were cheered on by many young French people who were also being held up, but when they reached the consulate they were told that no food or accommodation could be provided, and they must take the train back to Calais. This they refused to do and returned to Innsbruck station to find themselves surrounded by armed Austrian security police, and unable to get food or water. However, the young French who were being treated better by their consul came to the station bringing food and coffee to the beleaguered British, who thus had their first meal of the day. Following this, they staged an impromptu performance on the station platform, singing traditional folk songs while the Scots danced the Highland fling. And they sang an adaptation of a well-known music-hall song with words just written by one of the choir, Tina Davey. It ran as follows:

Verse 1	Farewell to cold winter, summer's come anew
	We've quarrelled with our consul and him and us are through;
	For now at last we've found him out and now at last we see
	A passport's no protection if in Berlin you would be.
Chorus	Let him go, let him tarry, let him sink or let him swim.
	He wants us in Calais, but we're wanted in Berlin
	For he's a Yankee Yesman, and the Yankee's day is done
	And we'll all get to Berlin with the rising of the sun
Verse 2	Our consul said I'll feed you if you go where I say
	But till that Berlin train arrives, we said, 'Its here we stay'
	'Oh no you won't, our forces will know how to deal with you'
	But we don't think that shifting us is a job they'll care to do.

Repeat Chorus

The next day, another attempt was made to travel through the American zone. This time, the contingent divided into groups and boarded five different local trains armed with tickets for Linz. But when they reached Saalfelden they were surrounded by American soldiers with bayonets; military police then boarded the trains and ordered all with British passports to get off; those who objected were forcibly thrown out receiving cuts and bruises. Though a group of Scottish delegates managed to remain on the train undetected, the others spent the rest of the day hemmed in by troops and were finally sent back to Innsbruck.

During the next few days, the contingent divided itself once more into small groups and, with the help of the Austrian Youth Movement, they were filtered through the barriers placed in their way. Some went for part of the journey by bus, others walked over the border at night with the help of local inhabitants, some went by train over the Brenner Pass into Italy and back through the British zone into the Russian zone where they were put on trains to Berlin. By 14 August, almost all of them had reached Berlin, and Morrison had failed in his attempts to stop them.

Ironically, in that month of August, Morrison had, in the columns of *Pravda*, (the Soviet Communist Party newspaper) boasted of the freedom of British citizens to travel abroad, and had said: 'Your government, for reasons I cannot understand, refuses to let you travel freely'.[11] The truth was that the British Government had no legal right whatever to prevent British passport holders from travelling to the festival, but had connived with other powers to stop them.

Later the National Council for Civil Liberties held an enquiry into the event and published the results in a pamphlet *Journey to Berlin* which showed how the government had arranged with the French, Belgians and Americans to do the job for them. In subsequent correspondence, the Foreign Office admitted that there had been an 'exchange of views and information' with other governments, but denied responsibility for the actions taken.

Meanwhile, for many of the young people involved, the Berlin Youth Festival was a highly enjoyable event. Some 26,000 from 104 countries participated. Each day, there were cultural programmes, sports events, receptions, outings and informal gatherings; at a conference held on the last day, a declaration was adopted stressing the need to prevent a new war, and to put an end to the arms race.

Not all the British participants reacted favourably to the event. As Monty Johnstone was later to recall, some of them objected to the obvious domination of it by communists. Thus there were many pictures of Lenin, Stalin and other communist leaders hanging on the walls of the hostels where they stayed which Johnstone had tried – unsuccessfully – to have removed. However, most of the British participants gained much from their contact with people from abroad, and came back inspired, determined to be active in the cause of peace.

THE FALL OF THE LABOUR GOVERNMENT

Just after the Youth Festival it was announced that a general election was to be held on 25 October 1951.

The Communist Party had already decided that, in view of the need to counteract the threat of a Tory government, the number of communist candidates must be severely limited this time. The rise in support for Conservatives was still very much in evidence; it was bolstered by dissatisfaction over continuing shortages of food, clothes and fuel, some of which were still rationed. Cuts in housebuilding meant that only about 200,000 new houses were being completed every year. The Tories promised that, if they won the election, the number would be raised to at least 300,000 a year.

So, this time, keeping the Tories out was seen as a priority by communists; as the Executive Committee said on 2 October 'in this hour of grave peril ... the Communist Party declares that it is the responsibility of all men and women who desire peace to prevent the return of a Tory government'.[12] In support of this aim, the party reduced the number of its candidates to no more than ten – four in Scotland, one in Wales, one in Sheffield, and four in London. The Party's election manifesto was headed 'Save Peace – Save Britain' and 'End American Domination'. In all other constituencies, party members were actively engaged in helping the return of the Labour candidate. In the end, all ten of the communist candidates failed to get one-eighth of the votes cast, and therefore lost their deposits.

The Liberals also reduced the number of their candidates from their previous 475 to 109, 66 of whom lost their deposits. However, this time, the Liberals managed to persuade the Conservatives to make anti-Labour pacts in constituencies where Labour had been previously elected on a minority vote. In return for this agreement, the Conservatives stood down in some constituencies to allow the Liberals to win a seat. Even so the number of Liberals elected went down from nine to six.

The division of seats in the new House of Commons illustrated the undemocratic nature of a 'first-past-the-post' electoral system and amply justified the party's declared aim of proportional representation, for which Gallacher had argued so vigorously in 1944. For Labour got more votes than the Tories, but lost the election. The Labour candidates received 13.9 million votes, or 48.8 per cent of the total poll. It was, in fact, the highest Labour vote ever recorded before or since. The Conservative candidates got fewer votes: 13.7 million or 48.1 per cent of the poll. Yet the Conservatives won more seats than Labour. They got 321, compared with Labour's 295. Even allowing for a handful of Liberals and others elected, the Conservatives achieved an overall majority of 17 seats.

So came the end of the post-war Labour Government, and with it the end of the hopes of millions of people.

23

WHICH ROAD TO SOCIALISM?

It was during the Labour Government's last term of office that the Communist Party drafted a new programme outlining the kind of socialist society for which it aimed and discussing how such an aim could be achieved. The proposal for such a programme was first mooted in the summer of 1950 following a visit by Harry Pollitt to the Soviet Union, during which he had a discussion about the British political situation with Stalin who had suggested that the British Party needed a long-term programme. In a report to the executive committee on 8 July 1950 in which the implications for the party of the general election results earlier that year were examined, Pollitt said: 'immediate issues and generalisations about socialism are not enough. Thinking people want a perspective. They want to see the line of march and the path ahead. We have to outline a programme for such people.' The report was endorsed by the executive committee and circulated for discussion by all party organisations.[1] Meanwhile, work on the new programme had begun.

Over the previous 15 years, the party's views about the way forward had greatly changed. Thus, in its programme *For Soviet Britain* adopted in 1935, it had been assumed that, if a socialist society was to come about, the existing parliamentary structure would have to be abolished and replaced by workers' councils or soviets. But, as noted in chapter 8, the idea that parliament must be abolished had been discarded in 1944 in the party's programme *Britain for the People* in which it was argued that the aim should be to *change* parliament and to democratise the state machine.

However, *Britain for the People* had been chiefly concerned with immediate post-war problems. It had been followed after the war ended by a book *Looking Ahead* by Harry Pollitt. Published in 1947, this contained a special chapter entitled 'The British Road to Socialism' which raised the possibilities of 'transition to socialism by other paths than those followed by the Russian Revolution'. 'The path, in any case, is necessarily different for each country' wrote Pollitt.

In 1950 work on the new draft programme caused some arguments within the Party's Political Committee. Moreover, as a result of a letter to Dutt from Pollitt, who was once more back in the Soviet Union in October of that year, it set out a much more critical view of the Labour Government and the Labour Party than previously.[2]

The first draft of the programme under the title *The British Road to Socialism* was in the end adopted by the Executive Committee and then issued for discussion in January 1951. Stressing the need for a lasting peace and for the restoration of Britain's independence, it made clear the party's long-term objectives: the kind of socialist society for which it aimed and how it could be reached. For 'only by the establishment of socialism can Britain's problems be finally solved and its people guaranteed a good life, lasting peace and steadily rising living standards.'

As Pollitt said in a political letter sent out in January 1951, the draft programme also answered the 'slanderous misrepresentations of our policy by which the enemies of the working class seek to isolate us from the rank and file of the Labour Movement.'

WHY LABOUR HAD FAILED

The programme began by looking back over the previous six years of Labour rule, recalling how, at the end of the war in 1945, people wanted to be certain that there would never be another war, and were determined that great social changes must be brought about. So they had rejected the Tories and had supported the Labour Party, who had declared that its aim was peace and friendship with the Soviet Union, and Socialism in Britain.

Contrary to what had been promised, the Labour Government had formed a war bloc with American imperialism against the Soviet Union, China and the Peoples Democracies of Eastern Europe, and against colonial peoples struggling for their national liberation. It had imposed a crushing rearmament programme at the expense of the social needs of the people.

The pretence that the Labour leaders aimed at socialism had proved to be untrue. The measures of 'capitalist nationalisation' introduced by the Labour Government had, according to the programme, 'nothing in common with socialism'. They covered only very limited sectors, leaving the bulk of industry in the hands of big business from which it drew its profits. Indeed, nationalisation had, for the most part, been directed at auxiliary services which, under previous capitalist management, had proved inefficient and even made losses, but were now providing cheap transport and power for the use of capitalist industry. The compensation paid to the former owners guaranteed them the continuance of their unearned incomes at the expense of the workers. The state-owned industries were bureaucratically administered and their governing boards were dominated by their former owners. So it was that the limited steps towards state ownership had benefited capitalism and in no way changed the capitalist character of the British economy. 'The lesson of the failure of the Labour Government is not the failure of Socialism' it said. 'It is the failure of Labour reformism and Labour imperialism, which is the servant of the big capitalist interests'.

'Socialism means the abolition of capitalism' it said. But 'the Labour leaders do not want to abolish capitalism. The so-called 'democratic socialism' is a screen behind which they justify their defence of the system of capitalist profit and exploitation, defend the position of the capitalists and monopolists, and seek to prop up the bankrupt capitalist social structure of riches for the few, poverty and low living standards for the many, and ever-recurring danger of slump and war.'

SOCIALISM – WHAT IT WOULD MEAN

Under socialist nationalisation *all* large scale industry and transport, together with the banks, the monopoly-owned wholesale and retail trading concerns, as well as large landed property, would be placed in the hands of the people. Social ownership meant that the governing boards would be composed of workers and technicians. All proposals, plans and targets would be placed before the workers in the industries and factories concerned, for joint discussion and joint decision. The democratic participation of the workers and their trade unions in management would thus be ensured at every level.

At the same time, cooperative-owned productive and consumer enterprises would be encouraged, while small shopkeepers and businessmen, and farmers in the countryside, would be freed from the restrictions imposed by the monopolists.

The ending of capitalist monopoly control of the country's economic, political and social life would generate tremendous forces for the rapid development of industry; the productive resources of the country would be reorganised and reequipped on the basis of a national plan, resulting in higher wages, reduced prices and the extension of social services. Socialism would mean an end to capitalist profit and exploitation, and would ensure that production was organised for the use of the people and not for the profit of a tiny minority.

'Socialism means freedom for the people, freedom from poverty and insecurity, freedom for men, women and children to develop their capacities to the full, without fear or favour. For women it means equal rights with men in the social, economic and political life of the nation; for young people, the opening of new opportunities ... for the family, a real home life, fuller interests and closer ties based on security and a new respect for the individual.'

Socialism would mean peace and an end to the danger of war; there would no longer be capitalists aiming to exploit the colonial peoples.

On the question of the party's attitude to the British Empire, the programme described the policies of the Tory and Labour leaders as 'a crime against the colonial peoples'. It said: 'All relations between the peoples of the present Empire which are based on political, economic and military enslavement must be ended and replaced by relations based on full national independence and equal rights. This requires the withdrawal of all armed forces from the colonial and dependent territories and the handing over of sovereignty to governments freely chosen by the peoples'. It suggested that the economic relations which would follow colonial independence would provide the basis for a 'new close fraternal association of the British people and the liberated peoples of the Empire'.

THE NEED FOR REAL DEMOCRACY

The programme also stressed the undemocratic nature of British society. The so-called 'free world', it said, was in fact one in which the capitalist class exercised a disguised dictatorship over the working class. Thus, despite democratic advances won by past struggles, the real power in Britain was still concentrated in the hands of a tiny section of rich property owners who controlled the land, large scale industry, finance and trade; their representatives held the commanding positions in the Civil Service and the Armed Forces, in the Judiciary, the Diplomatic and Colonial Services. They also controlled most of the newspapers, the BBC and the cinemas. Under such conditions, it alleged, democracy was restricted for the majority of the people, and was being further eroded by the attacks on the rights of free speech and organisation, and on the right to strike.

The people could not advance to socialism without real political power, which must be taken from the hands of the capitalist minority. 'Capitalist democracy' must be replaced by a real people's democracy. This involved 'transforming parliament, the product of Britain's historic struggle for democracy, into the democratic instrument of the will of the vast majority of the people.'

Such a transformation would depend on the united action of working people and their families, who formed over two-thirds of the population; to them must be added most professional workers, teachers, technicians, scientists, farmers, shopkeepers, small businessmen, whose future prospects were closely bound up with those of industrial workers. Together, they represented a mighty political force, fully capable of defeating the present exploiters and rulers and returning a majority to parliament representing the interests of all working people. To achieve this, a popular alliance was needed of all people determined to end the arbitrary power of the rich and to establish a Peoples Government truly representative of the people.

Such a government would not only introduce a planned economy based on socialist principles; it would bring about democratic electoral reform. This meant the introduction of proportional representation, and the extension of voting rights – at the time reserved to those aged 21 or over – to all young people aged 18 or more.

But electoral reform was seen only as a first step. The aim was to *change* the parliamentary system, to make it more democratic and to bring the state apparatus under democratic control. Thus the House of Commons would be made the sole national authority, freed from the restrictive influence of the House of Lords and the Monarchy; there would be democratic ownership of the press, people's control of the BBC, the democratic transformation of the Civil Service, the Foreign Office, the armed forces, the police, the law courts, the Judiciary.

ANSWERING THE ANTI-COMMUNIST ALLEGATIONS

There were three widespread misconceptions about the Communist Party and its aims which the programme dealt with.

One was the idea, constantly suggested in the newspapers and spread throughout the media, that the socialist countries presented a military threat to Britain, and to the capitalist world in general. The programme declared:

> The Communist Party rejects the theory of the inevitable war between the socialist and capitalist camps ... on the contrary, it declares that peaceful co-existence of socialism and capitalism is possible on the basis of mutual respect for national rights and independence.

And it went on:

> The Communist Party brands as a lie the charge that Communism is to be imposed by aggression and conquest, and declares that social transformation can only come through internal changes in actual conditions in each country.

Another myth was what Pollitt had described as the 'bogy of a bloody revolution'.[3] As the programme stressed, any danger to a peoples government determined to build socialism would arise from the 'capitalist warmongers and their agents' who would be most unlikely to give up voluntarily their property and their profits.

> It would be more correct to expect them to offer an active resistance to the decisions of the peoples government and to fight for the retention of their privileges by all means in their power, including force. Therefore, the British people and the peoples government should be ready decisively to rebuff such attempts.

The main misconception challenged was the allegation that the party aimed to abolish parliament, whereas, as shown above, the party aimed to change parliament so as to make it *more* democratic.

Emphasising that the way forward for Britain would be different from that of the Soviet Union, the programme said:

> The enemies of communism accuse the Communist Party of aiming to introduce Soviet power in Britain and abolish parliament. This is a slanderous misrepresentation of our policy. Experience has shown that in present conditions the advance to socialism can be made just as well by a different road ... Britain will reach socialism by her own road ... British Communists declare that the people of Britain can transform capitalist democracy into a real people's democracy.

Although the proposal to change parliament rather than abolish it had been accepted by the party as early as 1944, some members remained disturbed at the suggestion that the party no longer believed in 'soviets' or 'workers' councils' which were thought to be much *more* democratic than the British parliamentary system under which a cross on a ballot paper every few years was a substitute for peoples' participation in running the country. However, after much discussion among members of the party, the programme received overwhelming support; issued as a 3d pamphlet in January 1951 it had to be reprinted many times in the ensuing months. In the end, 200,000 copies were sold. In the Spring of 1952 it was to be adopted by the Party's 22nd Congress.

It was to remain the party's programme until 1957 when, at a Special Congress called following the 1956 revelations of Stalin's atrocities, some important changes to the programme were made. One of these concerned the statement that colonial independence would be followed by a 'close fraternal association of the British people and the liberated peoples of the Empire'. This formulation had been objected to by some West Indian members of the party, and by others from territories abroad, because it failed to recognise the right of their countries to complete autonomy. As a result of an amendment moved by Dutt, the words 'close fraternal association' were dropped in favour of 'close voluntary fraternal relations' with countries 'willing to develop such relations.'[4]

The most fundamental alteration to the programme in 1957 was the replacement of the term 'peoples government' by the term 'socialist government', making clear that this meant a government based on the Communist and Labour Parties, while for the first time it advocated the need for a multi-party system in a socialist society, and recognised 'the right of other political parties to maintain their organisations, party publications and propaganda and to take part in elections.

CONCLUSION

As noted in chapter 22, by the end of 1951, Labour had lost the General Election and a Tory Government had been installed. Over the years leading up to this defeat, Communist Party members had made various assumptions about the political situation which had turned out to be faulty. Thus, the proposal for a post-war coalition government in 1945 was put forward partly because the dramatic fall in support for the Tories demonstrated in the 1945 election had not been expected. In contrast, when the party decided to put up 100 candidates in the 1950 general election, it was assumed – quite wrongly – that Tory governments were a thing of the past. However, as discussed in Chapters 15 & 19 the main mistakes which the party made arose from its attitude to the Soviet Union – which continued to receive its uncritical support – and its acceptance of views put forward by the Cominform.

Despite these mistakes, the party throughout this period had many positive achievements to its credit. It had made a major contribution in building up workplace organisation in all the main industries including coal mining, engineering, building, transport, furniture, the docks and so on. It had agitated and organised – in many places successfully – on immediate issues such as a shorter working week, and against wage restraint; it had campaigned for equal pay for women, and taken the lead in the movement to defeat Order 1305 and in doing so regained democratic trade union rights, including the right to strike.

But its activities had not been confined to 'bread and butter' questions. It had consistently fought for freedom and independence for all colonial peoples and taken a stand against attempts by the Labour leaders to preserve the British Empire. It had bitterly opposed the subservient attitude to the United States, which had allowed Britain to become a war base for the Americans. Above all, it was chiefly responsible for inaugurating the first movement against nuclear weapons – indeed the petition to 'ban the bomb' was in the end signed by 1.3 million people in Britain.

Throughout all these endeavours, the Communist Party was targeted as 'the enemy' – not just by Conservatives, but by the right-wing Labour and trade union leaders. Its members had been subjected to witch-hunting and to special discriminatory rules. It is easy to see why this should have been so. For, despite its small size – about 35,000 members in 1952 – it had throughout offered the main challenge to the powers that be, seeking to spread the message: the need to replace the supremely unfair and undemocratic capitalist society with a socialist system which would rid the world of war, hunger, injustice and inequality, would replace the rule of the rich with the rule of the common people, and so guarantee a peaceful future, rising living standards, and a good life for all.

REFERENCES

1 A New Stage in the War

1. See *Way to Win*, 1942, Report of conference, pp58–9.
2. Information on the 1939 change of line is provided in *About Turn: The Communist Party and the Outbreak of the Second World War* edited by Francis King and George Matthews 1990. Information on the discussions after 22 June 1941 and the messages sent from Comintern is derived from material recently acquired by the Communist Party archive and supplied to the author by Monty Johnstone.
3. Winston Churchill, *Second World War*, Vol III 1950, p350.
4. Reported in *Industrial and General Information* (IGI) bulletin 9 July 1941.
5. IGI, *ibid*, 24 July 1941, 2 August 1941.
6. See *Ministry of Morale*, Ian McLaine, p197.
7. See Paul Addison, *The Road to 1945*, 1975, p135.
8. Clough and Amabel Williams Ellis, *Labour Monthly*, February 1942.
9. IGI, *ibid*, 16 September 1941, *op cit*.
10. See John Grigg, *1943: The Victory that never was*, 1980.
11. TUC Annual Report, 1941, p250.
12. See *Hansard*, September 9; September 11, 1941.
13. See *World News & Views*, 29 January 1944, p34.
14. House of Lords debate, 22 October 1941.
15. *Hansard*, 27 January 1942.
16. IGI, *ibid*, 24 February 1942.
17. See N. Branson, *History of the Communist party of Great Britain*, 1928-41, p316.
18. *Way to Win*, pp16, 17, *op cit*.
19. Branson, *ibid*, pp310-3.
20. *Hansard*, 28 January 1942.
21. *Labour Monthly*, October 1942.
22. *Hansard*, 4 June 1942.
23. See Vol 86, Labour Party NEC Minutes, 5 June, 24 June, 2 July, 1942.

2 Relations with the Labour Party and the Comintern 1941-3

1. Labour Party NEC Minutes, Vol 84, pp374, 375, 384.
2. A full list of 'proscribed organisations' before, during and after the war, is contained in a booklet 'Labour-Communist Relations', Part I by N. Branson and B. Moore 1990, CP History Group.
3. Labour Party Annual Report (LPAR), 1942, pp16-18.

4. *Industrial and General Information*, 1 November 1941.
5. LPAR, 1942, p107.
6. *Ibid*, p157.
7. See Vol 86, Labour Party NEC: Organisation Subcommittee minutes, 30 June 1942.
8. LPAR, 1942, p11.
9. LPAR 1943, pp47, 115.
10. Minutes of Labour Party NEC meeting, 27 January 1943, item 236; 60a (not circulated).
11. For correspondence see LPAR, 1943, pp9-16.
12. See N. Branson, *History of the Communist Party 1928-41*, pp154-5 and 313. According to Reuben Falber's recollections from 1958 onwards some money was donated via the Russian Embassy. But no evidence has yet come to light that this was happening during the 1940s.
13. *Daily Worker*, 17 April 1943.
14. LPAR 1943, pp161, 162, 165.
15. *Unity and Victory: Report of 16th Congress*, p3.
16. *Ibid*, p7.
17. *Ibid*, p29.

3 Industrial Work 1941-44

1. See *Arms and the Men*, a report of the Conference published by the Engineering and Allied Trades Shop Stewards National Council.
2. Wal Hannington, *Never on our Knees*,1967, p342.
3. See Hywel Francis and David Smith, *The Fed. History of the South Wales Miners*, p402.
4. Arthur L. Horner, *Coal and the Nation*, Communist Party pamphlet, 1943, p12.
5. See Margot Heinemann, *Britain's Coal*, 1944, p137.
6. A detailed account of the Barrow strike appears in *Engineers at War, 1939-45* by Richard Croucher 1982, p218-228. See also *Engineering Struggles* by Edmund and Ruth Frow 1982, pp189-192.
7. *Pollitt answers questions on Communist Policy*, March 1944.
8. See *World News and Views*, 22 April 1944.
9. *New Propellor*, April 1944.
10. James B. Jeffreys, *The Story of the Engineers*, 1945, p261.
11. Labour Party Annual Report, 1946, p172.
12. TUC Circular 89, 10 June 1943.
13. TUC Circular Report, 1943, p340; see also *Labour Research*, May 1942, p56; October 1942, p129; January 1943, p2; October 1943, p145.
14. *Daily Worker*, 20 October 1944.

4 The Fight for Equality for Women

1. See *Labour Monthly*, February 1942. Joan Beauchamp was author of a

book, *Women who Work*, published in 1937.

2. Palme Dutt, *Fascism and Social Revolution*, 1934, p218.
3. See Philip Bagwell, *The Railwaymen*, The History of the National Union of Railwaymen, 1963, p580-2.
4. See *Women who Work*, *ibid*, p26.
5. Wall Hannington, *The Rights of Engineers*, 1944, p40.
6. See *Labour Research*, November 1941; *Engineering Struggles*, *ibid*, p171.
7. See *Arms and the Men*; report of the conference.
8. These names are according to the recollections of Tamara Rust.
9. The proceedings were reported in *Industrial and General Information Bulletin* (IGI), 15 July 1941 and also in a pamphlet 'Parliament of Women'.
10. Proceedings of the 2nds session were reported in a pamphlet 'Calling all Women'; the 3rd session was dealt with in a pamphlet in June 1942 entitled 'Woman Power'.
11. *World News and Views*, 9 January 1943.
12. The proceedings were reported in a pamphlet, *Health and Housing*, issued by the Women's Parliament organisation.
13. *Daily Worker*, 23 November 1944. Bevin's speech, reported on 22 November, was made to a meeting of the joint industrial committee of the printing trades.
14. *World News and Views*, 11 November 1944.
15. *Ibid*, 4 November 1944.

5 The Party and the Armed Forces

1. See, The Autobiography of D.N. Pritt, Part II, *Brasshats and Bureaucrats*, 1966, p105-6.
2. Recollections of Jim Fyrth.
3. See Angus Calder, *The Peoples War*, 1969, p250.
4. See D.N. Pritt, *ibid*, pp85-99 in which he describes the bans put upon him and how he got round them.
5. See Winston Churchill, *Second World War*, Vol III (1950), p742; see also Paul Addison, *The Road to 1945*, 1977, p150-1.
6. See Bill Alexander, *Volunteers for Liberty*, 1982, p246.
7. Much of the information about individual experience was collected from participants in a conference called by the Communist Party History Group in 1986 to mark the publication of a book by Richard Kisch entitled *The Days of the Good Soldiers*, which names many Party members and describes their experiences. This was followed by a pamphlet edited by Bill Moore and George Barnsby entitled, *The Anti-Fascist Peoples Front in the Armed Forces*, based partly on letters subsequently received by the CP History Group. Carritt's experiences are printed in the above pamphlet, p23.
8. Material supplied to CP History Group.
9. Richard Kisch, *ibid*, p42.
10. See *Dictionary of Labour Biography*, edited by Joyce M. Bellamy & John Saville, Vol II, 1974.
11. See *Freedom for the Forces*, by ex-Staff Sergeant R.J. Spector, 1947, p10-11.

12. Letter to CP History Group.
13. *Ibid.*
14. See pamphlet by Moore and Barnsby, *ibid*, pp22-23.
15. Moore and Barnsby, *ibid*, pp19-20.
16. Letter to CP History Group. See also Moore & Barnsby, *ibid*, p20-1.
17. See Moore & Barnsby, *ibid*, p5.
18. *Hansard*, 25 July 1944.
19. See Moore & Barnsby, *ibid*, p30.

6 Wartime Struggles for Colonial Freedom

1. See R. Palme Dutt, *Labour Monthly*, September 1942 on 'India – What must be done'.
2. TUC Annual Report, 1942, p132.
3. *Ibid*, pp299-301.
4. See *Unity and Victory*, Report of 16th Congress of the Communist Party, pp26, 40.
5. See 'Mole in the Crown: memories of the Indian underground 1935-8' published in *Britain, Fascism and the Popular Front* (1986) edited by Jim Fyrth. See also booklet, 'Mole in the Crown', published 1985.
6. Letter to CP History Group, 1989.
7. *Ibid*, 1990.
8. *Daily Worker*, 30 January 1945.
9. See N. Branson, *History of the Communist Party of Great Britain 1928-1941*, 1985, pp319-320.
10. *Daily Worker*, 16 January 1945.
11. *Ibid*, 5 March 1945.

7 Friends or Enemies? 1943-4

1. Quoted in the *Daily Worker*, 29 July 1943.
2. See Nigel West, *MI5 British Security Service Operations 1909-1945*, pp218-280.
3. *Daily Worker, op cit.*
4. *Daily Worker*, 31 July 1943.
5. *Hansard*, 5 August 1943.
6. See '*I Claud*' by Claud Cockburn, Penguin edition, 1967, p235; See also, *The Week*, 22 July 1943.
7. *Daily Worker*, 19 January 1944.
8. See 'Anti Semitism' by John Gollan, *Labour Monthly*, June 1943.
9. *Labour Monthly*, January 1943.
10. *Labour Monthly*, June 1943.
11. Winston Churchill, *Second World War*, Vol 5, pp635-7.
12. See Bernard Donoughue and G.W. Jones, *Herbert Morrison; Portrait of a Politician*, 1973, pp303-306.
13. *Daily Worker*, 22 November 1243.

8 The Party's Post-War Aims

1. *Labour Monthly*, January 1944.
2. *World News & Views* (WN&V), 22 January 1944.
3. *'Communist Policy for Britain'*, Report of 18th Congress November, 1945, p7.
4. *WN&V*, 11 March, 18 March, 25 March 1944.
5. *WN&V*, 18 March 1944, p92.
6. This was Dutt's view, according to information supplied to the author by Monty Johnstone.
7. *WN&V*, 18 August 1945.
8. See *Communist Policy for Britain*, ibid, p39; *Daily Worker*, 26 November 1945.
9. See *Crimea Conference: Safeguard of the Future*, March 1945.
10. *WN&V*, 24 March 1945.
11. *Daily Worker*, 26 November 1945.

9 The Last Year of the War

1. See *Daily Worker*, 11 August 1944.
2. *World News & Views*, 4 November 1944.
3. *Daily Worker*, 17 March 1945; TUC Annual Report, 1944, p338; TUC Annual Report, 1945, p216.
4. *World News & Views* (WN&V), 17 June 1944.
5. Victor Rothwell, *Britain and the Cold War 1941-47*, 1982, p214.
6. Rothwell, *ibid*, pp203-7.
7. Labour Party Annual Report 1944, p147.
8. Statement issued 17 December 1944.
9. *Hansard*, 20 December 1944.
10. *Daily Worker*, 2 February 1945.
11. Rothwell, *ibid*, p92.
12. See D.F. Fleming, *The Cold War and its Origins*, 1961, Vol 1, pp159, 167.
13. Labour Party Annual Report 1945, pp81-2.
14. *World News & Views*, 4 August 1945.

10 The Labour Government and the Outside World, 1945-6

1. See D.F. Fleming, *The Cold War and its Origins*, 1961, p296.
2. *Hansard*, 16 August 1945.
3. For an account of what took place in Cabinet circles see Kenneth O. Morgan, *Labour in Power 1945-1951*, 1984, pp280-2.
4. See Communist Policy for Britain, Report of 18th National Congress in 1945, p68.
5. *Hansard*, 16 August 1945.
6. *Hansard*, 20 August 1945.

7. *Daily Worker*, 9 November 1945.
8. See Fleming, *ibid*, p670. See also, *World News & Views*, 20 October 1945.
9. *Daily Worker*, 2 April 1946.
10. *Daily Worker*, 21 September 1945.
11. Report of 18th Congress, *ibid*, p62.
12. *Ibid*, pp19, 36.
13. Speech reprinted in *Speeches of Winston Churchill*, Penguin, 1990, pp296-308.
14. See D.N. Pritt, *The Labour Government*, 1963, p66.
15. See Kenneth Harris, *Attlee*, 1982, p298.
16. *World News & Views*, 16 March 1946.
17. *Labour Monthly*, July 1946.
18. See *Challenge*, 11 May 1946, 8 June 1946.
19. See *World News & Views*, 14 December 1946 to 15 February 1947.
20. See *Daily Worker*, 24 February 1947 and Report of 19th Congress, p12.
21. *Daily Worker*, 7 October 1946.
22. TUC Annual Report 1946, pp436-440.
23. *Ibid*, pp469-472.
24. *Ibid*, p416.

11   1945-6 The Party's New Structure and Areas of Work: Relations with the Labour Party

1. *World News & Views* (WN&V), 19 February 1944, EC. Report to 17th Congress, p9.
2. *WN&V*, 20 January 1945; EC Report to 18th Congress p17.
3. *WN&V*, 22 January 1944.
4. *WN&V*, 26 February 1944.
5. See Documents for Congress, July 1943-August 1944, p46.
6. Proposals of Executive Committee on Party Organisation, 17 December 1944, para 5.
7. According to Peter Kerrigan in *WN&V*, 6 March 1948.
8. See *Daily Worker*, 1 May 1948.
9. Report of 18th Congress, p46.
10. *Ibid*, p55.
11. According to Hymie Fagan WN&V, 27 April 1946
12. *Ibid*.
13. *WN&V*, 22 September 1945.
14. Report of 18th Congress, p65.
15. *WN&V*, 26 January 1946.
16. *Labour Monthly*, January 1946.
17. A description of the articles in the Tory press appeared in a survey from Maire Norton in *World News and Views*, 18 May 1946; see also the *Daily Worker*, 7 June 1946.

12 1946: The Squatters Movement

1. Labour Party Annual Report 1946, p169.
2. *World News & Views*, 7 September 1946.
3. *Ibid*, 24 August 1946.
4. Letter from the Siddalls to the CP History Group, 1984.
5. Letter from Chapman to the C.P. History Group, 1984.
6. Letter from Bert Ward to the C.P. HIstory Group, 1984.
7. The Daws Hill events is described in material sent to the C.P. History Group by Jack Spector.
   For further information see James Hinton's article *Self-help and socialism: the Squatters Movement in 1946* in History Workshop 1988, No 25 which gives details of the takeover of army camps, particularly in Bristol and Birmingham. See also report of a conference on the squatters movement held by the Communist Party History Group which appeared in the March 1985 issue of *Our History Journal*.
8. Most of the ensuing information on the London Squatters is taken from a pamphlet, *London Squatters 1946*, August 1989, edited by Noreen Branson, based on the 1984 conference and published by the C.P. History Group.
9. Quoted in full in Ministry of Health Circular 174/46.
10. See 'The Squatters' published by the London District Committee of the Communist Party.
11. See Ministry of Health Circular 174/46 issued on 16 September.
12. Letter from Ivor Segal to C.P. History Group.
13. Quoted in *Labour Research*, November 1946.
14. See *London Squatters*, ibid.

13 Industrial Work and Attitudes to Nationalisation 1945-47

1. *Metal Worker*, November 1946.
2. *Ibid*, January 1947.
3. *Ibid*, February 1947.
4. *World News & Views*, 8 November 1947.
5. Reported in *Labour Research*, August 1946.
6. *Daily Worker*, 12 April 1946.
7. See *Daily Worker*, 6 June, 22 June 1946.
8. *Daily Worker*, 12 January 1946.
9. *Labour Monthly*, March 1946.
10. TUC Annual Report, 1946, p355-6.
11. *Ibid*, p456.
12. *Ibid*, pp416, 432.
13. *Labour Research*, February 1947, p29.
14. See Emile Burns, *World News and Views*, 4 January 1947.
15. *Daily Worker*, 4 January 1947.
16. See C.P. Executive Committee minutes, February 1947.
17. Arthur Horner, *Incorrigible Rebel*, 1960, p168.

18. *Ibid*, p182.
19. R. Page Arnot, *History of the Scottish Miners*, 1955, p279.
20. See Margot Heinemann, *Coal Must Come First*, 1948, p48-9.
21. Document printed in full in *World News & Views*, 21 August 1948.
22. *Labour Monthly*, July 1949, p201.
23. Report of 19th Congress, pp3-14.
24. *Daily Worker*, 24 February 1947.
25. *World News & Views*, 1 February 1947.
26. *Daily Worker*, 24 February 1947.

14 Post War Struggles for Colonial Freedom

1. *Times, Daily Telegraph*, 12 January 1946.
2. See Report of 18th Congress, p70.
3. *World News and Views*, 2 March 1946.
4. *Labour Monthly*, March 1946, p92.
5. Travel Notes, *Labour Monthly*, May 1946.
6. See Ramish Shangavi in *World News & Views*, 1 February 1947.
7. Reprinted in *World News & Views*, 25 January 1947.
8. See D.N. Pritt, *The Labour Government*, 1963, p216.
9. *Labour Monthly*, February 1946.
10. TUC Annual Report 1946, pp448, 475.
11. A full report of the conference is contained in a booklet, *We Speak for Freedom*, from which all the quotations are derived, together with the ensuing contributions.
12. *Labour Monthly*, July 1947.
13. *World News & Views*, 21 June 1947.
14. *World News & Views*, 24 July 1948.

15 1947 Economic Crisis: The Start of the Cold War: the Cominform

1. Trades Union Congress Annual Report, 1947, pp528-535.
2. *Hansard*, 13 November 1947.
3. *Labour Monthly*, April 1947.
4. John Collier, 8 November 1947; see also Elizabeth Gurley Flyn, *World News & Views*, 14 June 1947.
5. *World News & Views*, 14 June 1947.
6. *Labour Monthly*, July 1947, p194.
7. See for example, *The World Since 1945*, T.E. Vadney, 1987, p72.
8. TUC Annual Report 1947, p427.
9. *Ibid*, pp487-9.
10. *World News & Views*, 1 June 1946.
11. *Ibid*, 15 November 1947.
12. *Ibid*, 11 October 1947.
13. *Ibid*, 22 October 1947.
14. *Ibid*, 20 December 1947.

15. For Britain Free and Independent: Report of 20th Congress, p38.
16. *World News & Views*, 28 February 1948.
17. Ibid, 13 March 1948.

16 The Civil Service Purge

1. *Hansard*, 18 March 1948.
2. *World News & Views*, 10 April 1948.
3. Based on the recollections of Eddie Dare.
4. *Hansard*, 25 March 1948.
5. *Labour Research*, June 1948.
6. Trades Union Congress Annual Report, 1949, p279.
7. Information supplied by Steve Parsons.
8. See *Daily Worker*, 26 May 1948.
9. Reported in the *Daily Worker* 9 June, 18 June, 22 June 1948.
10. *Hansard*, 25 March1948.
11. See *Daily Worker*, 28 May, 21 May 1948.
12. Reported in the *Daily Worker*, 25 June, 30 July 1948.
13. TUC Annual Report 1948, p532-538.
14. See TUC Annual Report 1949, p278.
15. *Ibid*, pp502-3.
16. See Tony Bunyan, *The Political Police in Britain*, 1976, p165-6.

17 Professional Workers and Intellectuals

1. Information supplied by Steve Parsons. See also *Hansard* 26 April 1948 and 3 May 1948; also, *Science, Politics and the Cold War* by Greta Jones, p28.
2. See Charles Hobday, *Edgell Rickword: A Poet at War*, 1989, p231-246. See also E.P. Thompson in, *P.N. Review*, Vol 6, No 1, 1979.
3. See *Modern Quarterly*, Vol 3, p3; Vol 4, p3.
4. *World News & Views*, 20 March 1948, quoted by Sam Aaronovitch, p127.
5. See *World News & Views*, 24 April, 1 May, 15 May, 1948.
6. See J.D. Bernal, *Modern Quarterly*, Vol 4, No 1, p5.
7. *Ibid*, p8.
8. The Manifesto appeared in full in *Labour Monthly*, October 1948.
9. *Modern Quarterly*, Vol 2, No 4, pp336-356.
10. See Greta Jones, *Science Politics and the Cold War*, p18 et seq.
11. *Modern Quarterly*, Vol 2, No 4.
12. See Vittorio Vidali, *Diary of the Twentieth Congress*, first published in England in 1984, p192.
13. See *The Visible College: A Collective Biography of British Scientists and Socialists of the 1930s* by Gary Wersky, 1979, p293-304.
14. See article by Alan Bush, *Modern Quarterly*, Vol 4, No 1, pp38-47.
15. *Modern Quarterly*, Vol 3, No 3, pp20-41.

18 Trade Union Activities: Attacks from the Right 1948-9

1. *Daily Worker*, 10 June 1948.
2. *Ibid*, 22 December 1947.
3. *Ibid*, 5 January 1948.
4. *Ibid*, 2 February 1948.
5. See TUC Report of Special Conference, 24 March 1948, p47.
6. *Hansard*, 12 February 1948.
7. See *Britain Free and Independent*, Pollitt Report to 20th Congress, p47.
8. See *World News & Views*, 6 March 1948, p98; *Daily Worker*, 23 February 1948.
9. See *World News & Views*, 6 March 1948, p99.
10. According to a report in *Labour Research*, August 1948.
11. TUC Annual Report, 1948, pp78, 333.
12. *Ibid*, p337.
13. *Ibid*, p425.
14. See TUC Annual Report 1949, pp274-5.
15. Reprinted in *World News & Views*, 6 November 1948.
16. *Daily Worker*, 9 November 1948.
17. See *Daily Worker*, 23, 24 December 1948.
18. *World News & Views*, 2 April 1949.
19. A detailed examination of the ban on Communists in the T&GWU is made by Graham Stevenson in a booklet, *The Life and Times of Sid Easton, 1911-1991*, available from the T&GWU central office.
20. Reported in the *Daily Herald*, 18 September 1950.
21. See *Labour Research*, November 1945 and March 1948.
22. See *Labour Research*, January 1948; also *Labour Under the Marshall Plan* by Anthony Carew, 1987, p69.
23. See Alan Bullock, *Ernest Bevin: Foreign Secretary*, 1983, p235.
24. TUC Annual Report, 1948, p394, 448.

19 Eastern Europe and Stalin's Influence

1. See John Bloomfield in *Passive Revolution*, 1979, p232.
2. *World News & Views*, 10 July 1948.
3. *Ibid*, 17 July 1948.
4. For a detailed story of the events leading up to the trial, see *Truth Will Prevail* by Marian Slingova, the British wife of Otto Sling, who returned to Britain after her husband's execution and, in this book, published in 1968, describes not only her own experiences but the political background at the time.
5. Resolutions and Proceedings of 21st National Congress, p8.
6. *Ibid*, p4.

20 Events of 1949 and the 1950 Election

1. See TUC Annual Report, 1946, p240.
2. Reprinted in *World News and Views*, 2 April 1949.
3. See Kenneth O. Morgan, *Labour in Power*, 1984, pp273-7; also Alan Bullock, *Ernest Bevin: Foreign Secretary*, 1983, p529-30.
4. Reported in *World News & Views*, 9 October 1948.
5. According to D.F. Fleming in *The Cold War and its Origins*, 1961, pp522-5.
6. See *World News & Views*, 30 April 1949, 7 May 1949.
7. *Ibid*, 5 November 1949.
8. Labour Party Annual Report, 1949, p18.
9. *Hansard*, 21 March 1949, Home Secretary Chuter Ede.
10. TUC Annual Report 1950, p107, 294-8.
11. *World News & Views*, 6 August 1949.
12. See Kenneth O. Morgan, *Labour in Power*, 1984, p381. Also Jack Dash, *Good Morning Brothers*, 1969, p71.
13. See *Communist Policy to Meet the Crisis*, Report of 21st Congress, pp22, 24-6, 39.
14. Reported by Hymie Fagan, *World News & Views*, 11 March 1950.
15. See William Gallacher, *Last Memoirs*, 1966, p115.
16. TUC Annual Report, 1949, p391.

21 The Fight to Ban the Bomb: War in Korea

1. TUC Annual Report, 1950, p196, 411-425.
2. Quoted in *Daily Worker*, 28 September 1950.
3. Quoted in *Daily Worker*, 30 October 1950; see also *World News & Views*, 4 November 1950.
4. *Hansard*, 14 November 1950.
5. See D.N. Pritt, *The Labour Government*, 1963, p398.
6. A detailed description of the Sheffield events is provided by Bill Moore in a booklet *Cold War in Sheffield*, published by the Sheffield Trades Council Peace Sub-Committee in 1990. Moore visited the Public Records Office to examine Government documents relating to this event, but found them listed as 'not available for inspection'.
7. *Daily Worker*, 17 November 1950.
8. *World News & Views*, 2 December 1950.
9. See D.N. Pritt, *Light on Korea*, 1950.
10. T.E. Vadney, *The World Since 1945*, 1987, p143.
11. See Kenneth O. Morgan, *Labour in Power*, 1984, p423.
12. *Daily Worker*, 1 July 1950.
13. *World News & Views*, 15 July 1950.
14. TUC Annual Report, 1950, pp197, 414-6, 419-20, 576.
15. See Alan Winnington, *Breakfast with Mau*, 1986, p115-6.
16. *World News & Views*, 16 December 1950.
17. *Daily Worker*, 13 April 1951.

18. See Alan Winnington, *Breakfast With Mao*, pp115-6.
19. *Labour Monthly*, May 1951.

22 Campaigns for Democratic Rights 1950-51

1. See Kenneth O. Morgan, *Labour in Power*, 1984, p437.
2. See *World News & Views*, 2 December 1950; *Daily Worker*, 23 October 1950; Malcolm MacEwen in *Daily Worker*, 28 October 1950.
3. Source for most of this information comes from the *Daily Worker*, 10, 11 February 1951, which however stated that Harry Constable was *not* a Communist – an assertion contradicted by the recollections of others – see, for example, *Good Morning Brothers*, by Jack Dash, p71.
4. See TUC Annual Report, 1951, p232-3.
5. *Daily Worker*, 17 March 1951.
6. *Ibid.*
7. According to John Moss, *World News & Views*, 4 August 1951.
8. See pamphlet, *Journey to Berlin*, published by the National Council for Civil Liberties.
9. *Ibid.*
10. The experiences of this contingent were recounted in *The Innsbruck Story*, a pamphlet published by the Youth Festival Committee and also in *Journey to Berlin, ibid.*
11. Quoted in *The Innsbruck Story, ibid*, p4.
12. See *World News & Views*, 13 October 1951.

23 Which Road to Socialism?

1. See *The Fight for Peace and Working Class Unity*, p19.
2. For a detailed examination of how the programme was compiled and what is known about Stalin's influence, see article by George Matthews in *Changes*, 14-17 September 1991, which includes in full the letter from Pollitt.
3. See *Fight for Peace and Working Class Unity*, p18.
4. See Trevor Carter, *Shattering Illusions*, 1986, p59-60.

Appendix I

Communist Party Membership

These numbers show the total of Party cards issued between January and the month mentioned in the year concerned. Thus those listed for the month of March do not include new members recruited during the summer and autumn of that year. On the other hand, those listed in December do not allow for those members who failed to pay their dues and were lapsed or who could not continue membership while in the armed services.

1941 (December)	22,783
1942 (December)	56,000
1943 (July)	46,643
1944 (March)	47,513
1945 (March)	45,535
1946 (March)	42,123
1947 (June)	38,579
1948 (April)	43,000
1949 (March)	40,161
1950 (May)	38,853
1951 (March)	35,124

APPENDIX II
EXECUTIVE COMMITTEE
MEMBERS

16th Congress
July 1943

Abbott, Syd
Allison, George
Bartlett, Betty
Blackwell, Sam
Bramley, Ted
Burns, Elinor
Burns, Emile
Campbell, John Ross
Cox, Idris
Dutt, Rajani Palme
Gallacher, William
Giles, G.C.T.
Gollan, John
Haldane, J.B.S.
Hannington, Wal
Hanson, R.
Henderson, Sam
Henrotte, Esther
Horner, Arthur
Jeffery, Nora
Kerrigan, Peter
MacLennan, Bob
McMichael, Joan
Matthews, George
Moffat, Abe
Moore, Frank
Pollitt, Harry
Rust, William
Scott, Joe

17th Congress
October 1944

Abbott, Syd
Allison, George
Blackwell, Sam
Bramley, Ted
Brown, Isabel
Burns, Elinor
Burns, Emile
Burns, Tim (resigned)
Campbell, John Ross
Cox, Idris
Dutt, Rajani Palme
Devine, Pat
Gallacher, William
Giles, G.C.T.
Gollan, John
Haldane, J.B.S.
Hannington, Wal
Henderson, Sam
Henrotte, Esther
Horner, Arthur
Kerrigan, Peter
McMichael, Joan
MacLennan, Bob
Matthews, George
Montagu, Ivor
Papworth, Bert
Pollitt, Harry
Rust, Tamara
Rust, William
Scott, Joe
Coopted
Moore, Frank

18th Congress
November 1945

Abbott, Syd
Allison, George
Beauchamp, Kay
Blackwell, Sam
Bramley, Ted
Brown, Isabel
Burns, Elinor
Burns, Emile
Campbell, John Ross
Carritt, Gabriel
Cox, Idris
Devine, Pat
Dutt, Rajani Palme
Gallacher, William
Giles. G.C.T.
Gollan, John
Hannington, Wal
Henrotte, Esther
Horner, Arthur
Horner, John
Kerrigan, Peter
McMichael, Joan
Matthews, George
Montagu, Ivor
Papworth, Bert
Piratin, Phil
Pollitt, Harry
Rust, Tamara
Rust, William
Scott, Joe
Coopted
Clifford, Alf
Degnan, Tom
Kelly, Dan
Normanton, John
Potter, Tom
Warren, Dick

Executive Committee Members

NAMES INDEX

NAMES INDEX